DANTE'S GOLDEN LEGEND

MERCER UNIVERSITY

MERCER UNIVERSITY PRESS

Endowed by

TOM WATSON BROWN

and

THE WATSON-BROWN FOUNDATION, INC.

DANTE'S GOLDEN LEGEND

Auto-hagiography in the *Divine Comedy*

Mary Alexandra Watt

MERCER UNIVERSITY PRESS
Macon, Georgia
2021

Published 700 years after the Death of
Dante Alighieri
(1265–1321)

MUP/ H1011

Published by Mercer University Press
1501 Mercer University Drive
Macon, Georgia 31207

25 24 23 22 21 5 4 3 2 1

Books published by Mercer University Press are printed on acid-free paper that meets the requirements of the American National Standard for Information Sciences—Permanence of Paper for Printed Library Materials.

Printed and bound in the United States.

This book is set in Adobe Caslon Pro.

Cover/jacket design by Burt&Burt.

ISBN 978-0-88146-808-3
Cataloging-in-Publication Data is available from the Library of Congress

Contents

“Who do men say that I am?” (Mark 8:27)

Preface

The *Divine Comedy* as Auto-hagiography

IT MAY WELL be that all literature has an autobiographical dimension. It seems almost impossible to imagine that an author could distance himself so much from his own literary influences, from his own perceptions and beliefs, that his work would in no way reflect personal experience. Certainly, Dante's *Divine Comedy* has a readily discernible autobiographical aspect. Indeed, the pilgrim / protagonist is addressed as "Dante" at the summit of Mount Purgatory.[1] Throughout the *Comedy*, as well, Dante inserts his own opinions into the narrative, using not only his own voice, but also those of the souls he encounters: personal acquaintances, enemies, and heroes who wallow, trudge, and soar throughout its canticles. Moreover, Dante uses his own progression through the three realms of the afterworld to reflect upon his past experiences, to recount, contemplate, and understand the significance of the events of his life.

Yet the narrative structure, a prophetic journey, recounted

[1] "Dante, though Virgil's leaving you, do not / yet weep, do not weep yet; you'll need your tears / for what another sword must yet inflict" [Dante, perché Virgilio se ne vada, / non pianger anco, non piangere ancora; ché pianger ti conven per altra spada] (*Purg.* 30:55-57). All citations from the *Comedy* follow the Petrocchi edition unless otherwise noted. The translation follows Mandelbaum, again, unless otherwise noted.

in retrospect, takes the *Comedy* beyond a simple chronicle of Dante's life. There is a revelatory, mystical aspect that suggests to the reader that this is much more than a "bildungsroman," or a "portrait of the artist as a young man." Rather, if we look closely, we see that Dante himself is highly conscious of precisely what he is writing and uses the structure of his *Comedy* to present his own life as that of a saint, similar to those hagiographies collected in Voragine's *Golden Legend*.[2]

My approach is novel. While there have been numerous analyses of specific autobiographical aspects of the *Comedy*, such examinations are fragmentary. It has rarely been suggested, for example, that episodes that are obviously linked to Dante's life are important components of a greater autobiographical project. Amilcare Iannucci is one of the few scholars to consider that the autobiographical dimension of the *Comedy* might extend beyond the confines of specific episodes or cantos. Iannucci notes a link between certain episodes he calls "parallel episodes," which, he proposes, convey a personal revelation. But even Iannucci's approach is cursory in terms of examining the entire *Comedy* as a "life of Dante" told by the author himself.[3]

Accordingly, I do not offer a detailed study of individual episodes or cantos. Rather, I consider how they are integral to understanding the *Comedy*'s greater autobiographical structure. Moreover, it is not my intention to repeat the efforts of other scholars who have given such obviously personalized episodes an already invaluable inspection. Instead, I look at the entire *Comedy* as a continuous narrative intended to tell, among other

---

[2] de Voragine, comp., *The Golden Legend (Aurea Legenda)*.

[3] The structural role of parallel cantos has been the subject of the group study *Vertical Readings in Dante's* Comedy, edited by George Corbett and Heather Webb. This study explores how the relationship between similarly numbered cantos in each of the canticles creates a vertical structure within the *Comedy* that serves a hermeneutical function.

things, the autobiographical story of Dante's life. I will also argue that the *Comedy* not only presents the author's life but also urges us to read that life as a model of martyrdom, of salvation through suffering, and instructional in nature, hence, also hagiographical.

It is important to note, however, that this auto-hagiographical structure does not emerge spontaneously in the *Comedy*. Indeed, even the most cursory examinations of Dante's corpus of work reveals an author preoccupied almost from the start with the implications of his own experience. His earliest poetry and correspondence are deeply concerned with understanding the meaning of his dreams and visions, and they suggest a desire to find patterns in what might otherwise be perceived as random events.[4] In both the *Vita nuova* and the *Convivio*, for example, we find an author engrossed in the search for meaning and the struggle for self-expression. He combs through seemingly unrelated events looking for patterns—repetition of numbers, coincidence of names—and then tries to determine what these patterns signify. At the same time, he is experimenting with how to present the events of his life. In each of these aspects, Dante looks to earlier biographical, autobiographical, and hagiographical models as a means of explicating his life. There are some scholars who have taken a more comprehensive approach to the personal aspect of the *Comedy*, but such examinations have considered the issue primarily in terms of modelization. John Freccero, for example, in his pivotal work, *Dante: The Poetics of Conversion*, looks at the extent to which the *Comedy*'s structure borrows from Augustine's *Confessions*. But Freccero's approach focuses on discerning the presence of an earlier autobiographical model and fails to adequately examine the way in which Dante's story unfolds within and revises that model.

[4] See Barolini, "Dante and Cavalcanti," 31–63.

Moreover, Freccero's approach, with its focus on the Augustinian model, addresses neither the presence of other forms nor the way in which Dante revises them in order to tell his own life story.

This is not to say that I will disregard Dante's use of earlier models. However, the approach I take is considerably more expansive than Freccero's. I suggest that Dante draws upon not only the Augustinian prototype, but also on many others in composing the *Comedy.* Consequently, I will look at the way Dante appropriates a variety of narratives, not only autobiographical but more specifically, hagiographical, and revises them in such a way that they become vehicles for his own story aimed at including himself in the larger genre of "Lives of the Saints." Similarly, I will not be examining Dante's personal understanding of Augustine's work so much as how Dante uses Augustine's writing, and the writing of other authors, to create a new narrative form and to compel a specific reading of his own works. For that reason, I will not be studying, in the case of the Virgilian epic, for example, how many times we hear echoes of the *Aeneid*, but rather examining the purpose for which such echoes are inserted. In keeping with this broader approach, I will look at other works by Dante and consider the role that they play in the *Comedy*'s auto-hagiographical function.[5]

Just as much as the events of his own life provide Dante with source material for the narrative of the *Comedy*, so too do the *Vita nuova* and the *Convivio* furnish source material that is interwoven in the narrative fabric of the *Comedy.* The *Vita nuova* and the *Convivio*, as early attempts at life-writing,[6] I suggest, represent models that Dante glosses, absorbs, and rewrites

[5] Simone Marchesi provides a thorough study of Dante's engagement with some of his own poems, in particular, in the pilgrim's exchange with Bonagiunta da Lucca ("Epic Ironies," 99–117).

[6] Donald Winslow uses this term, explaining, "In the narrow sense this

as much as any of the other sources that contributed to his creation of the *Comedy.* While an autobiographical reading of the *Vita nuova* is by no means novel, the same cannot be said of the *Convivio*. Indeed, I am unaware of any scholars who read it this way. However, as I will show, such a reading is not only supportable but also indispensable to a full understanding of both the autobiographical and the auto-hagiographical dimensions of the *Comedy*.

The purpose of this study is to take a new look at the *Comedy*, a look which hopes to address this surprising void in the criticism. The comprehensive auto-hagiographical reading that I propose requires an awareness of the notion of self in the Middle Ages and the narratology of life-writing at the time of the *Comedy*'s composition.[7] It also requires an appreciation of how the medieval writer and reader perceived the notion of truth and its relationship to biography, autobiography, and hagiography. Most significantly, the reading that I propose requires that we understand how Dante approached these notions and recrafted them for his own purposes. In that regard, although the *Comedy* has been many things to many people, this book attempts to discover what it was to Dante. What I aim to show is that the *Comedy* is, above all else, Dante's story, or more precisely Dante's stor*ies*; the story of his love for Beatrice, and of his political vicissitudes, and of his spiritual evolution.

The first chapter, Life-Writing in the Middle Ages, appropriately, considers the medieval notion of self, as well as the

---

term means biography, but in general it may include autobiography as well, so that it is actually a more inclusive term than biography, even though some people may consider the word biography to include autobiographical works, letters, diaries and the like" (*Life-Writing*, 6).

[7] By *narratology*, I mean how a narrative is constructed, including the particular narrative models and meaning systems it employs.

representation of self in a variety of medieval putative autobiographical works. Concomitantly the first chapter also examines the narratology of medieval life-writing, both sacred and secular; that is, the requirements and the purpose of various life-writing models. In particular, it considers Voragine's *Golden Legend*, selected *razos* and *vidas*[8] of lyric poetry, together with writings by Augustine of Hippo, Abelard, and Suso,[9] and the co-called vision poem. At the same time, this exploration examines the medieval concept of truth and its literary expression, as well as how Dante's *Comedy* engages with these conventions. Given the nature of this study, the issue of whether autobiography existed as a genre in the Middle Ages is inevitable and indispensable. The answer is not a simple yes or no, especially if we think of autobiography in strictly modern terms. Rather this study, albeit brief, of self-expression and life-writing, as well as the purpose of both, considers the extent to which the external reception of a work and the exercise of introspection, both being earmarks of autobiography, mattered to the medieval life-writer. It is within that framework, that I begin my assessment of Dante's own exercises in life-writing.

Chapter 2, Dante's First Life: The *Vita nuova*, takes a close look at one of Dante's earliest attempts at writing his own life, the *Vita nuova*. With a particular focus on the mechanics and purpose of Dante's early literary eclecticism, I consider how and

[8] *Vidas* were short comments providing information about the author or alleged author of a poem or song. According to Paul Zumthor, through the intermingling of text and biographical information, "the interpreter poses an autobiographical reading of the song" ("Autobiography in the Middle Ages?," 42). *Razos* were brief interpretive commentaries intended to clarify the meaning of the poems. Amilcare Iannucci has noted that the "*ragionate cagioni*" of the *Vita nuova* bear a substantial resemblance to the Old Provençal *razos* (*Forma ed evento nella Divina Commedia*, 88).

[9] Suso, *Das Buch von dem Diener (The Life of the Servant)*, trans. Tobin in *The Exemplar*, 61–204.

why Dante emulates a variety of established literary models to recount his falling in love with Beatrice. Specifically, I propose that Dante starts with the framing metaphor of the "Book of Memory," and then adopts a variety of classical literary devices to present himself as an emerging literary presence, as an "*auctor*" in the classical sense. At the same time, I suggest that the *Vita nuova* evinces an early hint of the hagiographical stance that will color the *Comedy*, as Dante incorporates biblical analogy and religious imagery into his narrative to imply that this seemingly earthly love story might have a greater spiritual significance.

In chapter 3, The *Convivio*: Dante as Redeemer, I examine how Dante's *Convivio* engages with the *Vita nuova* as Dante rethinks the role of Beatrice and contemplates the meaning of his exile. As the *Convivio* expands upon the *Vita nuova*, going beyond the confines of the love story to commence Dante's political saga, Dante initiates his attempt at reconciling two disparate aspects of his life, the personal, or solitary, and the communal, or social. This chapter explores how this exercise allows Dante to distill, from his love story and from his political story, a common spiritual significance that establishes affinities between his life and the lives of the saints whose biographies were circulating widely in Dante's time. Although the *Convivio* remained unfinished, I argue that it represents, nonetheless, a crucial phase in Dante's auto-hagiographical project. As Dante continues the auto-exegetical experiment begun in the *Vita nuova*, we see a shift from his early sense that Beatrice is a type of Christ sent to save him, to an emerging awareness of his own salvific purpose. As Dante shifts his focus to a more comprehensive project, one that will encompass all that he has learned through such self-examination, the *Convivio* is abandoned. The break in the *Convivio* thus marks a moment similar to the earlier break in the *Vita nuova* and emulates the shift from "old man" to "new man" in St. Augustine's *Confessions.*[10]

The more comprehensive project is, of course, Dante's *Comedy*, which I consider in chapter 4, A Canticle of *Caritas.* In that chapter, I look at how Dante uses the *Comedy* to reimagine the *Vita nuova* and in so doing, transforms a story of carnal desire into a personal history of sacred love. It considers how the *Comedy*'s framing metaphor of the journey works symbiotically with Augustine's *nunc et tunc* paradigm to facilitate the reconciliation that Dante first attempted in the *Convivio.* As the *Comedy* condenses and retells the story of Dante's foray into the *dolce stil nuovo*, it also reveals Dante's evolving perception of himself as a writer. The *Comedy*, I propose, reflects a self-styled transformation from lyric poet to *auctor*[11] and from psalmist to evangelist, as the "book of memory" opened in the *Vita nuova* is absorbed into the book of the universe that is unveiled in *Paradiso.*

Just as in chapter 4, I looked at how Dante used the *Comedy* to reimagine his love story, in chapter 5, Exile: The Long Way Home, I consider how the *Comedy* effects a similar transformation in Dante's account of his political life. In this penultimate chapter I also examine how the *Comedy* positions Dante's particular political experience within a larger setting, that is, the unfolding of sacred history, to present his exile as a species of martyrdom.

In the epilogue, Dante Legend, I contend that reading the *Comedy* as auto-hagiography presents a much more accurate reading of a work that reflects the *zeitgeist* of the late Middle Ages, which was preoccupied with the relationship of life in the here and now to life in the hereafter. Moreover, Dante's auto-

---

[10] See Casadei, "Incipit Vita Nova," 179–86.

[11] The notions of *auctor* and *auctoritas* will be explored in greater depth below, but, for introductory purposes, *auctor* may be understood as connoting not just authorship but authority.

hagiographical impulse reveals an indomitable fascination with self-examination that will see its full expression in the Petrarchan obsession with self a generation later and that anticipates the humanist thought of the early Renaissance.

As the *Comedy* condenses and retells the story of Dante's literary career, both textually and intratextually, we discern a progression in Dante's perception of his literary significance. In the *Comedy*, for example, Dante critiques the *dolce stil nuovo*, narrates his forays into Aristotelian philosophy, and ultimately celebrates his achievement as a divinely appointed *auctor* whose works will be read by future readers.[12] By presenting his own encyclopedic vision of history, both sacred and profane, Dante is able to critique the lives of sinners and saints alike, and thus position himself as hagiographer. By evaluating his own life in that broader context, Dante simultaneously positions himself as autobiographer. Finally, by presenting his own life as the life of a saint, Dante becomes an auto-hagiographer. The *Comedy*, as a result, becomes the most accurate depiction of the man not so much as he was, but as he would have us read him, specifically, as a "legend."

---

[12] *Par.* 33:70-72: "and make my tongue so powerful that I / may leave to people of the future one / gleam of the glory that is Yours;" [e fa la lingua mia tanto possente, / ch'una favilla sol de la tua gloria / possa lasciare a la futura gente;]

Chapter 1

Life-Writing in the Middle Ages

UNSURPRISINGLY, THE presence of Dante, as both author and protagonist-pilgrim, looms large within the text of his *Comedy*. Dante scholarship is brimming with studies of those episodes that recall real events and people in the poet's life, together with theories as to the significance of the many geographical locators he includes. Notwithstanding their consciousness of these autobiographical aspects, modern scholars have shown a marked reluctance to categorize the *Comedy*, on the whole, as autobiography.

This reluctance is, in large part, attributable to a definition of biography and autobiography according to which the events forming the narrative must be true,[1] meaning that the events or experiences in the narrative occurred in actuality. As a result, much of the discussion in the modern era as to whether the *Comedy* is autobiographical has been co-opted by a debate as to

---

[1] Even those works that might have been considered autobiographical, such as St. Augustine's *Confessions*, differed vastly in structure from what we today might class as autobiography. Indeed, scholars have debated whether autobiography as a genre even existed before the Renaissance. See Paul Zumthor, "Autobiography in the Middle Ages?," for a summary of the unresolved debate.

whether or not the journey of the poet-pilgrim actually happened. Charles Singleton's and Robert Hollander's seminal studies of Dante's allegory framed the debate in terms of which allegorical mode Dante used when writing the *Comedy*; the allegory of the poets or the allegory of the theologians. Both studies focus on Dante's description in the *Convivio* of these two types of allegory and on Dante's statement that he is using the allegory of the poets in composing his poems.[2]

In the *Convivio* Dante tells us that the allegory of the poets uses a literal narrative that is not necessarily actual or historical, which he calls a "beautiful lie" ("*bella menzogna*"). In contrast, the literal narrative of the allegory of the theologians is historical, in other words, actual. In both cases, however, the allegorical meaning of the literal narrative is "true." In both cases, the allegorical truth may be expressed in multiple ways. Christian redemption, for example, could be expressed either by the historical escape of the Jews from Egypt or by Christ's crucifixion. Similarly, descent into the underworld and subsequent resurrection might be expressed by the story of Jonah being swallowed by a whale or by Christ descending into Hell after his crucifixion. Filial obedience found expression equally in Abraham's near sacrifice of Isaac or in Christ's acceptance of his crucifixion.

For the medieval reader, familiar with this kind of expression, events were interchangeable with other representations that might convey the truth of the event with equal effectiveness. Whether one was using the allegory of the poets or the allegory of the theologians, for the medieval reader, the truth of a poem or an account did not hinge on whether the episode had actually occurred. For the modern reader, "true" means actually

[2] *Convivio* II, i, 2-4.

happened (documentable, historical events), but for the medieval mind, "truth" signified that an event or assertion had meaning determined by God, that it was genuine, a revelation of truth, not an attempt to deceive. While this fluidity of image to express meaning has its roots in the biblical exegetical tradition, this signifying strategy was also used in theological prose and religious poetry.

From this perspective, the mere "implausibility" of the events described in the *Comedy* ought not to prevent us from reading them, as the medieval reader might have, that is, as "true." When Dante introduces the framing metaphor of the "the road of our life," he is not proposing that the reader contemplate whether the "road" is real.[3] Rather, he is forging a connection between two signifiers, giving the reader a clue as to the meaning of the work.[4] By taking an image that had long been used to signify one's lifespan, Dante tells us that what follows will be a life story. The reader is expected to know and accept the polysemy of the "road." In this signifying scheme, life is not merely *like* a road, it *is* a road. A road and a life have the same meaning. They share characteristics. They start. They have forks and curves. And ultimately, they end. Since the meanings are interchangeable, so too is their representation.

Within a narrative, meaning is further revealed by the similarity one event shares with other events. Hence, in the *Comedy*, the meaning of Dante's descent into the underworld is revealed and emphasized by its similarity to Aeneas's descent.

---

[3] *Inf.* 1:1: "cammin di nostra vita"

[4] Cesare Segre notes the distinction made by Saussure between "signifiers" and "signified" (or "meaning") and suggests that a narrative may be considered from at least two perspectives. The first is "*discorsivo*," in which the narrative is considered as a "signifier," and the second is in terms of contents, i.e., what is meant by the narrative, the signified (*Le strutture e il tempo*, 3). It is in this second sense that I use the term "signifier."

Since Aeneas's descent was revelatory, the reader can expect that Dante's descent will be also. At the same time, the similarities that Dante's descent bears to Christ's descent signals that Dante's event will, like Christ's, have redemptive value. It may be that Dante's revelation and redemption resulted from an actual event not described in the *Comedy*, but since actuality is of little importance to the truth of the medieval narrative, there is little need for Dante to include his actual experience. Instead, it is the adherence to an established pattern that enhances the truth of an episode.

Moreover, the fact that Dante's descent into the underworld has strong literary echoes of Aeneas's ought not to diminish the weight of Dante's account.[5] Quite the contrary—in Dante's time, Virgil's account of the founding of Rome, the *Aeneid*, was considered history,[6] and the revelatory power of a descent into the underworld was a given, so the similarities between Dante's journey and Aeneas's enhance the truth of Dante's revelation. The timing of Dante's journey to parallel Christ's descent into Hell and subsequent resurrection has the same effect.[7]

Although Dante clearly knew the distinction between actual and non-actual literal narratives, Singleton's statement "the fiction of the *Divine Comedy* is that it is not fiction," is not a necessary conclusion. Hollander, like Singleton, assumes that when Dante says his literal level is true, that Dante means "true" as in historical or actual.[8] Hollander concludes that Dante's insistence that the literal level is true is simply a ruse on Dante's

---

[5] For a thorough examination of the literary echoes of Virgil in the *Comedy* see Hollander, "Le opere di Virgilio nella *Commedia* di Dante," 247–343.

[6] Comparetti, *Vergil in the Middle Ages*, 202–203.

[7] The journey of the *Comedy* takes place over the Easter Triduum.

[8] Robert Hollander's gloss on Singleton's article, in which he concludes

part to gain broader acceptance of the poem's allegorical meaning.

While some scholars, including William Franke, have taken less categorical approaches to the question, the long entrenched conclusion that the literal narrative of the *Comedy* is a fiction essentially precludes its reception by modern scholars as autobiography.[9] Even more to the point here, focusing on the issue of the "truth" of the literal narrative unnecessarily detracts from a consideration of the autobiographical aspect that is rooted in the allegorical level of meaning.

Similarly, modern scholarship's inquiry into whether or not the *Comedy* is autobiography rarely takes full account of the multitude of signifying strategies used by medieval writers to write "true" life stories,[10] yet the use of commonly understood shared signifiers to represent a particular and idiosyncratic moment is an important feature of many medieval life-writing models.[11] Associating events from the author's life with events

that the *Comedy* is a "fiction which demands to be treated as literal truth," has been equally entrenched in Dante scholarship ("Dante's Poetics," 405).

[9] William Franke sidesteps the issue, noting that the discussion is ultimately fruitless given that the question of the truth of the *Comedy* comprises so many further questions. Is it a true story? Does the narrative relating Dante's journey through the three realms of the world to come purport to be literally true and so to be a historical account? Was Dante a prophet? Is his poem inspired? Is it supposed to be a true revelation of a metaphysical order of being or of an eschatological dimension of existence? And these formulations cover only what might be termed "religious truth", whereas the poem certainly has no less pretensions to disclosing philosophical, psychological, social, existential, etc., truth and truths, although a powerful compulsion to unity in Dante's Christian, semiologically centred universe would make all these appear as facets of the poem's Truth. ("Reader's Application and the Moment of Truth," 261)

[10] There are, of course, a few exceptions that I discuss throughout this study.

[11] Certainly, it can be argued that this continues to be the case. When

that have pre-existing meaning helped readers interpret the meaning of that life. Consequently, the departure from the confines of historicity or actuality as a narrative mode augmented the medieval biography or autobiography, elevating it from mere chronicle to didactic instrument.

The opening moments of the *Inferno* become more comprehensible when we bear this signifying strategy in mind. As Dante locates himself in a dark wood and then likens himself to a shipwreck survivor, we understand that he is describing his own experience—autobiographically—and expressing it as an event that others may have experienced as well. The modern mind understands and catalogues this mode of expression as "metaphor," but the modern reader makes a distinction between metaphoric and actual that the medieval reader did not. In essence, the modern reader does not equate the metaphoric representation with the event. For the medieval reader, however, events and their representations were easily conflated, as events themselves were considered mere representations of further meaning and were rarely considered as being limited to a specific time and space.

Dante's signifying strategy reflects this perception and ensures that his journey will serve not only as the story of his life but also as a lesson for others who are lost or who have only barely survived a catastrophe.[12] Moreover, Dante's choice of

---

an autobiographer, for example, says, "And so I was led to my Calvary...," we do not expect that the author was physically taken to a hill in Israel. Instead, we understand that the author believes himself to have been unjustly punished.

[12] In a similar way, the ninth-century English king Alfred, in the preface to his translation of St. Augustine's *Soliloquies*, describes himself as a forester cutting timbers in the wood of ancient knowledge. Presenting his task as physical labor, Alfred says, "Then I gathered for myself staves and props and bars, and handles for all the tools I knew how to use.... the fairest pieces of timber, as many as I could carry. I neither came home with a single

signifiers tells us both how Dante imagined himself and how he would have others imagine him and his life story.[13]

Singleton and Hollander, if I may be so bold, have unnecessarily restricted themselves to Dante's statements in the *Convivio* and in his *Epistle to Can Grande*.[14] Indeed, it seems that Hollander was so fixated on whether Dante considered himself a *poeta theologus* or *theologus poeta* that he did not consider the possibility that Dante did not restrict himself to the genres described in the *Convivio*, a work, it is important to note, that he abandoned. While Dante was certainly concerned with how historicity or actuality related to truth, confining the truth claims of the *Comedy* to a debate about which form of allegory the poet was using is unnecessarily limiting. Such a narrow approach fails to examine the extent to which Dante was familiar with and exploited a variety of biographical and autobiographical models to tell his own story. Concomitantly, it ignores the constant experimentation with genre and form in which Dante

---

load, nor did it suit me to bring home all the wood, even if I could have carried it." Further along in the preface he also uses an image that we find in the *Comedy*: "enlighten the eyes of my mind so that I can find out the straight road to the eternal home" (Brooke, *From Alfred to Henry III*, 48). See also Augustine, *King Alfred's Old English version of St. Augustine's Soliloquies*, 1–2.

[13] Giuseppe Ledda has recently begun to delve deeper into this aspect of the *Comedy*. Significantly, Ledda uses the term "autobiography" to explore "the modes Dante employs to speak about himself." Under the general term "autobiography," he includes not only all references to his real life, but "also the representation of the self as the protagonist of the poem, a character who undertakes a journey through the afterlife, during which he is ordered to put into a book all that which has been shown and revealed to him; and finally, the representation of the self as a poet engaged in the verse narration of this transcendent experience" ("Truth, Autobiography and the Poetry of Salvation," 251).

[14] Epistle XIII, *Epistole*, https://dante.princeton.edu/pdp/epistolae.html.

was engaged. Dante's explicit statements at the start of *Purgatorio*, that he is navigating better (and therefore, different) waters,[15] that he is resurrecting long dead poetry,[16] are clear signals of the experimental nature of the *Comedy*. Similarly, Dante's recognition in *Paradiso* that something in him has changed,[17] and that writing this new experience presents a considerable challenge, confirms that he was not prepared to restrict his *magnum opus* to a single form.[18] Indeed, Dante's entire *Comedy* is about newness: a new vision of the world, a new vision of poetry, and his own transformation from "old man" to "new man."[19] As such, it can be seen as much a continuation of the

---

[15] *Purg.* 1:1-3: "To course across more kindly waters now / my talent's little vessel lifts her sails, / leaving behind herself a sea so cruel;" [Per correr miglior acque alza le vele / omai la navicella del mio ingegno, / che lascia dietro a sé mar sì crudele;]

[16] *Purg.* 1:7-9: "But here, since I am yours, o holy Muses, / may this poem rise again from Hell's dead realm; / and may Calliope rise somewhat here," [Ma qui la morta poesì resurga, / o sante Muse, poi che vostro sono; / e qui Calïopè alquanto surga,]

[17] *Par.* 1:67-68: "within me I was changed / as Glaucus changed," [tal dentro mi fei, / qual si fé Glauco,]

[18] *Par.* 2:7: "The waves I take were never sailed before;" [L'acqua ch'io prendo già mai non si corse;]

Peter Hawkins's incisive study of Dante's engagement with a broad spectrum of sources examines the breadth of sources that Dante used to craft his *Comedy*, including the biblical canon, the ancient Latin poets, and Christian authorities such as Augustine and Benedict (*Dante's Testaments*, 111–14). See also Simone Marchesi who notes the amalgam of sources inherent in Dante's invocation of Apollo in the opening canto of *Paradiso*.

Par. 1:13-15: "O good Apollo, for this final task / make me the vessel of your excellence, / what you, to merit your loved laurel, ask." [O buono Appollo, a l'ultimo lavoro / fammi del tuo valor sì fatto vaso, / come dimandi a dar l'amato alloro.]

[19] In *Inferno* 26, Ulysses's voyage takes him to the brink of a "new land"; *Inf.* 26:137: "la nova terra." See also Dennis Looney on W. E. B. Du Bois's

Vita nuova and its autobiographical impulse as an opportunity to expand upon it.[20]

If we consider the *Comedy* is this regard, we must, I would argue, consider what use Dante makes of several other genres of life-writing with which he was clearly familiar: the *vidas* and *razos* of lyric poetry, the vision poem, the religious autobiography, and hagiography. When we do so, we find that Dante has amalgamated many of the elements of all of these while revisiting his earlier attempts at writing about his own life.

Let us start then, with the *vida* of the lyric poetry tradition. *Vidas* were short comments providing information about the author or alleged author of a poem or song. Through the intermingling of text and biographical information, "the interpreter poses an autobiographical reading of the song."[21]

Razos were brief interpretive commentaries intended to clarify the meaning of the poems. Both the *vida* and the *razo* take the form of a gloss, an "add on," as it were, to the text. Iannucci has noted that the "*ragionate cagioni*" of the *Vita nuova* bear a substantial resemblance to the Provençal *razos*.[22] In the *Vita nuova*, however, it is Dante himself who provides the annotation, becoming his own biographer and his own exegete. I will discuss this in further detail in the chapters that follow, but here we should note that in the *Comedy*, while the *vida* and the

---

view of Dante as a "protohumanist who prepares the way for those who follow," and who is at the vanguard of a "new vision of the world" (*Freedom Readers*, 68).

[20] Michelangelo Picone notes that of all Dante's works, the *Vita nuova* is the one most often categorized as autobiography ("La *Vita Nuova* fra autobiografia e tipologia," 59). This willingness to characterize the *Vita nuova*, as opposed to the problematic "vision" of the *Comedy*, as autobiographical, exemplifies the tendency to restrict autobiography to those works that recount "actual" events.

[21] Zumthor, "Autobiography in the Middle Ages?," 42.

[22] Iannucci, *Forma ed evento nella Divina Commedia*, 88.

razo components are still extant, they have been transformed. No longer external to the poem, details about the poet's life and the exegetical instructions are now embedded within the poem. Thus the author himself is transformed into autobiographer and auto-exegete, controlling how the life of the pilgrim is presented and how it is to be understood.

Additionally, in the *Vita nuova* Dante expands the scope of the *vida* and *razo* beyond lyric poetry, as he begins increasingly to experience and record the visions that form much of the work. As the poet transcends his identity as a mere *jongleur*, he begins more and more to insert himself into the vision poem tradition. While we may look to Piero Boitani's study of the dream vision for a full understanding of the genre, it suffices here to note that the vision or dream poem recounts a "penetration of the human spirit into a realm beyond the confines of ordinary experience, into a dimension where one discovers absolute truths and ontological realities, which appear only in veiled form in the sensible universe."[23] Most significantly, the dream or vision always carries an important message from the author to his audience. Boitani emphasizes that "nearly always there is a prophecy to be extracted and decoded."[24] Moreover,

---

[23] Boitani, "Dream and Vision," 71.

[24] Boitani provides a superb summary of the dream vision, defining it as a genre in which a dream or vision constituted the framework, in form and substance, of the work of art. It was inherited from the classics and from Scripture: the "Somnium Scipionis" in Cicero's *De Re Publica* and the commentary on it by Macrobius, the visions of Ezekiel, Paul and John, and Alain de Lille's *De Planctu Naturae* are examples of a tradition that did not die out until the end of the Middle Ages. The vision and the dream are artifices whereby the artistic ego can speak to the reader through two voices that may be quite different—that of the poet and that of the dreamer. These modes generally indicate a penetration of the human spirit into a realm beyond the confines of ordinary experience, into a dimension where one discovers absolute truths and ontological realities, which appear only in veiled form in the sensible universe. In the dream there is always an

as early as the first sonnet of the *Vita nuova*, "A ciascun'alma presa, e gentil core" ("To all besotted souls") Dante attributes to his dreams, in particular to his morning-dreams,[25] a prophetic quality. As Charles Speroni has pointed out, we gather from the prose commentary to this sonnet that the dream came true.[26]

In the *Convivio*, Dante continues to assert the prophetic quality of our dreams, stating that in them we see "continual proof of our immortality in the divinations of our dreams."[27] In the *Comedy*, Dante's assimilation of this genre is even more pervasive and includes five allusions to the morning-dream. Two

---

> underlying seriousness, which is not entirely cancelled even by a relatively light-weight subject. The vision always carries an important message from the author to his audience; nearly always there is a prophecy to be extracted and decoded. The genre is so elastic that, in the course of its development in the Middle Ages, it was not limited merely to themes of philosophical discussion, the experience of the other world and the mystic or apocalyptic vision. (Ibid., 71)

[25] *Vita nuova*, Chap. I: "Gia eran quasi che atterzate l'ore / del tempo che onne stella n'e lucente, / quando m'apparve Amor subitamente." [Already nearly over by a third were all those hours lit up by stars till morning, when Love appeared before me without warning.] Unless otherwise noted, all Italian citations are taken from the De Robertis edition, and all English translations are taken from the Frisardi translation.

[26] Speroni, "Dante's Prophetic Morning-Dreams," 51. *Vita nuova*, Chap. III, 15: "Lo verace giudicio del detto sogno non fue veduto allora per alcuno, ma ora e manifestissimo a li pi'u semplici." [The correct interpretation of my dream was not understood by anyone at first, but now it is clear to even the most simple-minded.]

[27] *Convivio* II, viii, 12-15: "Moreover, we see continual proof of our immortality in the divinations of our dreams, which we could not have if there were not some immortal part within us," [Ancora, vedemo continua esperienza de la nostra immortalitade ne le divinazioni de' nostri sogni, le quali essere non potrebbono se in noi alcuna parte immortale non fosse,]. Unless where otherwise noted, English citations from the *Convivio* are taken from the Lansing translation. All citations from the *Convivio* follow the Cudini edition unless otherwise noted. The translation follows Lansing, again, unless otherwise noted.

such references are found in the *Inferno*: in the invective against Florence at the beginning of the canto of Ulysses (*Inf.* 26:7-9), and in the episode of Count Ugolino (*Inf.* 33:26-27, 37-39, 43-45). The other three occur in *Purgatorio*: in the description of the pilgrim's awakening at the door of Purgatory (*Purg.* 9:13-20), in the dream of the "stuttering woman" (the *femmina balba*, *Purg.* 19:1-7), and in Dante's dream of Leah (*Purg.* 27:91-9.)[28]

By structuring the narrative of the *Comedy* as a vision poem and including references to prophetic dreams in all three of his autobiographical works, Dante does several things. First, he situates his story within a belief system shared by his readers.[29]

---

[28] Even so, while Dante's earliest commentators, familiar with the dream vision as a genre, approached the *Comedy* in this way, modern scholars have continued to conclude that the literal level is a conscious fiction. Theodolinda Barolini's assessment essentially concludes that Dante is using the "allegory of the poets." Although Dante cloaks "a truth in the guise of what appears to be a lie, or what Dante calls "*un ver c'ha faccia di menzogna*," Barolini argues that this "should not in any way detract from that truth." In her opinion it is merely a rhetorical device:

> Dante self-consciously used the means of fiction—poetic and narrative strategies—in the service of a vision he believed to be true, thus creating the hybrid he defined a "truth that has the face of a lie"—'*un ver c'ha faccia di menzogna.*' We should remember that the use of rhetorical techniques in the service of a divinely inspired message is explicitly defended by Augustine in the *De doctrina Christiana*, who furnishes examples of Paul's rhetorical prowess. (Undivine *Comedy*, 11)

Only Bruno Nardi explicitly denies that the *Comedy* is a literary fiction. Nardi, however, believes that Dante would have us receive the *Comedy* as a species of vision: "Chi considera la visione dantesca e il rapimento del poeta al cielo come finzione letteraria, travisa il senso" [Anyone who considers Dante's vision and the poet's rapture to heaven as literary fiction misrepresents the meaning] (*Dante e la cultura medievale*, 392).

[29] See Speroni, "Dante's Prophetic Morning-Dreams," for an overview of the medieval belief in prophetic dreams, including Michael Scotus's and Albertus Magnus's references to the timing of prophetic dreams. For more on the dreams found in *Purgatorio*, see also Basile, "Al mattin del ver si

Next, he links the three works in terms of genre. Most importantly perhaps, these techniques allow Dante to manipulate how his readers perceive him and is thus one of the most effective tools he has for constructing his autobiography. Indeed, in the moments before Dante experiences the final vision of the *Comedy*, St. Bernard says it is time to sleep.[30] Dante is a poet certainly,[31] but he is also a poet who has been endowed with a prophetic dream vision. As such, Dante's claims to truth are much more plausible.[32]

---

sogna," 41–68.

[30] *Par.* 32:139-44: "But time, which brings you sleep, takes flight, and now / we shall stop here—even as a good tailor / who cuts the garment as his cloth allows— / and turn our vision to the Primal Love, / that, gazing at Him, you may penetrate— / as far as that can be—His radiance." [Ma perché 'l tempo fugge che t'assonna, / qui farem punto, come buon sartore / che com' elli ha del panno fa la gonna; / e drizzeremo li occhi al primo amore, / sì che, guardando verso lui, penètri / quant' è possibil per lo suo fulgore.]

[31] In *Paradiso* Dante describes the very poem we are reading, on which he has toiled for many years. He expresses as well his hope that the poem might help him return to Florence as a poet and there put on the laurel crown.

Par. 25:1-9: "If it should happen... If this sacred poem— / this work so shared by heaven and by earth / that it has made me lean through these long years— / can ever overcome the cruelty / that bars me from the fair fold where I slept, / a lamb opposed to wolves that war on it, / by then with other voice, with other fleece, / I shall return as poet and put on, / at my baptismal font, the laurel crown;" [Se mai continga che 'l poema sacro / al quale ha posto mano e cielo e terra, / sì che m'ha fatto per molti anni macro, / vinca la crudeltà che fuor mi serra / del bello ovile ov' io dormi' agnello, / nimico ai lupi che li danno guerra; / con altra voce omai, con altro vello / ritornerò poeta, e in sul fonte / del mio battesmo prenderò 'l cappello;]

[32] Those, such as Giovanni Boccaccio, who followed Dante's instructions to look beneath the veil of the literal narrative (see *Inf.* 9:61-63 and *Purg.* 8:19-21) would surely have understood that the story beneath the veil was autobiographical. Boccaccio's "Life of Dante," the *Trattatello*, represents an attempt at interpreting the vision in the context of life-writing, but, as

It is notable also that Dante's assertions of truth are often coupled with his claim that he saw the thing being described.[33] This "seeing" thus becomes the central event in this "Life of Dante" and continues the visionary stance of the *Vita nuova*, in which Dante also "sees." Since the action of the *Comedy* consists of Dante "seeing," the central experience of the *Comedy* purports to be actual. And indeed, he *saw* these things, even if only in his poetic imagination. In structuring his narrative as a species of vision, Dante ensures that the veracity of the *Comedy*'s literal level cannot be disputed.

As Dante assumes the stance of visionary, avowing that he "saw" these things, he also insinuates himself into the ranks of the medieval visionaries familiar to his readers. Further, the apocalyptic nature of Dante's vision forges affinities between himself and John of Patmos, the putative author of the book of

---

Karen Gross notes, Boccaccio also writes as if he were composing a hagiography of Dante ("Scholar Saints and Boccaccio's *Trattatello in laude di Dante*," 66).

Gross also lists other critics who have made the same observation. Certainly, Boccaccio understood that vision the formed the narrative of the *Comedy* was a major event in the life of Dante. Moreover, Boccaccio, in recounting the anecdote of the two women of Verona, clearly intends his readers to believe that Dante's readers accepted the literal narrative as true. We know, of course, from the *Decameron* and the story of Ser Ciappelletto that Boccaccio was skilled in fabricating hagiographies. It is, therefore, not clear whether that is what he was doing with his "Life of Dante." (I shall leave that question to Boccaccio scholars.) What we can glean from this, however, is that Dante's *Comedy* resembles a vision poem, that the meaning of the vision might be understood as autobiographical, and that life recounted in the autobiography bore many affinities to the hagiographies that circulated broadly in the fourteenth century.

[33] For example, *Par.* 22:109-11: "more quickly than your finger can withdraw / from flame and be thrust into it, I saw, / and was within, the sign that follows Taurus." [tu non avresti in tanto tratto e messo / nel foco il dito, in quant' io vidi 'l segno / che segue il Tauro e fui dentro da esso.]

Revelation. Then, as Dante moves through the various realms of *Paradiso*, conversing with the saints, he positions himself as well, as one of them. Just as in the *Inferno* Dante included himself in the "splendid school" of the great writers of antiquity, here in heaven, he equates his life story with the "lives" of the saints.[34] As Dante's journey transforms him from lost sinner to exemplum of conversion, he follows an *iter* found in religious autobiographies (such as St. Augustine's *Confessions*), which was central to many of the biographies of saints circulating widely in the Middle Ages.

Variously called "lives" of saints or miracle stories, these biographies consisted of single stories or collections, such as the *Golden Legend* compiled by Jacobus de Voragine, and presented models of how a fledgling Christian might eventually ascend to heaven. In this respect, the life of a saint functioned as a travel guide or itinerary for the Christian on the road of life. The identity of the saint being celebrated is important, but the road map charted by the life of that saint is even more important. In the hagiographical model, events do not need to be verifiable to serve this function. Rather, they are found to be true by virtue of their capacity to provide the readers with an example to follow.[35] Hagiography thus used the life of the saint to lead sinners to God, by showing how God worked his will through that life.

---

[34] *Inf.* 4:94: "bella scola"

[35] As James Fraser notes, the

> celebration of a saint through devotional writing developed as a Christian literary phenomenon in Late Antiquity as an extension of the traditional *laudatio*, a partisan eulogistic biography inspired and shaped by *pietas*, the author's sense of duty. The primary object of the hagiographer's *pietas* was not the saint, of course, but God. Hagiography sought to venerate above all else his supreme power and majesty (made manifest through his having worked his will through the saint) and benevolence (in having inspired and empowered the saint to live a life of Christian goodness). ("Hagiography," 103)

It is not unusual then to find in the religious biographies and autobiographies, events that were experienced by someone else, rather than by the subject of the work. This phenomenon highlights again the essential difference in how "truth" is defined in medieval and in modern life-writing. It also complicates the question of whether autobiography existed as a genre in the Middle Ages. For the modern reader, the use of the first person carries the expectation that the events narrated have been experienced by the "I" recounting them.[36] In the Middle Ages, however, the use of first-person narration did not automatically signal that the events narrated should be understood as having been experienced by the narrator. The modern conception of the use of first-person narrative, particularly in the context of autobiography, has been so conditioned by the modern notion of selfhood and introspection, that imagining that "I" could actually refer to someone other than the narrator seems both ungrammatical and intellectually dishonest. For a narrator to recount, for example, that he was given certain privileges when in fact the privileges were granted to someone else seems inconceivable and inexplicable to the modern mind.[37] In the Middle Ages, however, such appropriation of actual events was commonplace because of the convention whereby such techniques were recognized as revelations of truth.[38] As Leo

[36] In his detailed discussion on the role of the narrator in narrating, Gerald Prince acknowledges several possible variations in first-person narration. Nowhere in his discussion, however, does he suggest that the narrating "I" might narrate events (using the first person) that were experienced by another (*Narratology*, 7–16).

[37] In the *Manuale de mysteriis ecclesiae*, Pierre de Roissy borrows so heavily from the twelfth-century *Poenitentiale* of Robert of Flamborough that he claims to have enjoyed certain dispensation privileges that were granted to Flamborough (Spitzer, "Note on the Poetic and Empirical 'I,'" 414).

[38] Anthony Cassell refers to these conventions as a "narratological

Spitzer has pointed out, "in medieval narrative, the notion of what we might call 'literary plagiarism' was commonly extended to include autobiographical facts which could not possibly apply to the author of a particular work."[39]

At first glance, the appropriation of the experiences of others might appear to be an extension of the process of appropriating narrative patterns found in other works. But, it is more than that. It is a genuine attempt to tell the events of someone else's life as if they were the author's, not simply to propose a relationship between two lives. Though the practice is related to the conception of "truth" as discussed above, it is probably more an aspect of the medieval sense of self which was profoundly different from that reflected in modern autobiography. In the Middle Ages, the self was given far less importance than it is in the post-Renaissance consciousness,[40] so its study was not considered to be a worthy subject except to the degree to which it might lead to a better understanding of God.[41] How-

---

grammar" ("Santa Lucia as Patroness of Sight," 72).

[39] Leo Spitzer cites three examples in particular: Pierre de Roissy's *Manuale de mysteriis ecclesiae*, Juan Ruiz's thirteenth-century *Libro de Buen amor*, and Marie de France's twelfth-century *Espurgatoire S. Patrice.* In the last of these, Marie substitutes her "I" for that of the monk whose work she was translating ("Note on the Poetic and Empirical 'I,'" 414–19).

[40] Arthur Melville Clark, for example, notes the marked paucity of "formulated aspirations" in the Middle Ages and suggests that where they did exist, they were "not of a kind to stimulate the individual's sense of individuality" (*Autobiography*, 26).

[41] Why medieval literature did not deal with the individual but was more concerned with humankind can only be answered with reference to sociological, psychological, and political factors, which do not form the basis of this book. According to Roy Pascal, in the Middle Ages, "the chaotic and violent unpredictability of life could scarcely be reduced by an individual to a meaningful coherence," which Pascal sees as the central defining characteristic of autobiography (*Design and Truth in Autobiography*, 25). Clark adds

ever, while medieval literature was not concerned with the experiences of the individual per se, it was interested in the individual experience as it related to the rest of mankind,[42] that is,

---

that the Renaissance and Reformation saw a "reaffirmation of individuality, which, though accepted in theory by the Church, had in practice been subordinated to ecclesiastical authority, to the fixed social gradation of feudalism and to the rigid castes of guild and community" (*Autobiography*, 31).

We can see early indications of this conception of individual worth in the writings of St. Augustine, which were so influential in the formation of theological and psychological thought in the Middle Ages and whose influence on personality is apparent in Dante, Petrarch, and Chaucer, in what Eugene Vance calls the "tension between the moral obligation to remember universals and the temptation to indulge in particulars" ("Augustine's *Confessions*," 12). For Augustine, the latter is a useless exercise and leads away from the truth, which is that God's meaning for us is found only in those things that are universal and common to us all.

[42] While Evelyn Birge Vitz suggests that this tendency can be traced to earlier classical biographies such as Suetonius's early second-century *Lives of the Caesars*, she nonetheless sees the influence of Christianity as the most significant contribution to this type of autobiography (*Medieval Narrative*, 18). As she suggests, the men who wrote about human nature, the faculties, and the appetites were primarily theologians whose basic concern lay not with individuation but with salvation and damnation, "the rise and fall of souls, their vertical movement in relation to God." Vitz sees this basic orientation as having pervaded almost all medieval thinking about human character and change. "Psychological movement is either exaltation or abasement (and abasement—humiliation—on *one* axis can be directly tied to exaltation on *another*); it is progress or regress: 'super-gress' or 'sub-gress.'" In particular this model was followed in the writing of the lives of Saints who were venerated not because of how different they were from the rest of humanity, but how high above humanity, how "super human" they were (19).

As Georges Gusdorf notes, the

> conscious singularity of each individual life is the late product of a specific civilisation. Throughout most of human history, the individual does not oppose himself to all others. He does not feel himself to exist outside of others and still less against others, but very much *with* others in an interdependent existence that asserts its rhythms everywhere in the community. No one is rightful possessor of his life or his death. Lives are so thoroughly

how it might stand as an exemplum for others. We may, therefore, conclude that consciousness of external reception was as integral to the medieval life-writer, as was the exercise of introspection.

More important than the view of an individual as separate from others was the view of the individual as one more piece in a great cosmic puzzle. The interpretive aspect of medieval autobiography, therefore, served two purposes: first, to determine the meaning of one's life in the grand scheme of the universe and, in particular, within God's divine will; second, to show how it might have meaning for others and how it might provide instruction to the members of its audience. Ironically, the diminished importance of self, as well as the implicit proscription against self-interest and the requirement that literature address more universal concerns, results in an expanded sense of "I" in medieval literature, one which contrasts enormously with the restricted conception that commonly exists in modern narrative. Thus, in the same way that a lack of historicity did not detract from the truth of the autobiography, whether the event described happened to the narrator or to someone else has equally little impact on the story's didactic value. What it does affect, however, is the breadth of application. Where an author is required to recount events that are uniquely his, it becomes a more difficult task to find a universal application. The freedom to appropriate events, however, broadens the selection process and permits the author to select events that convey a true meaning and may serve the exigencies of exemplum.

St. Augustine's *Confessions* demonstrates this combination

---

entangled that each of them has its center everywhere and its circumference nowhere. ("Conditions and Limits of Autobiography," 29–30) of a genuine attempt to interpret the meaning of the author-narrator's life in the context of God's divine will and, at the same time, to use that interpretation as a teaching device from which others might learn. What distinguishes *Confessions* from traditional sermonizing and, according to Spitzer, moves it into the realm of autobiography is that rather than drawing wholly on Scripture to explain God's truth, Augustine follows the general precept he often preached: "Go not out of doors; rather return into thyself; in the inner man dwelleth truth."[43] For those who espouse the modern definition of autobiography, this focus on introspection leads to a ready acceptance of Augustine's book as truly autobiographical. Roy Pascal, for example, notes the fact that it "could only have been written by the man engaged," that is, by the man who experienced the narrated events.[44] More important to Pascal than the fact that many of the events and feelings are such that only St. Augustine would know them is the fact that "it is only he who could link them and create out of them a coherence and growing intensity of meaning; only he could shape out of them the coherence of his moral personality."[45]

Pascal, however, ignores the subtle distinction that makes Augustine's work so clearly medieval as opposed to modern. The attempt to make sense out of the events is a mere precursor to the goal of finding a universal application for particular events. Augustine uses events that are uniquely his because they fit the requirement that the events narrated must have universal application. He uses his own events because they embody the

[43] "Do not go outside, the truth dwells in the interior of the soul" [Noli foras ire, in interiore anima habitat veritas] (Spitzer, "Note on the Poetic and Empirical 'I,'" 417). Augustine's *Confessiones* was likely written between AD 397 and 400.

[44] Pascal, *Design and Truth in Autobiography*, 71.

[45] Ibid., 23.

meaning he wishes to convey. But the use of his own events as the referent for a meaning that will have a universal application is incidental and is really a matter of choice. Augustine's events are not included simply because he experienced them, nor are they included primarily so that he can understand and tell his life story. Rather, he understands and tells his story, which has universal application, so that it may be used as an example of God's meaning. Augustine's interest in his life as an individual lies in his attempt to define that individuality as a reflection of God's will and in his attempt to see God's pattern in his life. Augustine is not looking to discover how he is different from other men. He is not looking to see what drives him and how his particular circumstances shaped him into the man he became. Augustine looks at his life instead in an attempt to see God's plan for him, to see the meaning, the sense of the events that occurred before he was graced with hindsight, not the meanings he thought they held before, but their "true" meaning as revealed by God after Augustine's conversion.

Because the events that Augustine chooses are mostly events from his own life, it is often difficult to see the extent to which his work is quintessentially medieval. However, as Eugene Vance observes, "in the *Confessions* the self is merely a 'contingent signifier'; the deictic 'I' a purely 'grammatical' sign pointing to an order of written signs identical with history."[46]

---

[46] Vance, "Augustine's *Confessions*," 13. As Vance also points out, there is in Virgil's *Aeneid* a long self-narrative "that can only have served as a poetic model—rather than as an example—for Augustine's *Confessions*" (14). He is referring to Aeneas's narrative of the fall of Troy in the court of Dido, which he calls an "auto-scopic narrative whose sincerity moves its audience" (14). Given Augustine's self-professed love of Virgil's work, it is not unreasonable to believe that Augustine knew this passage well. His use of it then as a model is not so much a borrowing but a recognition that the lesson of Virgil can also be learned from his own writing. As Vance says, Virgil shows us not

There are instances, for example, in which the reader discerns events and details that recall the lives of others. Augustine's conversion taking place in his thirty-third year, for example, may have been a fortuitous coincidence with Christ's age at crucifixion but could just as easily have been a fabrication intended to enhance the "truth" of his story. If Augustine repeats the lessons of earlier authors, appropriates their models to do so, or borrows elements from the lives of others, it is to serve the function of medieval autobiography, to seek meaning in one's life, inasmuch as it forms part of a universal truth. The likeness a work bore to another work would enhance its truthfulness as we have seen above. The likeness was also in keeping with a manner of self-definition that is highly prevalent in medieval autobiography, that is, the attempt to define oneself in terms of likeness to others. What gave a work credibility was its conformity to an established pattern. Yes, it should be better, it may even surpass the model work, but it ought not to deviate from recognized patterns.

A better example is perhaps the autobiography of Peter Abelard, the twelfth-century French cleric, in which the exemplary purpose is more pronounced.[47] As Evelyn Birge Vitz observes, "Abelard is not primarily narrating...he is speaking to others." The work raises no questions nor doubts about the author's past or present motivations or his nature nor is there any

---

only "the inherent dangers of epic (and perhaps Homeric) narrative by suggesting that epic actually nurtures violence within those cultures whose order its discourse purportedly preserves, but he shows us, just as importantly, the futility of man's attempts to know his own nature through his actions in history" (15). This is precisely the lesson being taught by Augustine.

[47] Pierre Abailard (Peter Abelard, 1079–1142) wrote *Historia calamitatum*, the story of his adversities, sometime in 1132 or soon after (Radice, trans., *Letters of Abelard and Heloise*, 25).

discovery of "who I am" through writing.[48] Abelard looks instead, to his place in the greater scheme of things and seeks "to understand the *meaning*—in an allegorical, or figural sense—of his life."[49] Abelard aims to teach his newly learned lesson to others by associating the meaning of his life with theirs.[50] At the same time Abelard typifies the medieval tendency to perceive oneself in terms of similarity to others, not in terms of individual distinction. Abelard, according to Vitz, never presents his philosophical or theological arguments as original, unusual, and different—only *better*: "His mind, his logic are not different, only greater than those of his adversaries."[51]

Abelard, like so many other medieval autobiographers, aligns himself continually with historical, biblical, and literary figures and often quotes, not what he said on any given occasion, but his own quotation of some warrior, saint, or philosopher.[52] Abelard, like Augustine, does not see himself or his life as *unique*, but rather *comparable* to other great men and their

---

[48] Abelard's life story then is aimed, not at expressing his innermost motivations and sense of self-worth, but at affecting his reader. Vitz says this is literature not of *ex*pression but of *im*pression and notes that Abelard is making of himself a sort of type: "He is delivering a sermon with his own life as the exemplum from which the lesson is to be learned" (*Medieval Narrative*, 33). The artistic impulse behind medieval autobiography could, therefore, be said to be the anticipated reception rather than the purging effect of self-expression.

[49] Ibid., 32–34.

[50] Vitz notes that Abelard "associates himself with his reader as the *destinataire* of his own sermon" (ibid., 34).

[51] Ibid., 12–13.

[52] Vitz refers to this as the "fascinating tendency of the Middle Ages and even, paradoxically, of medieval autobiography to be much less interested in the individual and his experiences and reactions, than in the time-honored experiences of all men—or rather of the great men and models from the past" (ibid., 19).

respective lives.[53] This convention leads to the mutability of form in the representation of the exemplum. It becomes especially pronounced in the religious autobiographies of the Middle Ages wherein the "religious experience is largely dissociated from the specific personality" and rapidly becomes accepted in the genre.[54] The life story of Frate Salimbene presents still another example of this tendency; he recounts personal experience in the form of episodes from the lives of the saints or associating personal experiences in his own life with significant historical events.[55]

Spitzer's suggestion that we must assume that the medieval public saw in the "poetic I" a representative of humankind is, therefore, tenable. According to Spitzer, the medieval listener would know that when a poet said "I," he was not necessarily referring only to himself.[56] Dante's juxtaposition of the first-person singular and plural in the first line of the *Comedy*[57] may,

---

[53] Ibid., 25.

[54] Pascal, *Design and Truth in Autobiography*, 24. See also Maddalena Carrasco, who notes the importance of conformity to a "standard formula" in the writing of saints' lives ("Sanctity and Experience in Pictorial Hagiography," 37–38).

While Carrasco's observations are made with respect to pictorial hagiography, her comments are equally valid in terms of narrative concepts. As Roland Barthes notes, "Among the vehicles of narrative are articulated language, whether oral or written, pictures, still or moving, gestures, and an ordered mixture of all those substances; narrative is present in myth, legend, fables, tales, short stories, epics, history, tragedy, *drame* [suspense drama], comedy, pantomime, paintings (in Santa Ursula by Carpaccio, for instance), stained-glass windows, movies, local news, conversation" ("An Introduction to the Structural Analysis of Narrative," 237).

[55] The Italian Frate Salimbene de Adam, also known as Salimbene da Parma (1221–1287), wrote the *Cronica*, his life story, in Latin sometime between 1280 and 1287 (Guglielminetti, *Memoria e scrittura*, 29).

[56] Spitzer, "Note on the Poetic and Empirical 'I,'" 421.

[57] *Inf.* 1:1-2: "In the middle of the road of our life, I found myself in a

therefore, be read as representing a metanarrative recognition of this understanding.[58] Where the first-person narrative was intended to teach, the empirical existence and experience of the narrator could have little interest except to emphasize that the narrated events did happen to an actual individual, who could just as easily have been the listener. The result, says Spitzer, is that the medieval public was interested only in the representative role of the poet. The listener was only concerned about the poet or writer to the extent that such poet or writer could represent the listener. Therefore, if an author borrowed someone else's events, it was of little consequence, since it "was a trifling matter who the empirical person behind this 'I' actually was."[59]

Because of the primacy of meaning over actuality and the relative unimportance of the individual qua individual, whether something happened or not was, therefore, not as important as what was to be learned from it. The Blessed Henry Suso, for example, presents himself explicitly as "an example of God's will."[60] Although Suso describes the stages of his spiritual growth as historical events, they appear more as exemplary devices than as actual occurrence and, according to Pascal, have significance "chiefly because they may be applied by others."[61]

---

dark wood," (translation mine) [Nel mezzo del cammin di nostra vita / mi ritrovai per una selva oscura,]

[58] According to Prince, "when the subject of a discourse is narrative, we may say that the discourse is metanarrative." He goes on to suggest that there are a number of ways in which discourse can be said to be "metanarrative." For example, "a particular narrative may refer to itself and to those elements by which it is constituted and communicated" (*Narratology*, 15). It is in this sense that I use the term "metanarrative."

[59] Spitzer, "Note on the Poetic and Empirical 'I,'" 416.

[60] *The Life of Blessed Henry Suso by Himself* is based on a late–fourteenth-century manuscript and probably was written between 1360 and 1365 (Suso, *Life of Blessed Henry Suso by Himself*, v).

[61] Pascal, *Design and Truth in Autobiography*, 25.

Medieval autobiography, not surprisingly then, tended to portray many experiences in terms of archetypes, to roll all experience into a greater picture and to see all of the events of one's life relative to the greater story of humankind. When speaking of himself, the writer was expected to transform himself "esthetically and morally, into a symbol of humanity as a whole, or at least of an entire class of men."[62] The writer, therefore, was not obliged to recount the actual events that engendered the understanding of his place in the universe. Since the events themselves were merely representative of a greater meaning, he needed only to relate their meaning in whatever symbolic fashion he might choose.[63]

Augustine, therefore, does not recount events simply because they occurred but, instead, because they represent spiritual growth. He treats the characters who populate his life story in a similar fashion so that in this representative mode, his mother is presented more as a symbol than as a real human being. We will see this same tendency in the *Comedy* where events and people are often included *because* of the meaning they convey. Just as medieval individuals did not matter except in terms of how they fit into the grand scheme of things, actual events had little relevance in the Middle Ages beyond the truth they might contain or represent. Accordingly, if a different event was experienced by another individual but shared the same meaning as an event experienced by the narrator, the former could be

[62] Vitz, *Medieval Narrative*, 40.

[63] In the case of the *Roman de la Rose*, a classic example of first-person narrative whose autobiographical value is dubious, human experience was typically presented in what Vitz refers to as "its archetypal aspect, not as an individualized sequence of actual events. From both the ontological and chronological standpoints, the symbolic, exemplary side of things takes precedence over the specific case, which, indeed, is not even represented narratively" (ibid., 40).

appropriated and commandeered at will so as to make the ultimate meaning of the narrated life more intelligible.

Naturally then, the modern definition of autobiography, with its insistence on historicity, often excludes the hagiographic and what I have called the "religious autobiography" models. But this restrictive focus on form over function loses sight of a common element in both medieval and modern life-writing models: the author's quest to determine the meaning of the life that is being recounted. By the time Dante wrote his *Comedy*, the exemplary function of life-writing had become so entrenched in medieval narrative that the writer's own voice was secondary to the initial universal focus of the story. The individual or particular—"I found myself"[64]—is subordinated to the universal in an implicit narrative reflection of the medieval sense of self. The particular is, of course, also a part of the universal, a microcosmic representation of the universal, and the task of the autobiographer is to find what portion of the universal truth his particular life represents and, conversely, how his particular life can be expressed in universal terms.

Universality, not actuality, is, therefore, the essence of truth in medieval life-writing. Sameness and recurrence attest to truth. Divergence from the norm detracted from the truthfulness of events. Accordingly, historicity, as we know it, was not a major determinant of whether a work was considered to be fiction or nonfiction. Consequently, fiction in the Middle Ages was not composed of that which was not actual, but rather, that which did not reflect God's plan and was, therefore, not true. Nonfiction was that which was used to reveal God's plan. As Paul Zumthor points out, "Medieval storytellers did not make

---

[64] *Inf.* 1:2: "mi ritrovai"

as clear a distinction between an account of real events and fiction as did those of other periods."[65]

Despite its insistence on historicity, the modern conception of autobiography is nonetheless cognizant of the autobiographer's necessarily subjective view and the problematic role of memory.[66] In particular, the necessarily retrospective approach of autobiography interprets events in light of subsequent events

---

[65] Zumthor, "Autobiography in the Middle Ages?," 29.

[66] Accordingly, autobiography and even biography have not generally been regarded as "historical." Francis West, in considering whether biography can be treated as history, notes that "biography is apt to be regarded as a branch of literature or literary criticism, rather than as history" (*Biography as History*, 5).

Franke, however, raises several issues that may cause one to reconsider the notion of "historicity" and that, if accepted, might very well justify including autobiography in history. As Franke suggests, "history can never be attained as an achieved fact, over and done with in the past. History always reaches us out of the past through the mediation of an interpretation in the present, an appropriation determined by what is meaningful in a new situation" ("Reader's Application and the Moment of Truth," 270).

Remo Bodei, in considering the issue of the role of time in historic narration, suggests an approach consistent with Franke's thinking. In Bodei's opinion, the narration of history may require a less rigid attention to timelines than that suggested by traditional historians. "La complessità della storia—in particolare del nostro tempo—richiede l'abbandono dei modelli narrativi ed intuitivi, perché deve spiegare fenomeni distanti dal suo comune spesso contro-intuitivi. Le storie sono così processi di trasformazione di sistemi sotto l'azione di stato nell'ambito sistemico, che hanno carattere contingente in relazione al funzionamento del sistema interessato" [The complexity of history—in particular of our time—requires the abandonment of narrative and intuitive models, because it must explain phenomena, far from one's commonplace, often counter-intuitive. Histories are, in this way, processes of transformation of systems underlying the action of the condition in the systemic scope, whose nature is contingent on and related to workings of the relevant system] (my translation) ("Riflessioni sul tempo e gli intrecci temporali," 341–43).

and may not, therefore, see earlier events as they actually were.[67] We must, however, here again differentiate between a modern and a medieval notion.[68] In medieval writing, historicity can also be derived from form, and truth may be revealed precisely through retrospection.

Although after the Renaissance, the reliance on memory inherent in retrospective interpretation is often seen as detracting from the reliability, and, therefore, the historicity of autobiography, in the Middle Ages, memory was afforded much more value. Rather than being the instrument of autobiography's demotion from "history," memory enables us, St. Augustine believed, to gain access to the immaterial essences. These include the highest essence through which a person's own image is to be perceived.[69] For Augustine, memory does have the potential to preserve truth, and autobiography does

[67] As Pascal observes, in "any worthwhile life there is a dominant direction that is not accidental, so that ultimately life is a sort of graph linking experiences" (*Design and Truth in Autobiography*, 17).

[68] Regarding the *Historia calamitatum* of Abelard, Zumthor comments that, although the work is "moral and didactic," it is "centered around events which are composed of controllable elements and can be defined in modern terms as historical" and reveals the modern notion of historicity to be tied to actuality ("Autobiography in the Middle Ages?," 30).

[69] Augustine believed that knowledge of the divine is innate in memory: "Thou has given me this honour to my memory to reside in it; but in what quarter of it are thou resident, that I am considering" (*Confessions* X, [1991] 25-26). Nonetheless, as Vance notes, St. Augustine was aware of the potential of the memory to be subject to contamination of a special sort, given that "the memory may ingest images that originate in sensual experience" ("Augustine's *Confessions*," 10): "The soul has loved these bodies outside of itself by means of the senses of the flesh, and it has become implicated through longstanding familiarity with them" [Et quia illa corpora sunt, quae foris per sensus carnis adamavit, eorumque diuturna quadam familiaritate implicata est] (*De trinitate* X, v, 7). One must, therefore, be careful in choosing between the truthful memory and the contaminated recollections.

have the potential for historicity. In his *De ordine*, Augustine notes the connection between grammar and history, suggesting that historicity is tied to the worthiness of the writing.[70] Accordingly, the modern arguments against characterizing autobiography (or for that matter, biography) as history simply cannot be applied to medieval life-writing.[71]

---

[70] Perhaps not surprisingly these, like truth, are derived from form. Augustine, for example, sees grammar as the fruit of reason in language and believes that grammar also serves as "the basis for an aesthetic order that can be free of error" (Vance, "Augustine's *Confessions*," 12). From *de Ordine* (English translation by Eugene Vance based on the original text and the French translation of that edition):

> But since its very name [grammar] proclaims that it professes letters,—hence, it is called "literature" in Latin—it resulted that whatever was committed to writing [*litteris*] as being worthy of memory necessarily passed into its domain. Thus to grammar was added the discipline of history, which is a single yet many-sided word, one which includes an infinity of things fuller of cares than of enjoyment or truth, and which is more burdensome for grammarians than for historians themselves. (Book II, 12, 37)

> Poterat iam perfecta esse grammatica sed, quia ipso nomine profiteri se littera clamat—unde etiam Latine litteratura dicitur—factum est, ut, quicquid dignum memoria litteris mandaretur, ad eam necessario pertineret. Itaque unum quidem nomen, sed res infinita multiplex curarum plenior quam iocunditatis aut ueritatis huic disciplinae accessit, historia non tam ipsis historicis quam grammaticis laboriosa. (Book II, 12, 37)

[71] Lewis Namier contends that biography ought not to be considered as "history" because biographers feared the "unbounded fields of history and preferred the boundaries of a single life." Namier's suggestion, therefore, is that biographers are not capable of "big picture thinking." Secondly, Namier suggests that the lack of professional standards for biographers might disqualify biography from the title of "history." Once again, however, this reflects that the modern definition of truth is based on provability and actuality. Concomitant with this objection, Namier suggests that biographers lack the necessary psychological qualifications to assess and interpret the acts of individuals. Thirdly, Namier suggests that biographers can "pick and choose among their subject's papers to illuminate the single human being, unlike the historian who must use all of the evidence and look at the lives of many

Inasmuch as the *Comedy* bears many of the earmarks of medieval life-writing projects, it can, I would argue, legitimately be categorized as autobiography. Its significative strategies, borrowing of events and imagery associated with other "lives," together with its function as an exemplum, are commensurate with medieval life-writing models. More than this, the conversion narrative of the *Comedy* borrows substantially from the hagiographical tradition.[72]

We understand, however, that this borrowing is not attributable to a simple lack of originality on Dante's part nor should it detract from the historicity of his account. Rather, it

---

men" ("History," 160–62).

[72] John Freccero submits, for example, that Dante looks to Augustine for much of his imagery and for many of his motifs, noting striking similarities between the Prologue scene in *Inferno* I and Augustine's *Confessions*. He points out that both writers experience thwarted attempts at conversion and that both experience the descent into humility as a necessary element of redemption. As well, the frequent use of wings imagery throughout the *Comedy* can be associated with Augustine's writings on the journey of the soul being associated with flight (*Dante*, 15). Similarly, the allegories of flight used throughout the *Comedy* extend as far back as Plato and Ulysses, according to Freccero, who says that "Autobiography is represented schematically in Dante's poem by this synthesis of Platonic allegory with traditional biblical motifs, just as it was in St. Augustine's *Confessions*" ("Introduction to *Inferno*," 173). Antonio Mastrobuono takes issue with this assessment of the *Comedy* in a detailed critique of Freccero's *Poetics of Conversion*. In response to his own question ("Are we to regard Dante's entire spiritual autobiography as essentially Augustinian in structure as Freccero claims?"), he answers with a decisive "Definitely not! Dante's entire spiritual journey is essentially Thomistic in structure" (*Dante's Journey of Sanctification*, 240). Among the many arguments he uses to support his position, Mastrobuono points out that seeing the problem of Dante's conversion in Augustinian terms cannot properly address the issue of Dante's spiritual progress. Freccero's insistence on an Augustinian conversion leaves him only with antinomies to explain the poet's gradual spiritual evolution. Freccero's solution, "a series of conversions," is simply not acceptable to Mastrobuono (238–39).

is merely intentional conformity to medieval convention in which borrowing events from the literary works of others emphasizes the truth and validity of the author's own story. Accordingly, by painting his conversion in a form reminiscent of Augustine's, for example, Dante's story is made more genuine, not less. Form, not actuality, therefore, is what determines truth and, by extension, historicity. Thus we may read Dante's frequent reminders of the importance of form, especially in the *Paradiso*, as giving metanarrative notice of the historicity and value of his work.[73]

Moreover, Dante's choice of which models to emulate suggests very strongly that he saw in his life story a conversion narrative coupled with a salvific purpose. As such, I would argue that Dante goes beyond autobiography and imbues it with a hagiographical aspect, hence auto-hagiography. We know from references in the *Vita nuova* and the *Comedy*,[74] that Dante was

---

[73] *Par.* 1:103-105: "All things, among themselves, / possess an order; and this order is / the form that makes the universe like God." [Le cose tutte quante / hanno ordine tra loro, e questo è forma / che l'universo a Dio fa simigliante,]

Par. 2:70-72: "But different powers must / be fruits of different formal principles; / were you correct, one only would be left," [Virtù diverse esser convegnon frutti / di principî formali, e quei, for ch'uno, / seguiteríeno a tua ragion distrutti,]

Par. 3:79-84: "The essence of this blessed life consists / in keeping to the boundaries of God's will, / through which our wills become one single will; / so that, as we are ranged from step to step / throughout this kingdom, all this kingdom wills / that which will please the King whose will is rule." [Anzi è formale ad esto beato esse / tenersi dentro a la divina voglia, / per ch'una fansi nostre voglie stesse; / sì come noi sem di soglia in soglia / per questo regno, a tutto il regno piace / com'a lo re ch 'n suo voler ne invoglia.]

[74] Cassell, examining the case of St. Lucy, notes the "the medieval tendency to link patronage and iconography to the saint's name." He further notes the "pattern of such legends as that of Saint Christopher as bearer of Christ, Saint Brendan as bearer of a brand or torch, or Saint Maurice as a

familiar with the hagiographical tradition and its attendant iconography. In his letter to Can grande, Dante highlights the didactic purpose of his *Comedy*, a purpose central to the composition of a "life" of a saint.[75] The *Comedy*, therefore, is constituted as hagiography, in both form and function.

As writer and subject of the hagiography, Dante is ideally positioned as self-exegete, a stance not possible where the author is expected to distinguish the recounting of events from his interpretation of them. However, when the actuality of events is not as crucial to the truth of the events as it is in the modern model, the writer can include commentary and interpretation by presenting the commentary, in essence, in the guise of an event. Dante, therefore, is not only writing autobiography but also writing how his autobiography ought to be interpreted. In so doing, he implicitly presents himself as an authority, at very least, with respect to the events that make up his story. Far from detracting from the truth and historicity of the work, the inclusion of commentary and interpretation confirms the authoritative nature of the account and thereby imbues it with historicity.

Dante's impulse is equally autobiographical in the sense that by inserting his life story into the hagiographical tradition,

---

Moorish soldier" ("Santa Lucia as Patroness of Sight," 72).

In *Vita nuova*, Chap. XIII, 4, Dante himself quotes the truism "nomina sunt consequentia rerum" [names are the consequence of things], indicating his awareness of one of the central elements of popular hagiography. One cannot help but note that Dante's own name, an abbreviation of "Durante" ("enduring"), is consistent with the aspiration he articulates throughout the *Comedy*, i.e., that his poetry should endure. For the role of the figure of Veronica in the *Vita nuova* and the *Comedy* as further evidence of Dante's familiarity with the cult of saints, see Vettori, "Veronica: Dante's Pilgrimage from Image to Vision," 43–63. Giuseppe Ledda's article "Truth, Autobiography and the Poetry of Salvation" explores in even greater depth Dante's knowledge of the hagiographic tradition.

[75] Epistle XIII, *Epistole*.

he dictates how he wishes his life story to be received. The expression of his desire to engineer how his life story will be received is the hallmark of autobiographical force. So while writing his life and writing it as the life of a saint, Dante creates another genre to add to the list of means by which life-writing was accomplished in the Middle Ages—that is, through the creation of auto-hagiography.

We may conclude, therefore, that notwithstanding differences in appearance, the *Comedy* is as much autobiography as is the *Vita nuova*. Differences in the form of the two works are attributable to the various stages of personal evolution they represent and to the different models each work emulates. The *Vita nuova* was written earlier than the *Comedy* and, as such, represents Dante's early forays into the world of lyric poetry.[76] Although the seeds of an evolution toward a less "medieval" model may be seen as early as Abelard,[77] the sense of self we find in Petrarch and in subsequent modern autobiographies may be more easily traced to the evolution of the poetic "I" in lyric poetry.[78] In its earliest stages, the lyric poems shared many of the

---

[76] See Prue Shaw's translation of the *Monarchia* for an exhaustive discussion on the issue of dating the *Vita nuova*.

[77] Roy Pascal writes that while Abelard's "ostensible reason for his account is to demonstrate submission to God's will[,] the unconscious reasons are truly autobiographical—to recapture the past, to see his life as a whole, to find within its vagaries its one rapture and the one indivisible personality" (*Design and Truth in Autobiography*, 24).

[78] With Petrarch and the emerging individualism of the humanists, autobiography moved toward the modern model when what Pascal calls "a startling change" came over men's thoughts with regard to themselves (*Design and Truth in Autobiography*, 26). The Renaissance saw for the first time a real interest in "what distinguishes one man from all others; an interest in the unusual, the different, the bizarre, the deviant" (Vitz, *Medieval Narrative*, 20). Pascal considers Petrarch's 1351 *Letter to Posterity* as expressive of a "new direction of interest and self-confidence" and introduces what Pascal

same aspects we saw at play in the religious autobiographies of Abelard and Augustine. For example, while, as Zumthor points out, "In narrative or didactic poems, the author often directly intervenes in the text through an apostrophe to his audience...[the] author's person, then appears in order to confirm the objectivity of the text—nothing more."[79] As Zumthor reminds us, "because of the transmission mode of these poems, mouth to ear, the speaker could always change and so if the author (who is perhaps one of the successive reciters) has made of the *I* the subject of the statement, then this *I* functions as a potential form whose actualization depends on the circumstances." Zumthor concludes, therefore, that it was unlikely that such poetry would have been interpreted in an autobiographical sense.[80] As was the case with Abelard's or Augustine's first-person accounts, in the early lyric poetry, since the poetic "I" is not

calls the theme of "untroubled concern for the inward dimensions of the self, springing not from any external necessity, self-defense or whatever it might be, but from a compulsion to meditate upon oneself" (*Design and Truth in Autobiography*, 26). By the fifteenth century, the poetic "I" had become more closely tied to the protagonist of the work in question and was so closely linked in the mind of the listener to the "exterior subject which these circumstances implicitly indicate" that there no longer existed an impediment to the "I" being identified with the person of the author.

[79] Zumthor, "Autobiography in the Middle Ages?," 31.

[80] In the case of the "grand chant courtois," observes Zumthor, "the absence of a perceptible referent for the *I*, as well as for narrative sequences, prohibits the introduction of the notion of autobiography" (ibid., 32). Zumthor also points to the use of "I" in the *pastourelles* and in Guillaume de Lorris's *Roman de la Rose*, suggesting that in the former the "spoken narrative merges grammatically with the act of enunciation itself. But is clear that the narration of which I is the subject in no way involves the story of a person." In the case of the *Roman de la Rose*, he says that the "I" has the "same nature as the personifications (*Doux regards* or *Courtoisie*), and for this reason he participates in the game with them; both the I and the personifications form the base of a metaphorical, universal and abstract meaning" (34–35).

constrained to signify an empirical narrator, the writer is similarly free to emphasize meaning to the point where events as actual occurrences have little value. However, as Zumthor observes, with the poet's gradual movement toward inclusion of himself in the text, vernacular poetry began to take on certain autobiographical aspects. Similarly, a late twelfth-century variant of the *grand chant courtois*, in which a series of songs were linked so as to suggest a linear succession of events,[81] lent itself easily to the perception of lyrical poetry as possibly autobiographical. At the same time the "*grands chants courtois*" were more and more frequently accompanied by *vidas* and *razos* to produce an intermingling of text and biographical interpretation. Ultimately, toward the end of the Middle Ages, what Zumthor calls "a narrative reconstruction of the lyrical statement with the 'I' taken seriously" came into being.[82] Symptomatic of Dante's lyrical stage in his writing career, the *Vita nuova* likely owes its form to this development, as opposed to the more spiritually focused Augustinian model with which the *Comedy* is frequently associated.

Given the divergent aims of what I shall call the "lyric" model and the "Augustinian" model, it is logical that both models would also exhibit differences in the use of the poetic "I." In the *Vita nuova*, the "I," while reminiscent of the Augustinian detachment of narrator from protagonist, is "hierarchically double," referring at once to an omniscient narrator and to the per-

---

[81] The twelfth-century troubadours Raimond de Miraval and Uc de Saint Circ composed a set of songs "linked by an artificial sequence of their dominant themes" so that the "fictitious references" constituted, "in linear succession, a kind of novelistic schema." The montage thus permitted the simulation of an "*aventure*" and created what Zumthor describes as a "projection into measurable time of successive and differentiated acts" (ibid., 36).

[82] Ibid., 43.

son whose memory evokes the moments of its own past existence.[83] The use of "I" in the *Comedy* is more akin to the "I" in the Augustinian model in which, according to William Spengemann, the narrative mode is "grounded ultimately in the conviction that the retrospective narrator can see his life from a point outside it, that his view is not subject to the limiting conditions of the life he is recounting."[84] Augustine's perspective is not so much one of hindsight (although temporally that may be the case) rather, Augustine contemplates past events from the perspective of what Spengemann calls "the point of immutable truth."[85] In the *Vita nuova*, Dante relocates the Augustinian perspective from somewhere outside that life to a point within the life of the narrator, taking the narrator from a "timeless ground above the protagonist's life to a point further along in the time of that life."[86] Dante's narrator in the *Vita nuova*, despite his claims of a "new life," remains temporally and spatially in the "here and now" as opposed to Augustine, who would have us believe that he has existentially altered his state of being and whose perspective is, therefore, one which should not be measured temporally or spatially along a mundane continuum. Augustine attempts to surmount the paradox that one cannot truly write autobiography until one's life has ended by suggesting that his conversion in essence has brought about a death of his former self. In his conversion, Augustine has begun a new life and

[83] Ibid.

[84] While the past self, the protagonist, can see each event in his life only in its everchanging relationship to a past which is being continuously reshaped by the addition of new experiences in the present and to future expectations, which experience is continually revising, the narrator can see each past event in its fixed relation to a past which has presumably reached its final form" (Spengemann, *Forms of Autobiography*, 7).

[85] Ibid., 6–7.

[86] Ibid., 34.

can look at the former life with the knowledge that comes from seeing a completed picture; he is able to assess events' proper weight, which are apparent only when a life is viewed in its totality. As Eugene Vance suggests, "the *Confessions* form a dialogue between the converted self and the self-as-other, the *vetus homo* of history."[87] The end of an old life and the start of a new is not only a result of conversion but also an essential element of "true" autobiography.

In the *Comedy*, in *Paradiso* specifically, however, Dante moves beyond the perspective of the *Vita nuova* and fulfils the promise its incipit offers.[88] When the pilgrim looks back to see how far he has come, the contemporaneous existence of "then" and "now" reveals that the removal necessary to review one's life is not so much temporal or linear but existential. Narratively, this perspective runs risks. Pascal speaks of the tendency to "make the line linking the past and present far too exactly continuous and logical" or to rationalize our lives, noting that memory "operates unconsciously to the same end."[89] We will see, however, that Dante, as a poet, was aware of such pitfalls and to a certain extent permits the narrator of the *Comedy* to withhold his ultimate interpretation and present knowledge of the meaning of events, and he instead permits the events to reveal their own meanings until ultimately all meaning is revealed in *Paradiso*. As Iannucci states, "Here, beyond space and time,

---

[87] Vance, "Augustine's *Confessions*," 5.

[88] *Par.* 27:76-78: "At this, my lady, seeing me set free / from gazing upward, told me: 'Let your eyes / look down and see how far you have revolved.'" [Onde la donna, che mi vide assolto de l'attendere in sù, mi disse: "Adima il viso, e guarda come tu se' volto."]

[89] "The consciousness of the outcome of an experience imposes itself on the experience and distorts it," Pascal writes; "the completed fact is substituted for the 'fact-in-the-making'" (*Design and Truth in Autobiography*, 15–16).

all meaning is gathered in and consummated."[90]

The distinction in the perspectives of the *Vita nuova* and the *Comedy* has a series of consequences, the first of which is the tone of narrative vis-à-vis the events of the past. As William Spengemann notes, in the *Vita nuova* Dante tends to view his past life far less harshly than does Augustine. Augustine professes no love for his past sins, but Dante's love of Beatrice "and the actions inspired by her provide the main impetus behind the *Vita nuova*."[91] Dante cannot help but retain some attachment to the events that have brought him to Beatrice. Augustine's events, on the other hand, were in no way conducive to his present position so they can be dismissed more easily. This is not to say, however, that Dante wholeheartedly adopts the Augustinian model in the *Comedy*. Indeed, Dante uses Augustine's model as merely one of many source models to which, as we saw above, he effects a series of revisions, annotations, and additions. Accordingly, while Beatrice's rebuke in *Purgatorio* 30 might suggest that Dante is emulating Augustine's rejection of the past, closer examination shows that the rebuke is not an absolute rejection of Dante's love for Beatrice but a rejection of *how* he loved her. While I examine this aspect in greater detail in the chapters that follow, the distinction is necessary here to show that the *Comedy*, while closer to Augustine's model than is the *Vita nuova*, is by no means a simple regurgitation of Augustinian thought.

Similarly, there are discernible differences in the relation of action to form between that found in the *Vita nuova* and that in the *Comedy*, which cannot be said to be entirely Augustinian. In the *Vita nuova*, the events of Dante's life share some of the value that Augustine had placed almost entirely on form. That is, the

---

[90] Iannucci, "*Paradiso* XXXI," 472.

[91] Spengemann, *Forms of Autobiography*, 34.

action in Dante's *Vita nuova* has a revelatory function. In Augustine's "life" the revelatory function is contained in the form through which the action is presented, that is, in the form of a retrospective.

According to William Spengemann, Augustine's life "only has value when contemplated through the form of truth, and even then, primarily as an example of error" and that "action and form are reconciled entirely on the ground of form."[92] Augustine explains the truth behind the protagonist's errors from his detached position and thereby highlights the distinction between the narrator and protagonist. In contrast, Dante, acting as narrator, allows the form of truth to emerge gradually from the protagonist's experiences, that is, from the action. As a result, the connection between the narrator and the protagonist in the *Vita nuova* is much closer to the modern conception of the poetic "I." In the *Vita nuova*, Dante sees the events as capable of revealing truth, whereas for Augustine, events have a hidden meaning that is only available from the outside perspective. Whether Dante's approach is intentional or not, he is moving toward the notion that a person can know themselves and that a person can interpret their own experiences from within their life. This approach accepts that events have a meaning in themselves as opposed to being meaningless except in what they represent. Later, in the *Comedy*, however, Dante will adjudge the approach of the *Vita nuova* not so much as wrongminded but as close-minded and limiting. Though he accepts Augustine's notion that the greater truth lies in the meaning revealed from a removed state, Dante does not reject outright the "lesser" truth of the actual event.

Finally, the differing perspectives of the *Vita nuova* and the

---

92 Ibid., 26.

Comedy, together with Dante's continuing concern for authentication, contribute to the difference in the representative styles of the two works. In the *Vita nuova* events are considerably less allegorical in their presentation than Augustine's events. In the sense that Augustine denies

> any ultimate spiritual significance to the temporal causal connections among the events of the faithless life, whatever divine meaning any particular event does possess stems entirely from its direct, vertical relation to the absolute truth, not from its place in a horizontal sequence of causes and effects; and that allegorical meaning is supplied entirely by the narrator, who alone is in a position to know it.[93]

For Augustine, all the events of his former life shared a common meaning (that is, that his faithlessness always resulted in error) and therefore were interchangeable.

In the *Vita nuova*, the empirical "I" does have some import, at least more than it does in Augustine's writing. For Augustine, the events of his former life shared the same meaning, so the choice of which events to include was not crucial. In fact, as we have seen above, the events described may not even have been culled from Augustine's own reality. In contrast, for Dante of the *Vita nuova*, the selection process is much more important and consists of selecting those events that were part of the pattern of meaning and dispensing with those that were not. Consequently, the role of editing is essential to the *Vita nuova* and distinguishes it from mere chronicle or journal.[94] The *Vita*

[93] Ibid., 36–37.

[94] Pascal notes that in autobiography as opposed to journal keeping, the autobiographer may revise the journal entry, omit it, or give it an emphasis different from it might have enjoyed when it was written and when its import in the overall picture of his life could not have been assessed (*Design and Truth in Autobiography*, 4).

nuova epitomizes this distinction in its metaphoric representation of the memory as a book written by the protagonist and from which the author now extracts those events that have meaning, copying them along with the necessary glosses into a smaller book he calls a *libello*. Dante, in writing his own *razos*, creates a product that bears some resemblance to the religious strain of medieval biography but, as was suggested above, is much closer to the secular lyric tradition of life-writing.

For Dante, in the *Vita nuova* at least, more than in the medieval minds before him, the events in their actuality and the concurrence of events contain meaning. It is then essential that he include in his account those events that have meaning. Since these events reveal a personal meaning, they cannot be so readily interchanged with events taken from the lives of others.

It is against this backdrop that we must assess Dante's work and the *Comedy* in particular. A product of the prevailing theology and an heir to the poetic tradition that gave birth to the *razos* and *vidas*, Dante, as Zumthor suggests, was aware of the inertia existing in "a language traditionally void of all avowals, of any aim of personal revelation."[95]

While the vision of the *Comedy* is still particular to its author, in it Dante has moved beyond the *Vita nuova* to fashion a narrative that incorporates and fuses a multitude of models to create a story with a broader application.[96] This shift accounts for the inclusion of the commentary within the text of the *Comedy*, the de-emphasis on actuality as the proof of events and, moreover, the move beyond the book of memory, which is markedly individual or particular, and toward the book of the universe. As such the *Comedy* does not closely resemble any of the previous autobiographical models. Rather, by appropriating

---

[95] Zumthor, "Autobiography in the Middle Ages?," 46.

[96] The narrative "I" is definitely linked to Dante. See *Purg.* 30:55-57.

various elements of many other sources, incorporating aspects of the lyric and vision poem traditions, and borrowing from the engrafting innovations of his own, he fashions a uniquely personal hagio-autobiographical model. [97]

The process through which he arrives at the model of the *Comedy* was, not surprisingly, also a gradual one; it was a product of Dante's own personal evolution. Although *Monarchia* and *De vulgari eloquentia* bear the stamp of Dante's personality and reflect the intellectual evolution in his life, it is most obviously in the *Vita nuova*, the *Convivio*, and, ultimately, the *Comedy* where we see Dante chart his own autobiographical path.[98] In these works, where he tries to make sense of the events of one man's life within God's divine plan, the "*sentenzia*"[99] rather than the occurrence, or "*littera*," is paramount.[100]

Even as the *Comedy* attaches importance to the exemplum, Dante is careful not to let the preeminence of meaning eclipse

---

[97] Giorgio Padoan suggests that there are at least three biblical visions that could have acted as models for Dante's vision: the abduction to heaven of St. Paul; the vision that St. Peter, St. James, and St. John had of the transfiguration of Christ; the vision of God's glory experienced by Ezekiel, "examples that in turn are buttressed with references to three authorities on visionary experience, Richard of St. Victor, St. Bernard, and St. Augustine" ("La 'mirabile visione,'" 44).

[98] Guglielminetti associates the *Convivio* with "*la liceità dell'autoritratto intellettuale*," which confronts the problem of "*parlare di se medesimo*" also found in the *Vita nuova* (*Memoria e scrittura*, 73).

[99] As John Freccero observes, "Dante's journey is neither a poetic fiction nor an historical account; it is exemplary and allegorical. Like Augustine's life it was meant to be both autobiographical and emblematic, a synthesis of the particular circumstances of an individual's life with paradigms of salvation history drawn from the Bible" ("Introduction to the *Inferno*," 179).

[100] According to Zumthor, the biographical "reality" is not the most important element in the *Vita nuova*; rather it is the "*sensus*" which prevails over the "*littera*" ("Autobiography in the Middle Ages?," 43).

the literal story being told. Barolini, for example, notes the great concern Dante had with authentication. Further, it is impossible to overlook the realism that emerges throughout both the *Vita nuova* and the *Comedy*. Eric Auerbach has written substantially on the issue of historicity and historical truth and the concomitant connection to realism and has drawn on the Judeo-Christian tradition to demonstrate examples of narrative that contain "absolute claim(s) to historical truth."[101] Auerbach suggests that, in contrast to the later narratives of the Middle Ages, not only was the meaning of the Old Testament stories "true" but the events occurred in actuality and were also "true." It is to this type of historicity that Dante aspires. Dante has included more details about himself than we have seen in any previous medieval writers, and the result is a greater appearance of truth—truth in the events themselves, not only in their meanings. In the *Comedy*, then, the actual events from Dante's life included in the narrative are not to be distinguished from archetypes or from the recall of events that befell others before him; rather, they should be viewed as enhancements, intended to add to the apparent historicity and reliability of Dante's message. Dante, it seems, is not content to rely exclusively on any single medieval model to authenticate the meaning of his life but expands his scope to include scriptural narrative patterns. For Dante, the events, not just their meaning, must also be authenticated and the actuality of his narrative confirmed.[102]

As a poet, Dante is much more adept at representing the

[101] Auerbach, *Mimesis*, 11.

[102] Dante's truth claims, coupled with his descriptive mode, have given birth to a whole debate as to the "truth" of actuality of the events described in the poem. Barolini, in commenting on the genesis of the debate, suggests that those who first propounded a view of the literal sense as a poetic construct may have done so to protect Dante from the charge of heresy (*Undivine Comedy*, 6).

revelatory and interpretive process than many of his models. The initial obscurity of the meaning of the *Comedy*'s prologue, for example, is only gradually elucidated through a variety of methods such as the echoing of its imagery and through allusion to it in subsequent "parallel episodes."[103] In this way, Dante addresses the difficulty noted by Pascal: "The greatest problem of autobiography is that the autobiographer is not relating facts, but experiences." Moreover, as Pascal notes, while autobiography must include "the meaning an event acquires when viewed in the perspective of a whole life," it must also give some of the other possible meanings, such as an aberrant meaning because the autobiography will be an "artistic failure if the end is assumed from the beginning."[104]

Poetically, Dante appears to have been more concerned with the aesthetics of the text than was Augustine, suggesting that Dante may have been prepared to blur the distinction between teaching and entertainment even if he was not prepared to impose in its place the distinction between fact and fiction. Accordingly, while the *Comedy* may be viewed as a move toward a more theological approach to life-writing than that taken in

---

[103] Iannucci discusses the division within the *Comedy* into "local" episodes and "structurally determining" episodes. The prologue is described as belonging to the latter category and, like other structurally determining episodes, will have its imagery and its significance repeated throughout the *Comedy* in episodes Iannucci calls "parallel episodes" ("*Paradiso* XXXI," 471). Iannucci has also suggested that parallel episodes not only are structurally determinant but also have an exegetical role. Used in the same way as the "parallel passages" or "testimonies" in the Scriptures, these passages are to be interpreted by comparison with others (*Forma ed evento nella Divina Commedia*, 92). This practice of comparing episodes to determine meaning is consistent with, and indeed represents a microcosm of, medieval autobiographical practices, which rely on comparison to other referents for interpretation.

[104] Pascal, *Design and Truth in Autobiography*, 16.

the *Vita nuova*, in many ways the *Comedy* also represents a departure from the traditional medieval autobiographical mode.[105] For example, Dante's adoption of traditional biblical exegetical methods goes beyond merely associating his life story with others from antiquity. Dante looks to hermeneutic methods associated with biblical exegesis[106] to propose that the historical

---

[105] Winslow uses the term "life-writing," which he defines as follows:

> In the narrow sense this term means biography, but in general it may include autobiography as well, so that it is actually a more inclusive term than biography, even though some people may consider the word biography to include autobiographical works, letters, diaries and the like. Life-writing has been used since the eighteenth century, although it has never been as widely current as biography and autobiography since these words came into the language. Some writers may prefer the Anglo-Saxon rooted phrase, life-writing, to those Latin and Greek based words. (Life-Writing, 6)

I have opted to use Winslow's term because it avoids many of the difficulties raised by the connotations attached to the term "autobiography."

[106] Corti gives a concise explanation of this method:

> L'*allegoria in factis* è fondamentalmente avantestuale, in quanto collega due referenti e non, come l'*allegoria in verbis*, due significati testuali: per essa gli episodi dell'Antico Testamento divengono prefigurazioni di episodi del Nuovo, da essa nasce la 'tipologia biblica', che riunisce in una corrispondenza tipologica la realtà storiche: lo storico re David è cosí un typos (*figura*) dell'*antitypus* Cristo. Il collegamento tra prefigurante e prefigurato non è un rapporto di origine retorica, ma divina; non dipende dall'esegeta del testo sacro, ma di Dio emittente dei messaggi, che ha messo in moto la catena dei rapporti fra gli eventi; donde consegue che *allegoria in factis* e *allegoria in verbis* non solo operano a due diversi livelli, della *res* e dei *verba*, ma appartengono a due diversi sistemi di segni: l'*allegoria in factis* è una grande unità di significato che va al di là dell'ambito semantico e ha una particolare funzione ermeneutica nei riguardi del testo sacro. ("Dante e la Torre di Babele," 245–46)

[Allegory *in factis* is fundamentally avant-textual, as it connects two referents and not, like allegory *in verbis*, two textual meanings: for it the episodes of the Old Testament become prefigurations of episodes of the New, from it the biblical typology is born, which brings together historical realities in a typological correspondence: the historian King David is thus a *typos* (figure) of the *antitypus* Christ. The connection between prefiguring and prefigured is not a relationship

value of his own narrative equals that of the Old and New Testament episodes. In this way, Dante's actuality, the source for the narrative, becomes the fulfillment of history and reveals, typologically, the "true meaning" of the *Comedy*.[107]

Dante also looks to epic poetry as a model for the *Comedy* and, as he did with other models, revises and amends it to serve his own project. The famous encounter with the poets of antiquity in *Inferno* 4 demonstrates a poetic impulse parallel to the spiritual impulse that drove Abelard and Augustine. However, while Augustine and Abelard assess themselves in terms of comparative saintliness, Dante's episode assesses himself in comparison with other poets. Dante has, therefore, in this case borrowed from the medieval methodology, thereby enabling himself to take his place amongst the poets of the past rather than merely paying homage to them.

Concomitantly, Dante follows the Augustinian model in that he takes great pains to present his poetic 'I' as a representative of humanity. Spitzer suggests, however, that Dante does include elements of his empirical personality (his feeling, speak-

---

of rhetorical origin, but divine; it does not depend on the exegete of the sacred text, but on the issuer of the messages of God, who set in motion the chain of relationships between events; whence it follows that allegory *in factis* and allegory *in verbis* not only operate on two different levels, of the res and verba, but belong to two different systems of signs: allegory in fact is a great unity of meaning that goes beyond semantic field and has a particular hermeneutic function with regard to the sacred text.] ("Dante e la Torre di Babele," 245–46)

[107] Barolini notes, for example, that in *Purgatorio* 29, John the Evangelist agrees with Dante on a visionary detail—"not the other way around!" (*Undivine Comedy*, 8). Barolini's observation acknowledge that in the *Comedy* the episodes of the Bible are used to buttress the truth of Dante's story as much as Dante's story buttresses biblical truths.

ing, gesticulating personality) in this "I."[108] Spitzer sees both of these aspects as necessary so that Dante can, on one hand, "transcend the limitations of individuality in order to gain an experience of universal experience" while, on the other, "an individual eye is necessary to perceive and to fix the matter of experience."[109] But Dante's inclusion of his empirical "I" is also necessary so that we know we are reading Dante Alighieri's life story which, despite his adherence to the models of universality, expresses its own meaning as well. The reasons for the imprinting of his empirical "I" on the poetic "I," a deviation from the medieval norm, are tied to his quest for authentication. Iannucci has suggested that the events of Dante's life represent a substantial component in the narrative structure of the *Comedy* and that the work tells the stories of Dante's love for Beatrice, his political vicissitudes, and, finally, of his evolution as a writer.[110]

Understanding form and function in the writing of one's life in the Middle Ages not only confirms Iannucci's proposition but also reveals a *Comedy* in which Dante's life provides the foundation of its entire narrative structure. By making his story the framework on which the other models are overlaid, from which the narrative pattern is fashioned, and from which the allegorical meanings emerge, Dante signals a subtle but important deviation from Augustine, Abelard, and the others. By making his actual life the major source of the *Comedy*, Dante, the writer, has become much more central to his own story than

---

[108] He cites, as an example, Dante "being jostled along in a procession of devils, now ascending toward Heaven magnetically attracted by the eyes of Beatrice" (Spitzer, "Note on the Poetic and Empirical 'I,'" 416).

[109] Ibid.

[110] Iannucci is one of the few who takes this view, suggesting that the *Comedy* is "an episodic work held together by Dante's story," that Dante's own life story is *the* driving narrative force behind the *Comedy*, with *Paradiso* XXXI as the ultimate justification of that life ("*Paradiso* XXXI," 470).

were any of his forerunners. The truth of Dante's stories is buttressed by the *sentenzia* of other lives, not vice versa, making Dante's life *the* exemplum and all others mere reflection.

Chapter 2

Dante's First Life: The *Vita nuova*

ALTHOUGH DANTE MAY not have had the *Comedy* in mind when writing the *Vita nuova*, nor when writing the *Convivio*, there is strong evidence to suggest that the *Comedy* is intended to posit an expanded, or at very least a more clearly defined reading of both of these earlier works. As a result, many aspects of these earlier works inform the signifying strategy and narrative structure of the *Comedy* and contribute to its hagiographical stance. To fully appreciate how the *Comedy* tells Dante's life story, we ought first to consider Dante's earlier attempts at life-writing.

It has been argued that using the *Comedy* to interpret the *Vita nuova* leads to the erroneous conclusion that when Dante wrote the latter, it could not have been fully understood by readers.[1] I would suggest that this is not a necessary conclusion and argue instead that the approach leads to the highly tenable conclusion that the *Vita nuova* could not, when first published, have been read in the way that Dante would later have us read it. In support of this approach, I would argue that the strong presence in the *Comedy* of patterns established in the *Vita nuova* demon-

[1] Dante, *Monarchia*, ed. Shaw, 180.

strates the interdependence of the two works, even if such interdependence was not perceptible when the *Vita nuova* was first published.

The inclusion and expansion of characters from the *Vita nuova* in the *Comedy* direct the reader to reflect upon and reconsider the significance of the earlier piece. Before the *Comedy*, Dante had already begun this process by including in the *Convivio* explicit references to the *Vita nuova* as well as clear attempts at reinterpreting it. Strong echoes of the *Convivio* in the *Comedy* suggest that Dante remained concerned with absorbing and revising his earlier works and then reconciling them within the greater context of the *Comedy*. A comprehensive reading of these "autobiographical" works in which we consider them as related components of a continuum as opposed to independent intellectual exercises would appear to be warranted.

This is not to say that the interpretation yielded by this approach is necessarily the one Dante intended when he first wrote the *Vita nuova* and the *Convivio*. It is, however, consistent with the implicit directive of the *Comedy* that prompts a retrospective interpretation of events and indicates that the first impression may not always be the true one. To understand how the *Comedy* compels a second look at, among other things, Dante's earlier attempts at life-writing, how the *Comedy* absorbs and reinterprets them, we should look first at precisely what he was absorbing.[2]

---

[2] Albert Ascoli addresses this specific issue and suggests that in much of Dante's writing, palinode constitutes "a powerful rhetorical device" that is used "as a tool for historicising Dante's writing career" ("Palinode and History," 26). Iannucci also suggests that Dante's use of palinode has structural implications: "The palinode can be seen in terms of Dante's intertextual strategy. The most recent scholarship on this subject has affirmed that the pattern of evocation and delimitation prevails not only in the interrelation among Dante's own works (and indeed within individual works), but also

Probably a stronger argument against a comprehensive approach is that it can lead to tenuous speculation when a particular work does not appear to conform to a pattern noted in other works. Luigi Pietrobono, for example, noting the differing treatment Dante affords the character of the "*donna gentile*" in the *Vita nuova* and in the *Convivio*, concludes that the *Vita nuova* (or at least the ending) must have been rewritten sometime after the *Convivio*.[3] Proceeding from the assumption that his theory of "*rifacimento*" is correct, Pietrobono goes so far as to suggest that the *Vita nuova* should be read as a prelude to the *Comedy* and that a complete understanding of either can only be gained from reading the other.[4] This conclusion was further endorsed by Bruno Nardi, who agreed that the issue of the *donna*

---

between Dante's texts and his classical and medieval precursors" (*Dante*, xv).

[3] According to Luigi Pietrobono, the two works "Si contraddicono apertamente e sostanzialmente. Accettar per vero e indiscutibile il contenuto dell'una e dell'altro non è possible." [They contradict each other openly and substantially. It is not possible to accept the content of both as true and indisputable.] The greatest difficulty he has arises from the fact that in the *Vita nuova* the love for the *donna gentile* is described as the "*avversario de la ragione*" whereas in the *Convivio* this love "*è la stessa ragione in persona*" (*Saggi danteschi*, 18).

[4] Pietrobono is of the opinion that "Se qualcuno non scorge per qual cagione Beatrice ha una parte cosí conspicua nel Poema Sacro legga *Vita nuova* e lo apprenderà. Se altri non immagina i fini per i quali Dante aveva fatto apparire per breve tempo in terra una giovinetta che per le virtú singolarissime e divine di cui l'aveva insignita ben meritava d'esser chiamata un miracolo, per saperlo ha da fare una cosa semplice, leggere la *Commedia*" [If anyone does not see why Beatrice plays such a conspicuous part in the Sacred Poem, read *Vita nuova* and he will find out. If others do not imagine the purposes for which Dante had made a young girl appear on earth for a short time, who for the very singular and divine virtues with which he had awarded her well deserved to be called a miracle, to find out he has to do a simple thing, read the *Comedy*] (*Saggi danteschi*, 6). This is in sharp contrast to Shaw, who holds that, although many critics take for granted that when Dante was writing the *Vita nuova* he already had the *Comedy* in mind, "there

gentile can be resolved only by concluding that Dante rewrote the ending of the *Vita nuova* subsequent to writing the *Convivio*.[5] Apart from the fact that this theory is unsupported by textual evidence, it fails to consider the distinct possibility that Dante started the *Convivio* in an attempt to effect a revision and to reflect a maturation in his thinking (for reasons I will explore below). That Dante later abandoned the *Convivio* and, instead, returned to and expanded upon the *Vita nuova* in the *Comedy* is evidence only that Dante was prepared to change his mind when his literary project so required. In contrast to Pietrobono's explanation for the apparent inconsistency, this possibility is not only commensurate with Dante's frequent use of subsequent writing to amend or enhance the meaning of an earlier work but also consistent with the textual evidence indicating that the *Convivio* remained unfinished.[6]

The best way perhaps to avoid the disadvantages of both approaches, that is, the comprehensive (Nardi's position) versus the independent intellectual exercise (that taken by James Shaw), is to recognize that the validity of either hinges on the

---

is not evidence to support this assumption" (*Monarchia*, ed. Shaw, 178).

[5] "La fine del *Vita nuova* cui Dante fa esplicito e preciso referimento nel trattato secondo del *Convivio* e che è presupposta dalla canzone 'Voi che 'ntendendo' era una cosa assai diversa da quella che ora vi si legge. Dunque è evidente che Dante stesso ebbe più tarde a dare al *Vita nuova* una conclusione diversa da quella che aveva in origine" [The ending of the *Vita nuova*, which Dante explicitly and precisely refers to in the second treatise of the *Convivio* and which is presupposed by the canzone "Voi che' intendendo," was something very different from what we now read there. Therefore, it is evident that Dante himself was later in giving the *Vita nuova* a different conclusion from the one he originally had] (Nardi, *Dal "Convivio" alla "Commedia"* [1960], 6).

[6] See Zingarelli, *La vita*, 5, on the *Convivio*, and the Petrocchi and Shaw editions, all of which provide substantial philological background on this issue.

purpose for which the earlier works are being examined and the perspective from which such an examination is taken. For the purposes of this book then, mindful of the pitfalls of both approaches, I begin with a review of the *Vita nuova*, independent of its absorption in subsequent projects and look specifically at Dante's intent in writing it and how his methodology serves that intent. In further chapters I will consider the *Vita nuova* in the expanded contexts Dante subsequently creates for it: the *Convivio* and, ultimately, the *Comedy*, with a view to understanding not so much how Dante reinterprets or rescinds certain portions of his earlier story but why he does so.

It is significant that Dante first attempts to order the events of his life by immediately imposing a metaphor. As I suggested above, medieval signifying schemes commonly employed images with pre-existing connotations to express a particular meaning. Dante's use of the image of memory as a book invokes a common medieval mnemonic aid,[7] but the metaphor here is more than a static image, for in the simple act of opening the book of memory, Dante expands the image and transforms it into a structural device. By opening the book, Dante gives it distinct chapters, provides it with content, and effects a transmutation in the memories it safeguards. Until this moment, those memories lay pristine and undisturbed, little more than a chronicle; the pages of the book had been filled with notations

[7] Mary J. Carruthers notes the persistence of the image of the "Book" in connection with memory. "In none of the evidence I have discovered is the art of writing itself regarded as a supplanter of memory, not even in Plato's *Phaedrus*," she writes. "Rather, Books are themselves memorial cues and aids, and memory is most like a Book, a written page or a wax tablet upon which something is written." She goes on to confirm that the "metaphor of the memory as a written surface is so ancient and so persistent in all Western cultures that it must, I think, be seen as a governing model or a 'cognitive archetype' in Max Black's phrase" (*Book of Memory*, 16).

of events and scribblings to commemorate them, unfiltered and devoid of enunciated meaning. By opening the book and transcribing into his *libello*, if not all the words written under the chapter heading "*Incipit vita nova*" (Here begins a new life), then at least what he believes they mean,[8] Dante is claiming the right to review, reinterpret, and essentially reinvent the events that left their traces on the pages of his memory. Now we see only those events selected by Dante, only those events he deems relevant to the meaning he wishes to express. Dante is, therefore, much more than a copyist; while his *libello* may recall the physical appearance of a medieval manuscript (a text, surrounded by a gloss), what we see is not the original book but Dante's rendition of its contents. Rather than an embellished manuscript, the product that emerges in the form of the *Vita nuova* is a rewriting of the original "Book of Memory." More than simple commentary on an existing text, Dante provides a complete overhaul of the source, surveying the events written thus far, interpreting them, and choosing those relevant to the meaning he wishes to convey. It is to this edition that he will add further commentary, including information about both the meaning of the events and the methods he uses to effect this rewriting. The perspective of Dante the copyist / editor is not the same as the perspective of Dante the chronicler who merely recorded events, unaware of their ultimate significance. Such knowledge and insight can be gained only after the events have

---

[8] *Vita nuova*, Chap. I, 1: "In quella parte del libro de la mia memoria dinanzi a la quale poco si potrebbe leggere, si trova una rubrica la quale dice: Incipit vita nova. Sotto la quale rubrica io trovo scritte le parole le quali è mio intendimento d'assemplare in questo libello; e se non tutte, almeno la loro sentenzia." [In my Book of Memory, in the early part where there is little to be read, there comes a chapter with the rubric: Incipit vita nova. It is my intention to copy into this little book the words I find written under that heading—if not all of them, at least the essence of their meaning.]

occurred, only after they have been viewed in the context of other events, and, most importantly, only after the death of Beatrice.

From the start then, we see that the *Vita nuova* reflects the defining characteristic of autobiography (modern or otherwise): the desire to reconcile the events of one's life and find meaning in them. The motivation behind this desire, however, while not immediately clear, can be gleaned from a number of elements, the most telling of which is the particular metaphor that Dante uses to frame his account. In Dante's use of the metaphor of the book, two objects share characteristics and may be understood as representations of the same meaning. Accordingly, Dante is not suggesting his memory is *like* a book but rather that it *is* a book. The distinction is important given that in the Middle Ages, the notion of a book was charged with significance beyond a mere physical description of an object. According to Michelangelo Picone, for Dante to consider a work a "*libro*" or "book," it had to carry the weight of "*auctoritas*," such as that he afforded the Bible or Virgil's *Aeneid*.[9] Not just any writer could produce a book. A book, in Dante's estimation, was the fulfillment of a divine mission to write what will eventually be considered history. Dante's decision to present his readers with

[9] Michelangelo Picone suggests that, in light of the research on the symbolism of the Book in the Middle Ages, Dante would have held the *libro* in high esteem and that for Dante few writings qualified as "Books." The term *libro* for Dante could only have been applied to those writings which imitated divine Scripture ("L'Ovidio di Dante," 108). Comparetti suggests that for Dante, "the history of the Latins begins with Aeneas and goes down to his own time." As Comparetti notes, Dante, as well as his medieval contemporaries, would have afforded Virgil's writings a historicity the modern reader would find unsupportable (*Vergil in the Middle Ages*, 202–203). Again, we ought to bear in mind the notion of truth and historicity as discussed in chapter 1 and recall that historicity was a function of form and reputation and that truth was a result of significance, not of probative value.

what is, in essence, a textual representation of a medieval manuscript clearly signals the reception Dante intended for the *Vita nuova*. Although he refers to the product of the transcription as a *libello*, he nonetheless terms his source document as a *libro*. In so doing, Dante imbues the contents of the source document with a certain historicity and credibility even if they might otherwise appear fictional. Equally important to bear in mind is that by defining the source document as a *libro*, Dante imputes to its writer a parallel elevation in status to that of *auctor*. The metaphor of the book not only establishes Dante as *auctor* but also provides him with a platform from which to expound upon what such status entails; an *auctor* does not confine himself to mere reporting but illuminates the significance of history and its events and rewrites them in accordance with this knowledge.

In rewriting these events, Dante looks predominantly to signifying schemes consistent with his putative status as *auctor*, the most immediately obvious of which is that used in the Bible. Just as in the Bible—the book of all books, written by the Divine Spirit—the allegorical meaning of the literal events of one testament are revealed in another written by the same author; so too is the meaning of Dante's "Book of Memory" revealed in the *libello*, or as Domenico De Robertis suggests, Dante's book of the *Vita nuova* "fulfills" the "Book of Memory."[10] De Robertis implies a relationship between the "Book of Memory" and

---

[10] De Robertis writes,

> O diciamo, nei termini dell'esegesi medievale e di chi li ha felicemente applicati all'opera dantesca, che il libro della *Vita nuova* adempie la figura del 'libro della memoria.' Col che si viene a fissare la natura di quell'altro rapporto, fra poesia e commento: rapporto storico. Dante ci sottopone la sua esperienza come un fatto storico, come esperienza appunto, e la commenta come tale, in termini non astratti o allegorici, ma di realtà vissuta, che pure racchiude un suo significato. (*Il libro della "Vita Nuova,"* 181)

the *Vita nuova* akin to that between the Old and New Testaments, which Erich Auerbach has described as figural. In the case of the *Vita nuova*, however, it could also be said that it "fulfills" the Bible since many of the events described in the *libello* echo events from both the Old and the New Testaments. It is almost as if Dante is writing a third testament in which the literal love story has an allegorical meaning common to all three. The literal text of the *Vita nuova* is a representation, an "*imitatio*" to use Auerbach's terminology, whereas the allegorical meaning, the "*adempimento*" (fulfillment), comprises the true meaning, which is not explicitly recorded in the literal text.[11]

The strategy behind this style with its patterns of imagery lies in the author's literary project. Dante starts with the meaning, the message he wishes to convey, and then uses an event to represent or justify it, thereby crafting the message into the allegorical or "true" meaning of the story. It is for this reason that in the *Vita nuova* the literal narration of events, the guise in which the meaning is cloaked, is clearly not paramount and is ineffectual without a secondary, underlying meaning. For Dante, the descriptive art is a construct, a mere choice of form to be given to a meaning. The continual references to meaning, starting with Dante's invitation in Chapter III to the other poets to explain his dream, can be taken as an invitation to his readers to do the same. The omission of the actual description

[Or let's say, in terms of medieval exegesis and those who have happily applied them to Dante's work, that the book of the new life fulfills the figure of the 'book of memory.' , between poetry and commentary: historical relationship. Dante submits his experience to us as a historical fact, precisely as an experience, and comments on it as such, in terms not abstract or allegorical, but of lived reality, which also contains its own meaning.] (*Il libro della "Vita Nuova,"* 181)

[11] In his essay "Figura," in *Studi su Dante*, Auerbach discusses this relationship at length, contrasting *figura* with *fulfillment* and suggesting a parallel relationship between *imitatio* and *veritas*, and between the literal level of meaning and the allegorical meaning in biblical exegesis (206).

of events such as Beatrice's death further suggests that meaning can be conveyed independent of the events. The importance of finding the underlying significance of what is written is so crucial to Dante that, as in the case of the repetition of the number nine in connection with Beatrice, he takes special pains, where the relation of the form to the meaning might be somewhat obscure, to ensure that we know what the signifiers represent.[12] At the same time, his inclusion of these dreams links the *Vita nuova* to the biblical dream and the dream vision traditions.

Notwithstanding the primacy Dante affords the allegorical meaning, the written narrative is remarkably realistic in its detail. The setting is realistic, and the characters, though stylized, are exceptionally human; the incident of the *gabbo* described in Chapter XIV, for example, has the same mimetic qualities as many of the biblical incidents noted by Auerbach in his pivotal work *Mimesis*. The purpose of such presentation is reasonably simple; it is necessary for the establishment of *auctoritas*, but how Dante accomplishes this is novel and complex.

If we bear in mind that what Dante presents as the allegorical meaning of the literal narration is, ironically, the actual progression of the events in Dante's literary evolution, we see that he has somehow inverted actual and figurative reality. We see this process on a smaller scale in Dante's use of the metaphor of the book, but it also pervades the entire work. The first step in the process is seen in Dante's visual representation of the *incipit*, which takes the reader away from the traditional ambit of likeness-based imagery and into a whole new sphere of representation. Dante does not say his mind is like a book; he says his mind is a book. To prove it, he shows us a part of what that

[12] In Chapter XXIX, 3, Dante explains the significance of the various confluences of nines in the Universe and in Beatrice's life and concludes that "she was a nine, that is, a miracle" [ella era uno nove, cioè uno miracolo].

book looks like. What is particularly significant in this approach is that it is the complete antithesis of the modern process where actual events are expressed as the literal narrative and their deeper meaning is expressed through metaphor, simile, and other devices. Dante transforms the actual events into what we might consider a figure of speech, and this figure of speech is presented as the literal narrative. From that literal representation the reader then culls the "figurative" meaning.

This process provides the foundation for much of the narrative structure of the *Vita nuova.* As in the case of his memory, likened to a book, Dante's literary progression is likened to his love for Beatrice and the turns it takes in the literal narrative. Rather than present the book or his love story as simile, he presents them as the reality, and the meaning from which he started becomes the hidden truth, or the allegorical meaning. Similarly, in Chapter XXIV where Dante recounts seeing Giovanna, Guido Cavalcanti's lady love, walking in front of Beatrice, rather than simply express an opinion which has its existence in actuality, Dante presents it as a narrative event. With this episode, Dante expresses his opinion that Guido is a mere precursor whom Dante will surpass as a writer.

While the literal narrative of the *Vita nuova* may have occurred in actuality and thus, may be "true," the allegorical level is also "true," for it contains both the meaning of those events and the message that Dante intends to convey. A further aspect of this significative scheme is the coincidence of the three roles of exegete, author, and protagonist. While the coincidence of the latter two roles is what moves the work into the autobiographical field, the presence of the first bears witness to the emphasis Dante places on self-exegesis.[13] This emphasis exemplifies the intention underlying the more obvious linear, temporal

[13] Iannucci, *Forma ed evento nella Divina Commedia*, 88.

movement of the narrative that purports to be Dante's story, and it is the form of this exegetical exercise, as much as its content, that expresses the meaning Dante takes from the events. As Picone has noted, the *Vita nuova*'s prosimetric form recalls Ovid's *Remedia amoris* and reiterates the affinity Dante hopes to forge between himself and the classical *auctores.*[14] The form can, therefore, be seen as another means of expressing the historicity of the work and the concomitant status of its author.

At the same time, the resemblance that the form bears to the *vidas* and *razos* of lyric poetry affirms the life-writing purpose of the work. The two readings are complementary as the latter provides an apparently actual accounting of the events that spawned the poetry, just as the former enhances their historicity. Accordingly, the exegetical form suggests the events not only happened but are also "true" in the medieval sense. It is this dual function of the narrative that must be understood before we can make sense of Dante's portrayal of the characters within the *Vita nuova* and of Beatrice in particular.

For Kenneth McKenzie (and James Shaw after him) "[t]here can be no reasonable doubt that Dante's Beatrice was a real woman."[15] Other scholars have spent long hours in search

---

[14] Picone, "L'Ovidio di Dante," 111.

[15] McKenzie, for example, offers the following logic in support of his argument that Beatrice was real:

> "We must remember that the Troubadours wrote about real ladies, not abstractions. Many realistic incidents in the *Vita nuova* were certainly derived from personal observation, and have no point unless they actually happened—a funeral, a wedding, the passage of a group of pilgrims on the way to Rome, etc. The scene is evidently laid in Florence, although the name of the city is not mentioned. In some cases Dante makes a special effort to have the circumstances conform to his scheme, as when he uses three calendars to connect the number nine with the death of Beatrice. If he had invented the story, he would have made the details conform to his scheme without such devices, just as he would have carried the symmetrical

of the historical Beatrice as if the truth of her historical existence would somehow answer the question of how Dante intended she be perceived. What is more important than her actuality, as Hollander has pointed out, is "Dante's treatment of her as actual."[16] Perceiving Beatrice as actual is essential to the perception that was she was divinely created. While the inclusion of purportedly actual events encourages an autobiographical reading, such a reading in turn ensures that the significance of Beatrice's divinity is associated with Dante himself. Beatrice's actuality precludes her from being merely a creation of Dante's imagination and instead confirms that her presence in Dante's life was the will of God. Just as the Bible and the *Aeneid* speak with authority because their events were divinely willed and their authors divinely inspired[17] so too does the *Vita nuova* recount similarly inspired events. So too is its author charged with the same important mission to interpret and rewrite these events in a manner that reflects their revealed meaning.

If Beatrice were simply presented as an ideal, a literary construct, both the historicity of the event and Dante's *auctoritas* would be compromised. Let us not forget that the greatest witness we, as readers, have that the Beatrice described in the *Vita nuova* was an actual person is Dante himself. Dante places her in the book of his memory and thereby imbues her existence with historicity. At the same time that

---

arrangement out more uniformly if he had composed all of the poems together. No satisfactory explanation can be given of many details, except on the supposition that they were real." (Dante, *La Vita Nuova*, ed. McKenzie, xviii)

Such thinking, however, does not allow for the possibility that Dante was likely a keen observer of human behavior with an eye for details. The incidents he described may very well have happened but not necessarily in the way he describes them, in the order in which he places them, or even to those described therein. See Shaw, *Essays on the* Vita Nuova, 163.

[16] Hollander, *Studies in Dante*, 21.

[17] See Comparetti, *Vergil in the Middle Ages*, for an examination of Virgil's reception the Middle Ages.

Dante incorporates Beatrice into his visions, he also locates her on the streets of his city and in people's homes. Dante, as author, also goes to considerable pains to ensure the veracity of the story. Just as later in the *Comedy*, Dante will admit that sometimes truth looks like a lie; in Chapter II, he recognizes that his story may be perceived as "*fabuloso*," or a "tall tale." Cleverly, Dante's inclusion of this recognition of his readers' doubt serves as an assertion of its actuality.[18]

Dante's lady, unlike the poetic object of so many of his contemporary lyric poets, would not be perceived, therefore, as some ideal construct formulated in the mind of the poet; instead, she would be seen as actual and imbued with meaning that can be revealed to Dante alone and only by reading her signs. Dante's status as *auctor* comes not from his being able to describe his lady love but in being chosen to receive her blessing and in being divinely inspired to interpret God's will at work in her. At the same time, Dante's presentation of Beatrice as actual in no way precludes her having allegorical significance.[19] Just as

---

[18] *Vita nuova*, Chap. II, 10: "Since dwelling on the passions and actions of one so young is like telling a tall tale, I will leave that behind; and passing over many things that could be copied from the same source, I come to words written in my memory under larger paragraphs" [E però che soprastare a le passioni e atti di tanta gioventudine pare alcuno parlare fabuloso, mi partirò da esse; e trapassando molte cose le quali si potrebbero trarre de l'essemplo onde nascono queste, verrò a quelle parole le quali sono scritte ne la mia memoria sotto maggiori paragrafi] (34, 35).

[19] De Robertis notes this apparent duality of Beatrice as both a poetic object and an historical reality: "La personificazione della Filosofia sarà pienamente assunta nel *Convivio*, ne contrassegnerà il movimento ispiratore; ma per esser distrutta proprio come 'persona' drammatica. Beatrice, invece, è figura e presenza reale: una realtà poetica, beninteso, che non ha nulla che fare con la sua eventuale identità storica, ma che implica una fede assoluta nell'oggetto..." [The personification of Philosophy will be completely fulfilled in the *Convivio*, of which it will mark its inspirational movement; but to be destroyed as a dramatic "character." Beatrice, on the other hand, is a real figure and presence: a poetic reality, of course, which has nothing to do with her eventual historical identity, but which implies absolute faith in

the events of the Bible are perceived as historical but at the same time have a significance revealed through interpretive tools, so too does Beatrice embody a meaning that was not immediately obvious to Dante the protagonist but that has gradually been made clear to Dante the narrator. To reveal this meaning Dante the narrator / commentator recreates for the reader the exegetical process by which he came to this understanding, keeping the reader in the same state of suspense we imagine the protagonist experienced.

Dante the commentator first looks to the biblical model of types, noting the many similarities Beatrice bears to other characters from the Bible, most notably, Christ. In the same way that Augustine paints himself in his pre-conversion state as typologically related to Adam,[20] Dante suggests that Beatrice is like Christ, or as Hollander terms the process, treating Beatrice as "'figurally' relevant to Christ."[21] Once Beatrice's resemblance

---

the object...] (*Il libro della "Vita Nuova,"* 19).

[20] In *Confessions*, Book II, vi, 12, Augustine tells of having stolen pears from a garden in his sixteenth year. The story places great emphasis on the elements of temptation and surrender to the pressure of others to sin. Further, Augustine explicitly states that he already had all of the pears he needed and that he wanted for nothing.

[21] Hollander, *Studies in Dante*, 55. Singleton has also made much of the many analogies Dante draws between Beatrice and Christ noting the singing of *Hosanna in excelsis* in *Purgatorio*, and in the *Vita nuova.* He cites the many images in Chapter XXIII that link Beatrice's death with Christ's death, such as a multitude of angels: "I imagined that I was looking toward the sky, and I seemed to see a multitude of angels ascending, and they had in front of them a little pure-white cloud. It seemed that these angels were singing in glory, and I seemed to hear the words of their song as 'Osanna in excelsis'—Hosanna in the highest—and it seemed I heard nothing else" [Io immaginava di guardare verso lo cielo, e pareami vedere moltitudine d'angeli li quali tornassero in suso, ed aveano dinanzi da loro una nebuletta bianchissima. A me pare che questi angeli cantassero gloriosamente e le parole del loro canto me parea udire che fossero queste: "Osanna in

excelsis"]; the sun growing dark: "And it seemed I saw the sun go dark" [e pareami, vedere lo sole oscurare]; the birds falling dead from the air: "and it seemed that the birds flying through the air were falling dead" [e pareami che li uccelli volando per l'aria cadessero morti]; and the occurrence of earthquakes: "and that there were tremendous earthquakes" [e che fossero grandissimi tremuoti]. The association of Beatrice's salutation with the term *salus* is often associated with Christ and, of course, the episode with Giovanna (Primavera) in Chapter XXIV (*Essay on the Vita Nuova*, 20–23). De Robertis provides substantial background with respect to the source of the images that accompany Dante's description of the dream in which Beatrice's death is announced, noting that each of them recalls at least one scene from the New Testament and often two or three Old Testament passages as well. In his commentary on the *Vita nuova*, he continues to consider the many analogies drawn between Beatrice and Christ produced by the image of the "*città dolente*" and in particular to the image of the pilgrims in chapter XL. *Vita nuova*, Chap. XL, 1: "After this tribulation, at that time when many people go to see the blessed image that Jesus Christ left us as an imprint of his beautiful visage, which my lady sees in glory, it happened that certain pilgrims were passing along a street that runs virtually straight through the middle of the city where that most gracious of women was born, lived, and died." [Dopo questa tribulazione avvenne, in quello tempo che molta gente va per vedere quella imagine benedetta la quale Iesu Cristo lasciò a noi per essemplo de la sua bellissima figura, la quale vede la mia donna gloriosamente....] De Robertis observes, "Cristo, *il* termine di ogni pellegrinaggio, diventa 'figura' di Beatrice (Cristo ci lasciò 'quella imagine benedetta'), la Veronica" [Christ, the destination of every pilgrimage, becomes a "figura" of Beatrice (Christ left to us "that blessed image"), the Veronica] (De Robertis, *Il libro della "Vita Nuova,"* 123).

Robert Harrison has also noted the profusion of images intended to evoke the image of Christ in the reader's mind and points first to the moment in Revelation when Christ appears to the Apostle: "*Vestitus erat veste aspersa sanguigno*" [He is dressed in a robe dipped in blood] (Rev 19:13; all Scripture quotations are from the NKJV unless otherwise noted.). Harrison notes further the blood in which Christ's shroud has been dipped, making it *sanguigno*. In short, the "*sanguigno* color of the cloth obliquely evokes the sacrificial blood of Christ, once offered up as wine to the disciples. Just as the rematerialization of Christ's body and blood in bread and wine represents the founding moment of Christian sacramentality by which the body to Christ is established, Dante extends her significance to himself by presenting us with a series of analogous relationships,[22] among the most obvious of which is the episode in Chapter XXIV, noted above, in which Giovanna (Primavera) precedes Beatrice.[23] By means of this episode, Dante establishes first that

---

of Christ maintains its historicity through time, so the crimson cloth wrapped around the body of Beatrice seems to repeat in its own way the moment of sacred metaphor, rendering Beatrice sacramental in nature" (*Body of Beatrice*, 26, 27).

[22] Corti offers an in-depth discussion of the various analogical models that were used in the Middle Ages, as well as their function. She noted that the analogical process in literature is one of the many ways of illustrating the rapport between a cultural setting and a literary one. In such an analogical process, the first of the two settings, the cultural, is assumed by the author to be well noted (in this case the biblical setting) and, therefore, familiar to the reader, who already belonging to a cultural community system; the second setting, the literary, is illuminated and sometimes directly created with the help of an analogical model assumed by the first. Corti sees the use in the medieval era of an analogical model that interacts between two differing cultural fields as tied to two factors: a) the conception of the world as "unico testo creato con coerente architettura da Dio, dove tutto è correlato a tutto" [a single text created with coherent architecture by God] and b) the resemblances of relations between the parts, i.e., formal, structural resemblances. Corti cites Perelman's caveat that unlike in mathematics, the analogous proportion "*a* is to *b* as *c* is to *d*" in literature does not posit equality of the two relationships but affirms a similarity of relationship ("Il modello analogico nel pensiero medievale e dantesco," 12–13).

[23] *Vita nuova*, Chap. XV: "And a little after these words, which my heart told me in Love's own language, I saw a gracious lady coming toward me, noted for her beauty, and she was already very much the lady-queen of my best friend. And this woman's name was Giovanna, except that she was given the name Primavera, or Spring—because of her beauty, as others believe—and was called accordingly. And coming along after her, as I watched, I saw the marvelous Beatrice." [E poco dopo queste parole, che lo cuore mi disse con la lingua d'Amore, io vidi venire verso me una gentile donna, la quale era di famosa bieltade, e fue già molto donna di questi primo mio amico. E lo nome di questa donna era Giovanna, salvo che per la sua

as John is to Christ, Giovanna is to Beatrice. He then establishes that as Giovanna is to Cavalcanti, Beatrice is to Dante.[24] Consequently, as John is to Christ, Cavalcanti is to Dante. What is implicit is that Christ, Beatrice, and Dante are on a certain level, analogous. The meaning of the episode and of the characters, one can deduce, extends beyond the words to pronounce that Dante is like the *verbum* whereas those who went before were like mere voices crying out in the wilderness and preparing the way. Here then we see the presence of a hagiographical narrative, in which miraculous interventions alert the sinner to the need to love as Christ does and the potential for him to do so.

The implication is clear: this is more than a simple love story. It is also more than a spiritual autobiography; this is also Dante's literary manifesto. Dante is stating unequivocally that he will surpass—or indeed may have already surpassed—the entire lyric tradition at the apex of which formerly stood Dante's "first friend," Guido Cavalcanti. Since Beatrice is the instrument of this revelation, her meaning and purpose are, therefore, not confined to Dante's spiritual salvation and growing understanding of love as God properly intended. She can also express Dante's literary destiny. Presenting the two meanings in the same form perpetuates the truth of each. Those who ask rhetorically who Beatrice is if not Beatrice, and what does she mean

---

bieltade, secondo che li altri crede, imposto l'era nome Primavera; e così era chiamata. E appresso lei, guardando, vidi venire la mirabile Beatrice.]

[24] Michelangelo Picone is among those who recognize this relationship, noting that "Giovanna (la poesia di Guido) precede Beatrice (la poesia di Dante), come Giovanni precede l'avvento di Cristo" (*'Vita Nuova' e tradizione romanza*, 70). There is little doubt that Cavalcanti is the *primo amico* referred to in the text given the number of other references we have and the biographical information that exists concerning their relationship.

if she does not mean Beatrice, have a point, for even the insertion of christological associations does not detract from her existence at the literal level of the narrative. However, the signifying scheme Dante inherits and employs in the *Vita nuova* in no way precludes literal characters from having an ulterior significance.

While Dante uses events and persons to tell the story of his love for Beatrice, he uses those same events to tell his story as a writer.[25] In Beatrice's refusal to grant Dante her salutation, we see not only the origin of Dante's praise of Beatrice without hope of reward but also an explanation for Dante's rejection of and challenge to the lyric tradition in favor of the more mystical experience as epitomized by the lauds of Iacopone da Todi and hinted at in the poetry of Guido Guinizelli. Just as Iacopone left behind the quest for worldly progress when his beloved died, so too is Dante's shift in aspiration attributable to Beatrice's death. Dante's independence from the hope of corporeal recompense is analogous to his independence from the tradition that engenders such hopes. Beatrice's true meaning, which is revealed only in hindsight, allows Dante to reconcile having earlier sought the input and approval of other poets[26] and justifies his shift in goals

[25] As Harrison notes, "[t]he story of Dante's disorientations, his false starts and breakthroughs, his continuous groping for the poetic voice and authentic idiom, makes the early work a space of encounter for the various poetic options that the poet adopts, abandons, transforms, or discovers. The story of these options is the implicit and still untold story of the *libello*" (*Body of Beatrice*, 36).

[26] The incident described in Chapter III, 9, where Dante the protagonist solicits the opinion of the other poets as to the meaning of his dream, is externally documentable. "Thinking over what had happened to me, I decided to relate it to several of the well-known poets of that time, and since I already had some experience in the art of writing verse, I decided to compose a sonnet in which I would greet all of Love's faithful. And asking them to interpret my vision, I wrote to them about what I had seen in my sleep."

from the hope of inclusion in the earthly school of courtly love to the hope of inclusion in a more lasting and more elevated communion with divine love.

Moreover, this literary manifesto, located as it is in the allegorical level, is interchangeable with the other representations or signifiers of Dante's role as an exemplum of conversion. In the *Vita nuova*, Dante lays the foundation for the salvific role he will perfect in the *Comedy*. In showing others how to write, he is also showing them that the path to God is his *Comedy*. In

---

[Pensando io a ciò che m'era apparuto, propuosi di farlo sentire a molti li quali erano famosi trovatori in quello tempo: e con ciò fosse cosa che io avesse già veduto per me medesimo l'arte del dire parole per rima, propuosi di fare uno sonetto, ne lo quale io salutasse tutti li fedeli d'Amore; e pregandoli che giudicassero la mia visione, scrissi a loro ciò che io avea nel mio sonno veduto.] As Dante notes in the next chapter, he did receive responses. "Many people responded to this sonnet and gave various interpretations of it. One of the responses came from somebody whom I consider my best friend, who wrote a sonnet beginning, 'You saw, it seems to me, the whole of worth.' His discovery that I was the one who had sent the poem was, so to speak, the beginning of our friendship." [A questo sonetto fue risposto da molti e di diverse sentenzie; tra li quali fue risponditore quelli cui io chiamo primo de li miei amici, e disse allora uno sonetto, lo quale comincia: Vedeste, al mio parere, onne valore. E questo fue quasi lo principio de l'amistà tra lui e me, quando elli seppe che io era quelli che li avea ciò mandato.] Cavalcanti's sonnet in response is still extant. See Avalle, ed., *Poeti del Duecento*, *La Letteratura Italiana*, 544.

The incident seems to carry a sense of false modesty with it. One can only imagine the intent of the young poet sending around his sonnet, inviting the opinions of more established writers. It seems like a wonderfully orchestrated attempt at self-promotion, announcing his arrival on the scene, requiring the acknowledgment of those who had already arrived. The incident is inconsistent, however, with Dante's later attempts to reject and surpass the very contemporaries whose approval he so obsequiously sought. Given that the incident would have been well known, Dante could not have ignored it and instead uses the episode in which Beatrice withdraws her salutation to contextualize and justify the incident.

charting a salvific itinerary, Dante creates an affinity between himself and St. Bonaventure[27] and imbues his life with the salvific quality found in the lives of the saints. By following Dante's lead, his readers, especially readers who are also writers, can also find salvation.

For the same reasons that Dante presents Beatrice as actual, so too does he present the *donna gentile* as actual. That is, he is creating a literal level that is "true," but which has an allegorical level that is also "true." As was the case with Beatrice, the significance of the *donna gentile*'s relationship to Dante is also revealed through analogy. However, in contrast to his treatment of Beatrice, Dante's treatment of the *donna gentile* draws on a secular work for an analogous model to draw the comparison, namely the relationship between Dido and Aeneas contained in Book 4 of the *Aeneid*. Aeneas has a destiny he must fulfill but allows himself to be sidetracked by Dido; so too does Dante allow himself to be distracted by the *donna gentile*. Just as Aeneas is brought back to his senses and put back on the path of his destiny by a message brought from the "exalted Father" and delivered by Mercury,[28] so too is Dante drawn away from the distractions of corporeal love to his destiny by a vision of Beatrice.[29] As Dido is to Aeneas, so is the *donna gentile* to

---

[27] In the mid 1200s, St. Bonaventure had used the itinerary or map motif in his *Itinerarium Mentis in Deum* to chart the course that the soul must take to reach God. In *Paradiso* 12, Dante has St. Bonaventure deliver an extended praise of St. Dominic and bemoan the decline in the Franciscan order. As for difficulties in dating its composition. see Davis, "Hierarchy and Excess," 433–53.

[28] *Aeneid*, Book IV, 238–41 "...Ille patris magni parere parabat imperio et primum pedibus talaria nectit aurea..." [He prepared to obey his great father's order; and first fastened the golden sandals to his feet...]

[29] *Vita nuova*, Chap. XXXIX, 1: "Against this adversary of reason there arose in me one day, at about the hour of nones, an intense imagining that seemed to see this glorious Beatrice wearing the same crimson clothes in

Dante. Further, the analogy also posits a relationship of likeness between Dante and Aeneas that once again emphasizes Dante's *auctoritas*. At the same time, and perhaps more significantly, his use of the secular *libro* to characterize his relationship with the *donna gentile*, emphasizes the distinction between it and his relationship with Beatrice that is described in biblical terms. As Michelangelo Picone points out, the nature of Dante's relationship with Beatrice also resembles the relationship between the mystic and God.[30] This resemblance further emphasizes the Christian nature of that relationship in contrast to that of his relationship with the *donna gentile*.

Dante's representation of *Amore* is also drawn from a Virgilian model as he explicitly states[31] and is punctuated with language echoing *Virgil*'s descriptions of love.[32] That such terminology was also highly common in the lyric poetry of the time

---

which she first appeared to my eyes. And she seemed young, roughly the same age as when I first saw her." [Contra questo avversario de la ragione si levoe un die, quasi ne l'ora de la nona, una forte imaginazione in me, che mi parve vedere questa gloriosa Beatrice con quelle vestimenta sanguigne co le quali apparve a li occhi miei;]

[30] Picone, "*Vita nuova* fra autobiografia e tipologia," 60.

[31] *Vita nuova*, Chap. XXV, 9: "That poets have written as stated here can be seen in Virgil, who writes that Juno—the goddess-enemy of the Trojans—spoke to Aeolus, lord of the winds, in book I of the *Aeneid*: 'Aeolus, to you...,' and that this lord responded, 'To settle on what you wish / Is all you need to do, your majesty. / I must perform it.' This same poet has an inanimate thing talk to animate things, in book III of the *Aeneid*: 'Tough sons of Dardanus.'" [Che li poete abbiano così parlato come detto è, appare per Virgilio; lo quale dice che Iuno, cioè una dea nemica de li Troiani, parloe ad Eolo, segnore de li venti, quivi nel primo de lo Eneida: Eole, nanque tibi, e che questo segnore le rispuose, quivi: Tuus, o regina, quid optes explorare labor; michi iussa capessere fas est. Per questo medesimo poeta parla la cosa che non è animata a le cose animate, nel terzo de lo Eneida, quivi: Dardanide duri.]

[32] In the *Aeneid*, love is often likened to fire: "et ora Cupido pro dulci Ascanio veniat donisque furentem incendat reginam atque ossibus implicet ignem" (I, 658-60); "Quocirca capere ante dolis et cingere flamma reginam meditor, ne quo se numine mutet" (I, 673-75); "At regina gravi jam dudum saucia cura volnus alit venis et caeco carpitur igni" (IV, 1-2); "Est mollis flamma medullas interea, et tacitum vivit

further underscores Dante's engagement with and examination of secular lyric that the *Vita nuova* represents. This anthropomorphic representation of love is consistent with Thomist thought concerning the representation of certain concepts in forms which are easier to comprehend.[33] It is important to note that, while Dante is using what is often considered an allegorical figure to represent love, love and its representation nonetheless still exist on the literal level of the narrative. We are still invited to look for a deeper meaning in terms of what love in the narrative means in Dante's own story; the "true" story whose meaning is being represented by the entire narrative plot. The

---

sub pectore volnus" (IV, 66-67). Similarly, in the *Vita nuova*, *Amore* is often accompanied by images of fire as in Chapter III, 3: "che me parea vedere ne la mia camera una nebula di colore di fuoco" [I seemed to see in my room a cloud the color of fire], and again in Chapter III, 6: "e tanto si sforzava per suo ingegno, che la facea mangiare questa cosa che in mano li ardea" [and he forced her cunningly to eat of that burning object in his hand], or in chapter XI, 1: "anzi mi giugnea una fiamma di caritade" [on the contrary, a flame of charity was lit within me].

[33] Iannucci points out that St. Thomas, within the context of biblical exegesis and specifically in terms of those instances where God is anthropomorphized, explains that the literal meaning of events lies not in the rhetorical figure used but in the content, in that which is figured: "Sensus parabolicus sub litterali continetur: nam per voces significatur aliquid proprie, et aliquid figurative, nec est litteralis sensus ipsa figura, sed id quod est figuratum. Non enim cum Scriptura nominat Dei brachium, est litteralis sensus quod in Deo sit membrum huiusmodi corporale: sed id quod per hoc membrum significatur, scilicet virtus operativ. In quo patet quod sensui litterali sacrae Scripturae nunquam potest subesse falsum" (*Summa Theologiae*, part 1, question 1, article 10, objection 3). [The parabolical sense is contained in the literal, for by words things are signified properly and figuratively. Nor is the figure itself, but that which is figured, the literal sense. When Scripture speaks of God's arm, the literal sense is not that God has such a member, but only what is signified by this member, namely operative power. Hence it is plain that nothing false can ever underlie the literal sense of Holy Writ.] Iannucci points out that, in the *Comedy*, Dante has Beatrice paraphrase St. Thomas to explain this notion to Dante the Pilgrim (*Forma ed evento nella Divina Commedia*, 86).

fact that, as in the case of the *donna gentile*, Dante uses a secular paradigm as a point of comparison, coupled with the fact that, like the *donna gentile*, *Amore* ultimately disappears from the text, suggests that Dante's destiny lies outside of secular love and instead is drawn to its Christian counterpart. When we consider this meaning in conjunction with the earlier analogy that Dante draws between himself and Guido Cavalcanti, we understand the way Dante sees himself as destined to surpass his contemporaries. Dante's writing will not only be divinely inspired but will also carry a divine truth absent in the secular love poetry.

Dante's portrait of himself as protagonist provides a further example of the importance of establishing historicity to the notion of *auctoritas*. To confirm Dante as an *auctor* we must believe both that Beatrice was a miracle of God and that it was to Dante she was sent. Dante's inclusion of himself in the text allows him to convince us that he is not writing fiction, that he is writing history and, therefore, truth. In the same way as Beatrice's actuality was essential to her divinity, Dante's actuality is important to establishing the historicity of the divine mission he claims and the challenge it inspires. Here too we see that Dante follows a pattern commonly found in the hagiographical models. In the *Life of St. Lucy* for, example, we see that Lucy's life is linked to St. Agatha's and thereby is infused with her sanctity. As Dante associates himself with "St. Beatrice," he will similarly be infused with her sanctity.[34] In the *Comedy*, Dante will take

[34] Dante is clearly familiar not only with the hagiographical tradition but also with the mechanics of construction a life of a saint with its attendant iconography. In particular, the figure of Beatrice, who name is associated with beatitude, or blessing, reflects the medieval tendency to link patronage and iconography to a saint's name. (St. Lucy's name, linked to *lux*, *luce*, meaning *light*, is also associated with vision.) As Anthony Cassell points out, "in Vita nuova XIII Dante himself quotes the truism that '*nomina sunt consequentia rerum*'" ("Santa Lucia as Patroness of Sight," 72–73).

this strategy even further. In *Inferno* 2, we learn that Beatrice has been sent to Dante by Rachel, who was sent to Beatrice by St. Lucy, who in turn was sent by St. Mary. Dante is thus included in this continuum of sainthood.

Given the extent to which the *Vita nuova* suggests that Dante's life is akin to that of a saint, it is surprising how little it borrows from the medieval Christian autobiographical model epitomized by St. Augustine's *Confessions*. Notwithstanding apparent similarities between the works, closer inspection reveals these similarities to be little more than superficial. For example, while Dante's inclusion of events from his own life and his insistence on actuality might appear at first consistent with Augustine's accounting of events from his own life, an examination of the purpose for which each author includes himself reveals the use of the first-person voice as little more than a formal similarity. In the Augustinian model, for example, the author's actuality enhances the exemplum function of the story. In the *Vita nuova*, however, Dante's assertion of his actuality establishes his own particular importance. In the Augustinian model, the actuality of events is important to the value of the lesson they express. In the *Vita nuova*, as we have seen, the reliability of the events contributes to the historicity and authority of the work and by extension, to the authority of the writer. In the *Vita nuova*, Dante's actuality serves his attempt to step outside of the normal course and find a meaning particular to him in both his love for Beatrice and in his literary journey. In contrast to the later project of the *Comedy*, in Dante's earliest attempt at life-writing there is little in the way of a discernible attempt to discover a universal application for its lessons.

The hope he expresses toward the close of the *Vita nuova*, that he may live long enough to say things about Beatrice that have never been said about any other woman, expresses Dante's literary aspirations and distills the ultimate significance of the work.[35] Dante's use of language reminiscent of Virgil indicates the manner in which he plans to write, while the desire to differentiate himself, to write as no one before him, marks a departure from the Augustinian model.[36] Unlike Augustine, Dante does not here present himself as an exemplum for others; instead, he sets himself apart from his contemporaries. Everything in his *Vita nuova* tells us that Dante is different from them; he is an *auctor*.[37] He alone has been selected to receive this lady's salutation, and it will be his personal mission to follow the path that has been pointed out to him.

Similarly, while the opposition of "then and now" in the *Vita nuova* appears at first to signal adherence to the Augustinian model, it is little more than a passing resemblance. In Augustine's *Confessions*, the two separate narrative perspectives, "then and now," are produced by the occurrence in which a piv-

---

[35] *Vita nuova*, Chap. XXXI: "So that, if it be pleasing to Him who is that for which all things live, and if my life is long enough, I hope to say things about her that have never been said about any woman. [Sì che, se piacere sarà di colui a cui tutte le cose vivono, che la mia vita duri per alquanti anni, io spero di dicer di lei quello che mai non fue detto d'alcuna.]

[36] De Robertis, in his commentary on the *Vita nuova*, notes that this language is almost certainly adapted from that used by Virgil in his 4th Eclogue: "O mihi tum longae maneat pars ultima vitae, / spiritus et quantum sat erit tua dicere facta: / non me carminibus vincet…" (*Eclogue* IV, 53-55) (*Il libro della "Vita Nuova,"* 247).

[37] Michelangelo Picone notes that the events recounted in the *Vita nuova* are those that demonstrate the shining sign of distinction and the belonging of the poet (fusion of the protagonist with the exegete) to a highly restricted canon of the romance "*auctores*" ("Fra autobiografia e tipologia," 64).

otal event (a conversion or figural death) in the life of the protagonist lends new insight to the events of the past.[38] The pivotal event concomitantly produces a related feature, the contrast between "old man" and "new man" occasioned by the spiritual death of the former self as the result of the cataclysmic event.

Certainly, the *Vita nuova* contains a pivotal event that engenders a new perspective on the events of the past. That Dante distinguishes between "then and now" (that is, before and after the cataclysmic event) and reflects on past events from such a perspective is made clear in the first chapter of the *Vita nuova*, where he notes, "Nine times, the heaven of the light had returned to where it was at my birth, almost to the very same point of its orbit, when the glorious lady of my mind first appeared before my eyes—she whom many called Beatrice without even knowing that was her name."[39]

The word glorious ("*gloriosa*") makes it clear that Beatrice is already dead. This perspective is reiterated in the next chapter where, discussing the meaning of a poem, Dante says the "correct interpretation of my dream was not understood by anyone at first, but now it is clear to even the most simple-minded."[40]

---

[38] In the *Confessions* the turning points are marked by Augustine's baptism and the death of Augustine's mother Monica in Book 9, chapters 6 and 9 respectively.

[39] *Vita nuova*, Chap. II, 1: "Nine times, the heaven of the light had returned to where it was at my birth, almost to the very same point of its orbit, when the glorious lady of my mind first appeared before my eyes—she whom many called Beatrice without even knowing that was her name." [Nove fiate già appresso lo mio nascimento era tornato lo cielo de la luce quasi uno medesimo punto, quanto a la sua propria girazione, quando a li miei occhi apparve prima la gloriosa donna de la mia mente, la quali fu chiamata da molti Beatrice li quali non sapeano che si chiamare.]

[40] *Vita nuova*, Chap. III, 9: "The correct interpretation of my dream was not understood by anyone at first, but now it is clear to even the most simple-minded." [Lo verace giudicio del detto sogno non fue veduto allora

As Domenico De Robertis points out, this comment recalls the Gospel of John, which recounts how the disciples of Christ did not immediately understand the prophecy of his death, but once he was dead, "*glorificatus*," they saw its meaning.[41] The allusion immediately introduces an analogy between Beatrice and Christ and signals the pivotal event, the death of Beatrice, that triggers the distinction between "then and now."

Moreover, although Dante's use of the title "*Vita nuova*" might suggest adherence to the Augustinian paradigm, a closer look reveals that Dante's perspective is gained neither from his own conversion nor through a figurative death of the self, but is tied instead to an external event, that is, the death of Beatrice. It is this event that permits him, indeed forces him, to turn from the old way of writing, the lyric tradition, to the new way of writing, one in which the object of the poet's adoration, selected by divine destiny, continues to inspire from her exalted position in heaven. Just as the death of Christ made Christian redemption possible, so too will Beatrice's death, the death of a Christ-

---

per alcuno, ma ora è manifestissimo a li più semplici.]

[41] In his notes to the *Vita nuova*, De Robertis points out that "L'intera frase ricorda le parole da Giovanni, XII, 16: 'Haec non cognoverunt discipuli eius primum; sed quando glorifactus est Iesus, tunc recordati sunt quia haec erant scripta da eo' riferentisi appunto all'oscurità delle profezie di Cristo circa la propria morte (oscure anche ai suoi 'fedeli,') ma ripete insieme il paradosso evangelico della verità nascosta ai sapienti e rivelata ai semplici e ai fanciulli" [The entire sentence recalls the words from John, XII, 16: "Haec non cognoverunt discipuli eius primum; sed when glorifactus est Iesus, tunc recordati sunt quia haec erant scripta da eo," referring precisely to the obscurity of Christ's prophecies about his own death (obscure even to his "faithful,") but repeats together the evangelical paradox of the truth hidden from the wise and revealed to the simple and to children] (*Il libro della "Vita Nuova,"* 44). ("His disciples did not understand these things at first; but when Jesus was glorified, then they remembered that these things were written about Him and *that* they had done these things to him" [John 12:16]).

like figure, make possible Dante's literary and spiritual redemption. Dante's omission of the details of her death demonstrates the primacy he gives to the meaning of events rather than to their literal expression. The reader is meant to focus on the meaning of the event, not its literal details, for to have Beatrice die in any way other than crucifixion would detract from the christological association Dante has so carefully created. Dante's explanation for this omission, that her death is not part of his present topic, therefore, is quite correct, especially since the *libello* is not really about Beatrice's corporeal existence.[42] This event signals the literary redemption Dante uses to explain his presumptuous claim to elevated status as an *auctor*. At the same time, the event grants him the perspective he needs to maintain that status.

But Dante, the "old man," has not died, at least not in the Augustinian sense. Dante is still evolving, and, as we shall see below, the *Vita nuova* not only looks back but also looks forward to the continuation of his life and fulfillment of the possibility of redemption. The protagonist of the *Vita nuova* is still very much in the same life, his first life. He differs from the Augustinian protagonist who sees life, removed from it not so much by time and space but by an existential shift. Accordingly, while the *Vita nuova* may share a few superficial characteristics with the Augustinian model, it is probably more accurate to suggest that elements of the Augustinian models are integrated along with elements from a variety of models in order to fashion a narrative that reflects a uniquely personal project.[43]

---

[42] *Vita nuova*, Chap. XXVIII, 2: "It is not part of the present topic, if we look back at the proem that precedes this little book." [ciò non è del presente proposito, se volemo guardare nel proemio che precede questo libello; la seconda è che, posto che fosse del presente proposito.]

[43] Picone addresses this hybrid feature of the *Vita nuova*, noting that

The *Vita nuova* is, in this way, much more than an annotated anthology; it is a conscious attempt at self-promotion and constitutes a definitive statement of literary intent. The entire work is fashioned so as to effect the desired reception and present a particular image of its author. Dante's use of the metaphor of the book, his redefining of the traditional role of copyist and commentator, and his reinterpreting the events found in the book of memory show readers the value that Dante places on his own writing and what he perceives as his place as writer even at this early stage in his career. His discussion of the poets of antiquity leaves us with no doubt that Dante is prepared to use the classical *auctores* to go beyond the vernacular literary tradition of which he was a part.[44]

Toward the end of the *Vita nuova* we catch a glimpse of where he might be heading. As Dante considers the pilgrims who head to Rome to see the Veronica,[45] he presents the very

---

Dante, especially at this early stage of his writing career, was heavily influenced by several sources. The *Vita nuova*, he suggests, seems to resolve the tension inherent in the double cultural articulation of the thirteenth century, that is between "esemplare e personale, agiografica e autobiografica" but at the same time seems tied to the "modello dinamico dell'*imitatio auctorum*" ("*Vita nuova* fra autobiografia e tipologia," 59).

[44] *Vita nuova*, Chap. XXV, 10: "And in order that some coarse person does not get presumptuous about these things, I will add that the ancient poets did not write in this manner without reason, nor should vernacular poets write like this without having some understanding of what they are saying." [Cap. XXV: E acciò che non ne pigli alcuna baldanza persona grossa, dico che né li poete parlavano così sanza ragione, né quelli che rìmano dèono parlare così, non avendo alcuno ragionamento in loro di quello che dicono.]

[45] *Vita nuova*, Chap. XL, 1: "After this tribulation, at that time when many people go to see the blessed image that Jesus Christ left us as an imprint of his beautiful visage, which my lady sees in glory, it happened that certain pilgrims were passing along a street that runs virtually straight through the middle of the city where that most gracious of women was born,

motif that will frame the *Comedy*: pilgrimage to that "Rome where Christ is a Roman."[46]

While at first, Dante is merely an observer of these pilgrims (as opposed to a fellow traveler), in the following chapter he proposes the idea of a journey that he himself, or at least his spirit, will take:[47] a pilgrimage to see "she who blessed the city."[48] Here Dante uses a device common to hagiography, the confluence of name and attribute, to present Beatrice as a saint. But he goes further, employing what Cassell calls "narratological grammar" of hagiography, through which, Dante, by associating himself with a particular saint, shares in that sainthood.[49]

In the context of his literary evolution—or perhaps we may call it conversion at this point—Dante signals to his readers that

---

lived, and died." [Cap. XL: Dopo questa tribulazione avvenne, in quello tempo che molta gente va per vedere quella imagine benedetta la quale Jesu Cristo lasciò a noi per esemplo de la sua bellissima figura, la quale vede la mia donna gloriosamente, che alquanti peregrini passavano per una via la quale è quasi mezzo de la cittade ove nacque e vivette e morìo la gentilissima donna.] The Veil of Veronica, or simply the Veronica, is a Christian relic consisting of a piece of cloth said to bear an image of the face of Christ.

[46] *Purg.* 32:102: "quella Roma onde Cristo è romano." Alessandro Vettori has noted how the Veronica reference in the *Vita nuova* and in *Paradiso* functions both as the beginning of his journey and the end of it ("Veronica," 52).

[47] *Vita nuova*, Chap. XLI, 11: "When he has reached the site of his desire / he sees a woman there, an honored name / whose splendor is so luminous a flame the pilgrim-spirit's rapt, his gaze entire." [Cap. XLI: Quand'elli è giunto là dove disira, / vede una donna che riceve onore, / e luce sì che per lo suo splendore / lo peregrino spirito la mira.]

[48] *Vita nuova*, Chap. XL, 10: "For she who blessed the city is nowhere / in sight." [Ell'ha perduta la sua Beatrice.]

[49] Cassell, "Santa Lucia as Patroness of Sight," 72. Later in the *Comedy*, Dante will build upon this "grammar" to expand and associate his life with that of Saint Lucy. Indeed, in *Inferno* 2:94-96, we learn that Lucy has joined the list of saints who have willed his journey.

he will henceforth be writing both hagiography and auto-hagiography since the journey to St. Beatrice will be his own.

The *Vita nuova*, therefore, affirms the authority Dante the writer seeks and offers an explanation for his literary and spiritual redemption. It presents Dante as particularly blessed, elevated above his contemporaries, poised to enter the ranks of the sainted elite.

As the *Vita nuova* nears its close, we see, if only through a glass darkly, the seeds of further self-inspection.[50] The poet speaks of a vision he is not yet ready to transcribe, and it becomes evident that Dante, in writing his own story, has begun to see an even greater role for himself.[51] In a very Pauline sense, Dante begins to move beyond childish things, which explains why he has abandoned the distractions and dead ends of secular poetry together with the love it celebrates, and looks instead to the greater glory that awaits the truly Christian poet and lover.

---

[50] 1 Cor 13:11-12.

[51] *Vita nuova*, Chap. XLII, 1: "After writing this sonnet a marvelous vision appeared to me, in which I saw things that made me decide not to say anything more about this blessed lady until I was capable of writing about her more worthily." [Cap. XLII: Appresso questo sonetto, apparve a me una mirabile visione, ne la quale io vidi cose che mi fecero proporre di non dire più di questa benedetta, infino a tanto che io potesse più degnamente trattare di lei.]

Chapter 3

The *Convivio*: Dante as Redeemer

IF THE *VITA NUOVA* launched Dante's literary challenge, it is in the *Convivio* that we see the first battle. In the *Convivio* Dante aggressively advances, surpassing the lyric tradition and staking out new territory. At the same time, the love story continues as the narrative focal point, though in this later endeavor Dante approaches the ladies in his life from a different perspective and continues the quest to identify a broader significance to his interaction with them. Further, while its narrative, like that of the *Vita nuova*, examines the meaning of his own life, the *Convivio* looks even further and seeks to comprehend and communicate the societal implications of his existence.

Though Dante explicitly mentions the *Vita nuova* in the *Convivio* and makes it clear that he intends to continue that project in the *Convivio*, the connection between the two works is much more intricate than one of mere continuity.[1] Indeed,

---

[1] *Convivio* I, i, 16: "If in the present work, which is called *The Banquet*, as I wish it to be, the subject is treated more maturely than in the *Vita nuova*, I do not intend by this in any way to disparage that book but rather more greatly to support it with this one, seeing that it understandably suits that one to be fervid and passionate, and this one tempered and mature." [E se ne la presente opera, la quale è Convivio nominata e vo' che sia, più virilmente si trattasse che ne la Vita nuova, non intendo però a quella in parte

while a project of continuation may be discernible on the basis of external form,[2] the *Convivio*'s internal form reveals a relationship between the two works that is by no means simple. Relying on a number of strategies, Dante uses the *Convivio* not

---

derogare, ma maggiormente giovare per questa quella; veggendo sì come ragionevolmente quella fervida e passionata, questa temperata e virile esser conviene.] and *Convivio* II, ii, 1: "To begin, then, I say that after the passing of that blessed Beatrice who lives in heaven with the angels and on earth with my soul, the star of Venus had twice revolved in that circle of hers, which at different times of the year makes her appear in the evening or in the morning, when that gentle lady, of whom I made mention at the end of the *New Life*, first appeared before my eyes, accompanied by Love, and took a place within my mind." [Cominciando adunque, dico che la Stella di Venere due fiate rivolta era in quello suo cerchio che la fa parere serotina e matutina, secondo diversi tempi, appresso lo trapassamento di quelle Beatrice beata che vive in cielo con gli angeli e in terra con la mia anima, quando quella gentile donna, cui feci menzione ne la fine de la *Vita nuova*, parve primamente, accompagnata d'Amore, a li occhi miei e prese luogo alcuno ne la mia mente.]

[2] Although the *Convivio* commences with the impersonal third person as the narrative voice, while still in the first chapter it shifts to the first-person singular, which dominates the remainder of the work, indicating that Dante intended it to be perceived as having a personal connection to its author. Further, the prosimetric form also suggests, in two ways, a personal aspect. Dante's insertion of poems already known to be his work combined with the first-person voice practically demands an autobiographical reading. Nardi confirms that a number of the poems would have been well known as Dante's work, suggesting that "Dante propone il testo di quattordici sue canzoni, delli quali alcune già note ai lettori…." [Dante proposes the text of fourteen of his songs, some of which are already known to readers.] The evident desire to elucidate the meaning of the poems along with the discussion as to why such an explanation is necessary further emphasizes the project's personal nature. Additionally, the prosimetric form recalls the use of the same form in the *Vita nuova* and suggests a connection to it, if not a continuation (or sequel), as Vasoli suggests of the earlier prosimetric and highly personal offering (Dante, *Convivio*, ed. Vasoli, xvi; Nardi, *Dal "Convivio" alla "Commedia"* [1960], 23).

only to continue writing his life story but also to revise and expand the scope of the earlier and less mature work.[3]

Among the many devices used to this end, no other is as integral or as essential as the framing metaphor of the banquet. Given that Dante used the framing metaphor of the book in the *Vita nuova* to establish a structure upon which his entire literary project might rest, it would appear at first that the use of a similar method for a similar purpose suggests a close connection between the two works. A closer inspection, however, reveals that the choice of metaphor introduces an important distinction between the two works. Whereas the book of one's memory, a chronicle of one's life, seems almost by definition to require the recounting of a series of events, a banquet is a self-contained, single event. Indeed, we see very quickly that the framing metaphor used in the *Convivio* does not lend itself as easily to a progressive narrative structure, that is, one that is diachronic, as does the book metaphor of the *Vita nuova.* The metaphor of the *Convivio* engenders instead a more static, synchronic narrative mode. This distinction is crucial to understanding the *Convivio* in its relationship to the *Vita nuova* and to understanding its autobiographical dimension. For example, whereas the commentary in the *Vita nuova* bore a resemblance to the Provençal *vidas* and its very title was evocative of a biographical work, the *Convivio* more closely resembles a self-portrait produced at a

[3] *Convivio* I, i, 16: "For it is proper to speak and act differently at different ages, because certain manners are fitting and praiseworthy at one age which at another are unbecoming and blameworthy, as will be shown below with appropriate reasoning in the fourth book. I wrote the former work at the threshold of my youth, and this one after I had already passed through it." [Ché altro si conviene e dire e operare ad una etade che ad altra; perché certi costumi sono idonei e laudabili ad una etade che sono sconci e biasimevoli ad altra, sì come di sotto nel quarto trattato di questo libro, sarà propria ragione mostrata. E io in quella dinanzi, a l'entrata de la mia gioventute parlai, e in questa dipoi, quella già trapassata.]

single moment in time.

Consequently, the author of the *Convivio* is much closer to the events narrated in the text than the author of the *Vita nuova* is to the events narrated in that text. The protagonist of the *Vita nuova* did not understand the meaning of the events as they occurred, unlike its author who existed on a different plane of cognizance because of the intervening event of Beatrice's death. In the *Convivio*, however, the protagonist exists on the same plane as does the author of the work. Both the protagonist and the author were aware of the allegorical significance of the poems it contains and the events they narrate when the poems were written.[4] The perspective of the *Convivio* is, as a result, mostly

[4] This is confirmed in *Convivio* II, xii, 5: "so I who sought to console myself found not only a remedy for my tears but also the words of authors, sciences, and books. Pondering these, I quickly determined that Philosophy, who was the lady of these authors, sciences, and books, was a great thing. I imagined her fashioned as a gentle lady...." [io, che cercava di consolarme, trovai non solamente a le mie lagrime rimedio, ma vocabuli d'autori e di scienze e di libri: li quali considerando, giudicava bene che la filosofia, che era donna di questi autori di queste scienze e di questi libri, fosse somma cosa. E imaginava lei fatta come una *donna gentile*....]

Convivio II, xii, 8: "Consequently, feeling myself raised from the thought of that first love to the virtue of this one, almost in amazement I opened my mouth to speak the words of the canzone before us, revealing my condition beneath the figure of other things...." [Per che io, sentendomi levare dal pensiero del primo amore a la virtù di questo, quasi maravigliandomi apersi la bocca nel parlare de la proposta canzone, mostrando la mia condizione sotto figura d'altre cose....] Whether Dante originally composed the poem as allegory has been the subject of much debate. Francis Fergusson, for example, does not believe Dante, saying, "But I think she was a real woman, and I cannot believe that *Voi che intendendo* [*sic*] was originally written to celebrate philosophia, the love of wisdom, genuine though that love was in Dante" (*Dante*, 41). What is more important is not so much what the truth was but what Dante intended us to accept as the truth.

rooted in the present tense and is substantially devoid of an earlier, unseeing, unenlightened past.

These distinctions in narrative mode are further emphasized by the hermeneutic strategies of the *Convivio*. The emphasis that the *Convivio* gives to allegorical meaning (what Piero Cudini refers to as the qualitatively clear and decisive dominance of the allegorical supra meaning[5]), together with the concomitant diminution in the importance of the literal narration, further detract from the possibility of a progressive narrative, what we might call a "story." The resulting "nonstory" of the *Convivio* is, however, precisely what characterizes the nature of Dante's message at this stage of his career. What the framing metaphor highlights, and the hermeneutic strategies echo, is the fact that the commentary in the *Convivio* is neither a chronicle of a journey of self-discovery nor an attempt to clarify what was not clear when the "book of memory" was first opened. It is instead a public exposition of what Dante presents as a demonstrable and decisive truth that seems to have been visible to the author and protagonist, if not all along, then certainly prior to the commencement of the banquet. In contrast to the *Vita nuova*, the *Convivio* greatly lacks narrative progression. As well, the opposition between "then and now," typical of many hagiographies and evident in the *Vita nuova*, seems notably absent from the *Convivio*. Yet, as we shall see, such an opposition very much informs the *Convivio*. Dante's continual references to the *Vita nuova* and his characterization of it as a product of his youth combine to create a continuity and a clear linear progression in which the *Convivio* may be viewed as continuing the project commenced in the *Vita nuova* where *Convivio* has become "now" and the *Vita nuova* has been relegated to "then."

---

[5] "predominio qualitivamente netto e deciso al sovra significato allegorico" (*Convivio*, ed. Cudini, 131).

In an even more fundamental way, the vision of the *Convivio* is closely linked to that of the *Vita nuova*. In neither account can Dante truly be said to be looking back from "without" or outside of his life. He has not yet experienced the death of self necessary to the Augustinian model and, accordingly, from an exegetical perspective is not able to properly understand all the events of his life. In the *Convivio* he is closer to such a perspective, having been exiled physically, even if he is still within his own life. The *nunc et tunc* aspect of the Augustinian model is, therefore, most effectively achieved through its relationship to the *Vita nuova*. By juxtaposing the youthfulness of the *libello* with the more mature *Convivio*, Dante in essence absorbs the earlier work, transforming it into a first chapter, making it merely part of an even greater book. By framing the two works in such a way as to create a contrast, Dante has, paradoxically, persuaded us that the two parts are complements.[6] Moreover, the two parts will interact symbiotically, the *Vita nuova* providing the rudiments of the project that is continued in the *Convivio*, and the *Convivio* in turn furnishing a revised significance to the *Vita nuova*.

Not only is the *Convivio*'s framing metaphor essential to repositioning the *Vita nuova* in the context of Dante's subsequent evolution, but it is also crucial to expressing the revised role Dante has fashioned for himself. Dante uses the banquet metaphor to paint himself as a Christ figure, an image only hinted at in the *Vita nuova* that will see its full development in the *Comedy*. Therefore, as was the case with the *Vita nuova*, the framing metaphor signals the reception Dante intends for the work and the way in which he, as its author, should be regarded.

---

[6] Cudini refers to this alternatively as a "legame di continuità—opposizione" [bond of continuity-opposition] and a "rapporto di continuità-diversità" [relationship of continuity and difference], but he stops short of exploring the symbiotic nature of this rapport (*Convivio*, ed. Cudini, 133).

As the host of the *Convivio*, a supper at which Dante announces that the bread he offers will provide a new light, Dante creates a stunning, if not immediately obvious, analogy between himself and Christ.[7]

Here then is where we see Dante at his most unabashedly auto-hagiographical. Adopting a distinctly hieratic pose to create this affinity, Dante recalls the same relationship implied in Chapter XXIV of the *Vita nuova*, in which Giovanna (Primavera) preceded Beatrice. Here, however, Dante has adeptly chosen an image that represents a later Christ than that alluded to in the *Vita nuova*. The analogy in the *Vita nuova* was to a Christ whose mission and, therefore, Dante's as well, was still mere prophecy. In the *Convivio* the analogy is to a more mature Christ on the brink of fulfillment of that prophecy. (In the *Comedy*, Dante will continue to follow the life of Christ, timing his journey to coincide with the triduum.) The metaphor of the *Convivio* in which Dante, the host, breaking bread and teaching those who are his disciples allows Dante to fulfill the prophecy of the *Vita nuova* and create a new covenant. Just as the New Testament fulfilled the Old Testament scripture, so too will Dante's new testament fulfill and rely on the old scriptures, those of others and his own. Dante has created a further relationship of analogy, that is, between the two allusions and the

[7] *Convivio* I, xiii, 12: "This shall be a new light, a new sun which shall rise where the old sun shall set and which shall give light to those who lie in shadows and in darkness because the old sun no longer sheds its light upon them." [Questo sarà luce nuova, sole nuovo, lo quale surgerà là dove l'usato tramonterà, e darà lume a coloro che sono in tenebre e in oscuritade per lo usato sole che a loro non luce.] While many critics have noted the biblically allusive nature of this language, surprisingly the relationship between Jesus, host of the Last Supper, surrounded by his disciples (or as the provider of light and bread in general), and Dante, host of this new banquet where bread and new light will be offered, appears in none of the authorities I have consulted. See Matt 26:17-29; Mark 14:12-25; Luke 22:7-38.

two works. In so doing he continues to transform the *Vita nuova* into "then" while presenting the *Convivio* as "now" and, therefore, by implication, the truer perspective. Thus we see the beginnings of a strategy that will figure prominently in the *Comedy*; the absorption of one work into the greater corpus of a later work. In another sense, the transformation of the *Vita nuova* into "then" also presents the two works as parallel episodes and illustrates one of Dante's earliest attempts at a strategy that will inform much of the *Comedy*.

It is through this temporal posteriority with its attendant "truer" perspective, combined with the analogous relationship to Jesus Christ, that Dante expresses the new and truer role in which we are to envision him. No longer simply an *auctor*, he is now also a redeemer. The Christ of the *Convivio*, however, is somewhat different from that of the *Vita nuova*. Dante's new wisdom and love for philosophy have resulted in an intellectual Christ who metes out not only Augustine's wisdom but also Aristotle's. Here in the *Convivio* we see one of Dante's earliest efforts at reconciling pre-Christian and post-Christian wisdom, a project that occupied much of late medieval thought. If the inspiration for the *Vita nuova* was mystical or spiritual, then certainly the inspiration for the *Convivio* was rational, but the goal of both works is, nonetheless, consistently redemption. Dante will redeem those who sit at his banquet by serving them the new light and offering them the bread of this new communion.

The analogy is reinforced throughout the *Convivio* with other references suggesting that Dante is like Jesus. Dante, for example, as the "*io*" ("I") of the narrative, espouses attitudes similar to those of Christ toward those in positions of authority.[8] Moreover, Dante, the writer adopts a style that recalls

---

[8] Dante continually associates his audience with sheep, recalling the image of Christ and by analogy, Dante as the Good Shepherd. *Convivio* I,

Christ's manner of expression. According to the Gospels, Jesus spoke in parables in order to fulfill the words of the prophets.[9] Dante's frequent reliance on analogy, therefore, constitutes yet another way he associates himself with Christ and underlines his authority as redeemer.

While the framing metaphor is crucial to the expression of Dante's expanded role, it is also the descriptive device through which the genesis of this enhanced role finds expression. Just as in the *Vita nuova*, a specific event caused Dante to rethink his position vis-à-vis his field of endeavor, in the *Convivio* too, a specific event, in this case exile, reveals the "true" and broader

i, 7: "Blessed are the few who sit at the table where the bread of the angels is eaten, and most unfortunate those who share the food of sheep!" [Oh beati quelli pochi che seggiono a quella mensa dove lo pane de li angeli si manuca! e miseri quelli che con le pecore hanno comune cibo!] Just as Jesus held the Saducees and priests in disdain, so too does Dante reject the priests and lawmakers and speaks instead to the common people for they, like him, have been rejected and oppressed by the authorities. The Gospels contain examples of Jesus' rejection of the authority of the scribes, Saducees, and Pharisees. Matthew 5:20, for example, encapsulates the sentiments of Christ toward these lawmakers and enforcers of the law: "For I say to you, that unless your righteousness exceeds the righteousness of the scribes and Pharisees, you will by no means enter the kingdom of heaven." See also Matthew 15:14 ("Let them alone. They are blind leaders of the blind. And if the blind leads the blind, both will fall into a ditch.") and the entirety of Matthew 16, which further underlines Christ's attitude toward the Pharisees and Saducees. Dante is equally scathing in his treatment of these groups. A particular focus of his disdain is he who is "a friend of wisdom for the sake of utility, as are jurists, physicians, and almost all those belonging to religious orders" [*Conv.* III, xi, 10: colui che è amico di sapienza per utilitade, sì come li legisti, [li] medici e quasi tutti i religiosi].

[9] "All these things Jesus spoke to the multitude in parables; and without a parable He did not speak to them, that it might be fulfilled which was spoken by the prophet, saying: 'I will open My mouth in parables; I will utter things kept secret from the foundation of the world'" (Matt 13:34-38).

direction he is to follow. The new direction creates a new context within which other previous events are then reconciled. In the *Vita nuova*, the withdrawal of Beatrice's salutation and her death caused Dante to resituate himself in relation to the lyric poets and look to a new kind of poetry, one that praises without seeking recompense. Similarly, Dante's exile resituates him with respect to the entire field of "*litterari*" and "jurists" and opens the way for the challenge to their authority he mounts in the *Convivio*.[10] Nonetheless, given that the initial role upon which Dante now expands was first established in the *Vita nuova*, it is imperative that Dante deny neither the *Vita nuova* nor the meaning of its events. The *Convivio*, therefore, requires a difficult narrative balance on Dante's part. He must look forward, yet also keep the past in mind. Accordingly, in the *Convivio*, Dante takes great pains not to negate the divine selection revealed in the events of the *Vita nuova.* He states quite clearly that this work will not detract from the earlier piece and implicitly recognizes that he remains obliged to the authority established therein.[11] Even though the *Convivio* suggests that at the end of the *Vita nuova* Dante did not see his true destiny, it does not suggest that he was mistaken as to its divine nature. The error of the *Vita nuova* can be corrected, for it was only a misperception. It is perception, then, that is corrected in the *Convivio*, not the object perceived. Dante is by no means denying a

---

[10] Dante makes no secret of his disdain for the so-called "litterari" or "learned" and implicitly distinguishes himself from them. He holds lawmakers in a similar disdain. *Convivio* I, ix, 3: "To their shame I say that they should not be called learned, because they do not acquire learning for its own use but only insofar as through it they may gain money or honor," [E a vituperio di loro dico che non si deono chiamare litterari, però che non acquistano la lettera per lo suo uso, ma in quanto per quella guadagnano denari o dignitate,]

[11] *Convivio* I, i, 16.

divine destiny and does not want to be seen as turning away from such destiny to embrace either a worldly female or a profane doctrine. Accordingly, reason and the pursuit of knowledge in the *Convivio* are at all times linked to God and are essentially Christian in nature, just as his exile is expressed in Christian terminology.[12]

Dante hints at the true nature and extent of the redemption he will bring in a variety of ways. One of the earliest and perhaps most complex examples is found in the opening chapter where Dante refers to those who sit at the feet of the banquet guests, waiting to gather what falls.[13] The image recalls Matthew 15:26-27 wherein a Canaanite woman asks Christ's mercy for her sick daughter. Though Christ tells the woman, "It is not good to take the children's bread and throw it to the little dogs," she quickly responds that even the little "dogs eat the crumbs that fall from their masters' table." Seeing the woman's great faith, Christ concedes that although she is not a Hebrew, she is faithful, and he accedes to her request (v. 28). The episode is generally interpreted as Christ's anticipation of the conversion of the Gentiles, considered by the Hebrews to be unworthy "dogs."[14]

---

[12] As indicated above, the framing metaphor forged an affinity between Dante and Christ, thereby establishing a Christian context for Dante's marginalization.

[13] *Convivio* I, i, 10: "Therefore I (who do not sit at the blessed table, but, having fled the pasture of the common herd, gather up a part of what falls to the feet of those who do sit there…" [E io adunque, che non seggio a la beata mensa, ma, fuggito de la pastura del vulgo, a' piedi di coloro che seggiono ricolgo di quello che da loro cade…]

[14] The Jews historically referred to themselves as the "sons of God" because they were the chosen people who had preserved the true religion of the world and to whom God had entrusted God's promises. The Gentiles were called "dogs" for their idolatry and their deep moral corruption (Sales, *La Sacra Bibbia*, 70).

The combination of this image with that of Dante as the host of the banquet, mirrors the grammatical duality produced by Dante's undulation between first-person singular and first-person plural at the beginning of Book 1. The effect is one of inclusion and differentiation at the same time and conveys to the reader that Dante is like those who were excluded but whose faith will ultimately be rewarded with redemption. At the same time the dual role tells the reader that it is Dante who will bring this redemption. The role of redeemer is probably Dante's most significant expansion of the *Vita nuova*, for while there he was being redeemed, here he is both redeemed and redeemer. If we remember that the *Convivio* is to be read as a further development of the *Vita nuova* through which Dante told his literary story and hinted at his own *literary* redemption, then we see that Dante is now painting himself as the literary redeemer of those to whom redemption was not originally extended but who may eventually be proved worthy. The redemption starts with his own work, but, as we shall see by Book 4, the project has expanded to the redemption of pagan writers. The events of the *Convivio*, the circumstances of Dante's exile and unjust accusation, result in his mission being extended beyond that revealed in the *Vita nuova*. Now his mission goes beyond simply ordering and giving a Christian interpretation to his own history and writing. Now the task includes the history and writing of other authors. While Dante's study of philosophy has given him the tools to read and understand the ancient authors, his exile assures him of his divinely appointed authority to interpret them and to place them within a Christian context.

Nowhere is this expanded authority as pronounced as in the case of Dante's treatment of Cato of Utica, to whom he refers as "most hallowed"[15] and of whom he asks, "What man on

---

[15] *Convivio* IV, v, 16: "sacratissimo."

earth was more worthy to signify God than Cato? Surely none."[16] To further underscore the extent of this redemptive mission, Dante evokes the words of the Apostle Paul, immediately before and after both references to Cato. In the latter of the two citations, Dante invokes the same doctrine used by Paul (circumcision "of the heart") to justify preaching to the Gentiles[17] and by the church in its interpretation of the story in Matthew noted above.[18] Just as Paul showed the Gentiles the way to redemption, so too will Dante bring the possibility of redemption to the pagan writers whom he deems worthy. If, as Michelangelo Picone suggests, the *Vita nuova* represented opposing ideological worlds (classicism and Christianity) en route to reconciliation[19] then surely the *Convivio* continues the effort.[20] But here the emphasis is different. As Picone observes, in

---

[16] *Convivio* IV, xxviii, 15: "E quale uomo terreno più degno fu di significare Iddio, che Catone?"

[17] "For he is not a Jew who is one outwardly, nor is circumcision that which is outward in the flesh; but he is a Jew who is one inwardly; and circumcision is that of the heart, in the Spirit, not in the letter; whose praise is not from men but from God" (Rom 2:28-29).

[18] *Convivio* IV, xxviii, 10: "This is why St. Paul says to the Romans: 'He is not a Jew who is one outwardly, nor is that circumcision which is outwardly manifested in the flesh; but he is a Jew who is one inwardly, and circumcision is that of the heart, in spirit and not in the letter, whose praise comes not from men but from God.'" [E però dice santo Paulo alli Romani: "Non quelli ch'è manifestamente, è Giudeo, né quella ch'è manifesta [in] carne è circuncisione; ma quelli ch'è in ascoso è Giudeo, e la circuncisione del cuore, in ispirito non in littera, è circuncisione: la loda della quale [è] non dalli uomini ma da Dio."]

[19] Picone sees the *Vita nuova* as an amalgam of classical text and Christian commentary that represents the encounter of opposing ideological worlds (classicism and Christianity) en route to reconciliation ("La *Vita nuova* fra autobiografia e tipologia," 112).

[20] Dante's interpretation of the Gospel of Mark (that portion which narrates the appearance of the angel outside Christ's empty tomb) is just one of the many examples of Dante's efforts to integrate and give a Christian

the *Vita nuova* Dante's relationship to the classical authors was rooted in *imitatio*, that Dante, in writing his *libello*, integrates "the theory of pagan love (*eros*) into the vision of Christian charity (*caritas*)."[21] The reconciliation process in the earlier work was essentially one of absorption. In the *Convivio*, Picone points out, the classical authors are treated in a different way. Picone suggests that Chapters 25 through 28 of Book 4 illustrate most clearly Dante's reconciliation process at work in the *Convivio*. Here Dante ranks the quotations of classical authors "within an encyclopedic Christian system. For him there does not seem to be a rupture between pagan truth and Christian truth, but continuity. Thus the classical fables and myths are fully capable of being restored to modern learning."[22] Here then is where we see Dante at his most Pauline. He is not supplanting the classical authors but instead including them and converting their work into Christian literature. At the same time as Dante includes the pagan authors within a Christian rubric, he adopts forms not typically associated with Christian theological writing, such as Boethius's *De Consolatione Philosophiae* and the use of the "allegory of the poets"[23] to give structure to his own

---

context to the secular sciences. *Convivio* IV, xxii, 15: "By these three ladies may be understood the three schools of the active life: namely the Epicureans, the Stoics, and the Peripatetics, who go to the sepulcher (that is, the present world, which is a receptacle of corruptible things) and seek out the Savior (that is, blessedness)..." [Per queste tre donne si possono intendere le tre sette de la vita attiva, cioè li Epicurei, li Stoici e li Peripatetici, che vanno al monimento, cioè al mondo presente che è recettaculo di corruttibili cose, e domandano lo Salvatore, cioè la beatitudine...]

[21] Picone, "Dante and the Classics," 58.

[22] Ibid., 60.

[23] For example, Dante's noting the choice between allegory of the poets and allegory of the theologians in the *Convivio*. *Convivio* II, i, 3: "The first is called the literal, and this is the sense that does not go beyond the surface of the letter, as in the fables of the poets. The next is called the allegorical,

work. Dante's decisive statement on the issue of *auctoritas*, that an *auctor* is one who is not only to be believed but also obeyed,[24] helps legitimize his adoption of such forms. *Auctoritas* in Dante's hands suggests that a particular model of writing is to be followed by those aspiring to *auctoritas* and, conversely, that a form used by an *auctor* is legitimate. By using the forms of acknowledged *auctores*, Dante continues to present himself as an *auctor* while the lending of his Christian authority to the non-Christian forms continues his project of redemption of

---

and this is the one that is hidden beneath the cloak of these fables, and is a truth hidden beneath a beautiful fiction." [L'uno si chiama litterale, (e questo è quello che non si stende più oltre che la lettera de le parole fittizie, sì come sono le favole de li poeti. L'altro si chiama allegorico,) e questo è quello che si nasconde sotto 'l manto di queste favole, ed è una veritade ascosa sotto bella menzogna.]; *Convivio* II, i, 4: "Indeed the theologians take this sense otherwise than do the poets; but since it is my intention here to follow the method of the poets, I shall take the allegorical sense according to the usage of the poets." [Veramente li teologi questo senso prendono altrimenti che li poeti; ma però che mia intenzione è qui lo modo de li poeti seguitare, prendo lo senso allegorico secondo che per li poeti è usato.] As Hollander points out, the mixing of the two types of allegory was frowned upon (*Studies in Dante*, 41–46). Yet Dante has mixed the two types of allegory. Although, for Hollander, the significance of the introduction of this option lies in the fact that it buttresses Dante's claim to truthfulness of his poem, I would suggest that in the context of this book the import lies in the fact that it legitimizes the mixing of what was previously considered a secular format with that of a Christian format. Dante is fashioning a new role for the Christian poet, setting parameters that previously had not been sanctioned though in practice may have occurred. Antonio d'Andrea has also noted the novelty of this mixing, suggesting that Dante's attempts to combine the allegory of the poets and of the theologians, however, produce the result that "Lo statuto del senso letterale rimane così in sospeso e riflette la sua ambiguità sulla stessa" [The status of the literal sense thus remains suspended and reflects the ambiguity of the same] ("L' 'Allegoria dei poeti,'" 72).

[24] *Convivio* IV, vi, 5: "hence we can see that authority means "pronouncement worthy of faith and obedience." [E così 'autore', quinci derivato, si prende per ogni persona degna d'essere creduta e obedita.]

non-Christian authors.

Dante's exile, however, affects his literary story and engenders another narrative thread, that is, his political evolution. The inclusion of this story marks a decisive expansion of the *Vita nuova* and very much characterizes the *Convivio* as a second chapter. As Picone notes, the final aspiration of the *Vita nuova* was not to seek an historical reintegration into the *civitas terrena*, the earthly city, but to find an intellectual route that leads to his absolute integration into the *civitas eterna*, the eternal city.[25] The *Convivio*, on the other hand, is a book intentionally destined to restore its author in the esteem of the Florentine *civitas* from which he believes he was unjustly estranged.[26] In addition to effecting this reintegration, the *Convivio* seeks to vindicate Dante and redeem him in the eyes of his detractors. The inclusion of civic engagement in hagiography is by no means out of place when we consider that "the celebration of a saint...developed as an extension of the traditional *laudatio*, a partisan eulogistic biography."[27] As James Fraser has noted, "the goal of the hagiographer was rarely, if ever, to convince the incredulous...but to transform disinterested credulity into admiration, and even partisan devotion."[28] Dante thus positions himself as a patron saint of Florence, a latter-day saint whose redemption will extend to the wrong-minded Florentines.

---

[25] Picone notes, "iter intellettuale che conduce alla integrazione assoluta nella civitas eterna" ("La *Vita Nuova* fra autobiografia e tipologia," 63).

[26] In March 1302, when Dante was outside of Florence, he was accused of corruption by his political opponents and exiled. In the early days of his exile Dante, a member of the Guelph party, together with other exiled Guelphs, attempted to join up with members of the opposing Ghibelline party. See Watt, *The Cross that Dante Bears*, 206, and Browning, *Dante*, 31–32. In *Epistole* III, V, VI, VII, Dante refers to himself as exiled undeservedly, without merit, unjustly.

[27] Fraser, "Hagiography," 103.

[28] Ibid., 105.

Dante will save them from themselves.

Notwithstanding the apparent disparity such a divergent narrative thread might otherwise introduce, the adaptability of the framing metaphor of the banquet permits Dante to maintain a sense of internal cohesiveness throughout. The metaphor is ideally suited to the expression of Dante's literary progress and, in its implicit analogy between Christ and Dante, ideal for framing his political story since Dante, like Christ, has been unjustly accused. Just as the analogy between himself and Christ permitted Dante to assume the role of redeemer of the non-Christian writers, his role as an exile and, therefore, an external observer in this narrative thread justifies another role as teacher and redeemer of society.[29] Without offering us an explicit exegetical explanation, Dante has audaciously created an image that represents his perception of reality. It is almost as if he had written "And so I imagined my life, the false accusations and marginalization, as the life of Christ." Just as the true story of his literary evolution lay in the allegorical interpretation, here too the true story is also located in the allegorical meaning of the metaphor he uses to give form to his story.

Using the framing metaphor of the banquet as the principal representation of the events that impelled his political mission, Dante introduces a variety of strategies within that framework to express his reaction and his proposed solutions to the cataclysmic event of his exile. Dante's continuing desire to reintegrate himself into society, for example, is expressed not only in the content of the *Convivio* but also in its form. By commencing in the impersonal third person, Dante compels the reader to focus first on a universal or general notion not particular to

---

[29] As Cudini suggests, although the exile experience was a negative one, it serves to imbue Dante with an "eccezionalità" (exceptionality) and confirms the novelty of his cultural mission (*Convivio*, ed. Cudini, 56, 57).

anyone. The shift to the second-person plural refocuses the reader on a specific object, one in which the writer is addressing the reader and creating a common bond that is more intimate than the preceding generality.[30] When Dante ultimately shifts to the first-person singular,[31] the reader is finally made aware that the common bond is shared not with just a nameless writer, but the *io* (the "I"), which, for the reasons set out above, soon becomes identified with Dante, author and protagonist of the *Vita nuova*. Yet Dante does not maintain this distinction between *io* and the audience, the purpose of its insertion having been served. Instead, he alternates between the first-person plural and the first-person singular, making it clear that while he sees himself as outside of the existence of those whom he addresses, he is seeking ways to reintegrate himself.[32] However,

---

[30] *Convivio* I, i, 1: "As the Philosopher says at the beginning of the *First Philosophy*, all men by nature desire to know. The reason for this can be and is that each thing, impelled by a force provided by its own nature, inclines toward its own perfection. Since knowledge is the ultimate perfection of our soul, in which resides our ultimate happiness, we are all therefore by nature subject to a desire for it." [Sì come dice lo Filosofo nel principio de la Prima Filosofia, tutti li uomini naturalmente desiderano di sapere. La ragione di che puote essere ed è che ciascuna cosa, da providenza di prima natura impinta, è inclinabile a la sua propria perfezione; onde acciò che la scienza è ultima perfezione de la nostra anima, ne la quale sta la nostra ultima felicitade, tutti naturalmente al suo desiderio semo subietti.]

[31] *Convivio* I, i, 10: "Therefore I (who do not sit at the blessed table...)" [E io adunque, che non seggio a la beata mensa...]

[32] Cudini also notes this vacillation found in *Convivio* I, i, 1: "Così, i due periodi di cui si compone il paragrafo si chiudono sostanzialmente allo stesso modo, 'tutti li uomini naturalmente desiderano di sapere'/ 'tutti naturalmente al suo desiderio semo subietti': muta il soggetto, che da impersonale, dopo lo scorrere dell'argomentazione, si è personalizzato ('tutti...*semo* subietti')" [Thus, the two periods of which the paragraph is composed end substantially in the same way, "all men naturally desire to know" / "all of them naturally subject to their own desire": the subject changes, from the impersonal, after the flow of the 'argument, it is

Dante does not rely on form alone to express his desire for re-integration; the content of the *Convivio* confirms what the form suggested. Dante identifies his circumstances with those of the audience which he addresses. He paints himself as part of a collective and tells us why he should be considered part of that collective, part of the "us" of "*nostra anima*" (our soul).[33]

Dante uses the same fusion of form and content to express his desire to vindicate his name. He uses as a model, Boethius's *De Consolatione philosophiae*, a work explicitly designed to facilitate speaking of oneself to clear one's reputation.[34] Similarities

---

personalized ("we are all...subject")] (*Convivio*, ed. Cudini, 50–51).

[33] Cudini notes that Dante did not consider himself a scholar by profession, that he is not one "di quelli pochi che seggiono" [the few who are sit] but flees also from the "pastura del vulgo" [the common herd] and thereby becomes a scholar of the truly wise, from whom he gathers "di quello che da loro cade" [that which falls]. Cudini suggests that Dante is declaring his desire that the "miseri" share what he has learned or rather what he has already shown. In this way he alludes to the *canzoni* on which he will comment, which he has evidently already completely or partly divulged (*Convivio*, ed. Cudini, 7, 8). See *Convivio* I, i, 10-11:

"Therefore I (who do not sit at the blessed table, but, having fled the pasture of the common herd, gather up a part of what falls to the feet of those who do sit there, and who know the unfortunate life of those I have left behind, for the sweetness that I taste in what I gather up piece by piece, and moved by compassion, though not forgetting myself) have set aside for those who are unfortunate something that I placed before their eyes some time ago, by which I have increased their desire."

[E io adunque, che non seggio a la beata mensa, ma, fuggito de la pastura del vulgo, a' piedi di coloro che seggiono ricolgo di quello che da loro cade, e conosco la misera vita di quelli che dietro m'ho lasciati, per la dolcezza ch'io sento in quello che a poco a poco ricolgo, misericordievolmente mosso, non me dimenticando, per li miseri alcuna cosa ho riservata, la quale a li occhi loro, già è più tempo, ho dimostrata; e in ciò li ho fatti maggiormente vogliosi.]

[34] Picone suggests that Dante uses Boethius's *De Consolatione philosophiae* as one of the models for the *Convivio* (notwithstanding that it was not typically considered a "Christian" work) because it so readily accommodated its self-explanatory purpose ("La *Vita nuova* fra autobiografia e tipologia,"

in the form of both works would suggest that Dante's *Convivio* will have the same goal. However, Dante cites Boethius directly as authority to speak on his own behalf[35] so that the literal narrative also bears witness to this desire.[36]

It is in the expression of a third objective of the work, redemption, that the effectiveness of form combined with literal content is most evident. The narrative structure provided by the framing metaphor permits Dante to exploit a series of images, which in turn accommodate multiple allegorical meanings. The initial analogy between Dante and Christ, for example, is continually affirmed by metaphors that present society as a flock of sheep that has strayed from the right path.[37] Dante as the teacher and host of the supper will light the way, the right way, back to the fold. At the same time, the continual use of the path

63).

[35] *Convivio* I, ii, 13: "This necessity moved Boethius to speak of himself, so that under the pretext of consolation he might defend himself against the perpetual infamy of his exile, by showing it to be unjust, since no other apologist came forward." [E questa necessitate mosse Boezio di sé medesimo a parlare, acciò che sotto pretesto di consolazione escusasse la perpetuale infamia del suo esilio, mostrando quello essere ingiusto, poi che altro escusatore non si levava.]

[36] *Convivio*, ed. Cudini, vviii; Nardi, *Dal "Convivio" alla "Comedia,"* 21; *Convivio*, ed. Vasoli, xviii.

[37] "I am the good shepherd. The good shepherd gives His life for the sheep" (John 10:11); "But go rather to the lost sheep of the house of Israel" (Matt 10:6).

imagery[38] also recalls Christ's use of similar imagery.[39]

In this respect, the narrative of the *Convivio* bears much in common with the hagiographical tradition. As an attempt at creating an itinerary that will lead the sinner to redemption, the *Convivio* is related to the pilgrimage of the mind that Dante introduced in the *Vita nuova*. As this pilgrimage of the mind reenacts events from biblical history (as physical pilgrimages do), Dante employs another element common to the medieval hagiographical traditional: an arduous journey or pilgrimage undertaken by the saint.

Finally, Dante's representation of himself as the host of the banquet at which the new light will be given recalls Christ's characterizations of himself as the light that would bring people out of the darkness, the provider of bread, and redeemer of the

---

[38] *Convivio* IV, i, 9: "…iproposi di gridare a la gente che per mal cammino andavano, acciò che per diritto calle si dirizzassero" [I resolved that I would cry out to those who were walking along this evil path so that they might place themselves back on the right way.]; IV, xii, 19: "…lo buono camminatore giugne a termine e a posa; lo erroneo mai non l'aggiugne…" [A wise traveler reaches his goal and rests; the wanderer never reaches it,]; IV, xvi, 10: "E per lo cammino dritto è da vedere…" [So the straight way leads us]; IV, xxii, 6: "…così questi umani appetiti per diversi calli dal principio se ne vanno, e uno solo calle è quello che noi mena a la nostra pace" [so these human appetites proceed from the beginning along different paths, and there is but one path alone that leads us to our peace.]; IV, xxiv, 12: "…che entra ne la selva erronea di questa vita, non saprebbe tenere lo buono cammino…" [who enters into the meandering forest of this life would not know how to keep to the right path]; IV, xxviii, 2: "…l'altra si è, che ella benedice lo cammino che ha fatto…"[that it blesses the journey that it has made, because it has been straight and good].

[39] "Enter by the narrow gate; for wide is the gate and broad is the way that leads to destruction, and there are many who go in by it. Because narrow is the gate and difficult is the way which leads to life, and there are few who find it" (Matt 7:13-14).

faithful.[40] Dante's new role as savior extends, therefore, not only to literature but also to the society that wrongfully rejected him. Such redemption, it ought to be remembered, is not exclusively spiritual in nature. Certainly, Dante considers secular wisdom in a Christian context, but Dante, unlike Christ,[41] is not only attempting to bring about the kingdom of heaven; he is also attempting civic redemption, in essence, good government, through Aristotelian rationalism.

In choosing a framing metaphor that lends itself as easily to one narrative thread as to the other, Dante mirrors a technique that has its beginnings in the *Vita nuova*: the suggestion of one story by the imagery of the other. As in the *Vita nuova*,

---

[40] Jesus is frequently portrayed as the light that will bring the people out of the shadows: "That it might be fulfilled which was spoken by Isaiah the prophet, saying: 'The land of Zebulun and the land of Naphtali / By way of the sea, beyond the Jordan, / Galilee of the Gentiles: / The people who sat in darkness have seen a great light, / And upon those who sat in the region and shadow of death / Light has dawned" (Matt 4:14-16); "And this is the condemnation, that the light has come into the world, and men loved darkness more than light, because their deeds were evil" (John 3:19); "I am the light of the world. He who follows Me shall not walk in darkness but have the light of life" (John 8:12); "I have come as a light into the world, that whoever believes in Me should not abide in darkness" (John 12:46). The association of bread with life and salvation is also omnipresent in the New Testament. Christ offers bread (Matt 26:26), multiplies bread (Matt 14:19-20;), and characterizes himself as bread (John 6:35). Dante recalls many of these associations in presenting his banquet as one at which he will also serve bread. His general invitation of the "*miseri*" to his banquet recalls Christ's practice of eating with those most despised by society: "'Why does your Teacher eat with tax collectors and sinners?' When Jesus heard that, He said to them, 'Those who are well have no need of a physician, but those who are sick'" (Matt 9:11-12). Dante's reiteration that the knowledge he is imparting is divine in nature completes the association in recalling Christ's words to Satan: "It is written, 'Man shall not live by bread alone, but by every word that proceeds from the mouth of God'" (Matt 4:4).

[41] "Jesus said, 'My kingdom is not of this world'" (John 18:36).

where the same imagery lent itself as easily to the writer's story as to the love story, here too the imagery and structure of the *Convivio* are equally adept conveying the political story and the writer's story, both of which, in turn, share redemption as one of their goals. While at times the political message is distinct, as in Dante's use of invective,[42] and at others, his literary story is distinct (as in the digression on the meaning of *auctor*), often both stories overlap, making his role as *auctor* intrinsic to his political role. This overlap is most evident in the fourth book. What we see throughout the last completed *trattato* is that this layering is not simple coincidence in the sense that the two stories are parallel; rather, the narratives are linked such that the authority of one story is contingent on the other and each narrative thread provides the basis for the other.

It is in this fourth book, for example, that Dante cites Virgil's *Aeneid* as authority for his political views with respect to the divine authority of the Roman Empire.[43] In order to do so,

[42] One example of this appears in *Convivio* IV, xxvii, 11: "O my miserable, miserable homeland! What pity for you constrains me whenever I read or whenever I write anything that has to do with civil government!" [Oh misera, misera patria mia! quanta pietà mi stringe per te, qual volta leggo, qual volta scrivo cosa che a reggimento civile abbia rispetto!] See also *Convivio* IV, vi, 19-20: "I am speaking to you, Charles and Frederick…" [E dico a voi Carlo e Federigo regi…]

[43] *Convivio* IV, iv, 11: "Virgil concurs in this in the first book of the *Aeneid* when, speaking in the person of God, he says: 'To these (namely the Romans) I set no bounds, either in space or time; to these I have given empire without end.'" [E in ciò s'accorda Virgilio nel primo de lo Eneida, quando dice, in persona di Dio parlando: "A costoro—cioè a li Romani—né termine di cose né termine di tempo pongo; a loro ho dato impero sanza fine."] The reference is from *Aeneid* I, 278-79: "His ego nec metas rerum nec tempora pono: / imperium sine fine dedi" [To the Romans I set no boundary in space or time. I have granted them Dominion, and it has no end] (Virgil, *Aeneid*, 36). Dante's opinion in this respect is not expressed only in the *Convivio* but rather appears in Ep., VII, 11-12 in which Dante states that

Dante must first rewrite the relevant section of the *Aeneid* by attributing the words of Jupiter to "*Dio*" (God). Having thus redeemed and Christianized the work, Dante relies on it in support of his argument. His literary story and revised literary mission, therefore, become intrinsic to his political story, for only in redeeming a pagan authority can he legitimately set that author's works alongside the "Scriptures" whose prophecies will be fulfilled by Dante's political mission. Similarly, he poses a coincidence of Aeneas's arrival in Italy with the birth of King David, both of which he uses to confirm the historic basis of his argument that the world was at optimal disposition for the birth of Christ during the reign of the Roman Empire. Dante thereby assigns to the *Aeneid* the same historical value as he affords Orosio and the Old Testament.[44] That Dante's calculation as to the coincidence of the two events is dubious[45] only confirms the

---

the "glorious dominion of the Romans is confined neither by the frontiers of Italy, nor by the coast-line of three-cornered Europe. For although it has been constrained by violence to narrow the bounds of its government, yet by indefeasible right it everywhere stretches as far as the waves of Amphitrite, and scarce deigns to be circumscribed by the ineffectual waters of Ocean. [Romanorum gloriosa potestas nec metas Ytalie nec tricornis Europe margine coarctatur... Nam etsi vim passa in angustum gubernacula sua contraxerit, undique tamen de inviolabili iure fluctus Amphitritis attingens vix ab inutili unda Oceani se circumcingi dignatur.]

[44] *Convivio* IV, v, 6: "All this occurred at one point in time: David was born when Rome was born—that is, when Aeneas came to Italy from Troy, which was the origin of the Roman city, according to written records." [E tutto questo fu in uno temporale che David nacque e nacque Roma, cioè che Enea venne di Troia in Italia che fu origine de la cittade romana, sì come testimoniano le scritture.] As Vasoli points out, the "scritture" to which Dante refers are, for the foundation of Rome, *Aeneid* I, I, sgg. and for the birth of King David, Orosio, Eusebio di Cesarea and Livio (Vasoli, ed., *Convivio*).

[45] With respect to the dubious conclusion drawn by Dante in this regard, Vasoli cites Busnelli and Vandelli, both of whom note that any of the

importance of his insertion of the Virgil reference to his project. Dante has had to substantially revise either the biblical history or the "history" according to Virgil in order to locate the latter amongst the writings that confirm the fulfillment of the messianic prophecies. In Dante's hands, Virgil's *Aeneid* becomes intrinsic, along with the Gospel of Luke,[46] to his political expression.

The confluence of the two narrative threads is also accomplished stylistically, particularly in Dante's incessant and often tedious reliance on ordinal and hierarchical structure. Each argument on every topic he addresses is broken into parts of a whole and then again into sub-parts. The conspicuous use of reasoning and logic[47] makes it clear that Dante is seeking to depict himself in the commentary as a philosophical thinker capable of creating order and harmony out of an apparently chaotic world. When Dante suggests that if only the present-day

---

authorities available to Dante at the time of the *Convivio*'s writing would reveal a difference of almost a century between the two events.

[46] *Convivio* IV, v, 8:

> "Nor was the world ever, nor will it be, so perfectly disposed as at the time when it was guided by the voice of the one sole prince and commander of the Roman people, as Luke the Evangelist testifies." [Né 'l mondo mai non fu né sarà sì perfettamente disposto come allora che a la voce d'un solo, principe del roman popolo e comandatore, fu ordinato, sì come testimonia Luca evangelista.] In fact, Luke merely attests to the existence of such a ruler and does not conclude that this implies that the world was perfectly disposed at that time to the birth of Christ. ("And it came to pass in those days that a decree went out from Caesar Augustus that all the world should be registered" [Luke 2:1].)

[47] Aldo Vallone points out that much of Dante's didactic style reflects the structure of the medieval Latin prose in which Dante had immersed himself at the time of writing the *Convivio*, as opposed to the love poetry of his contemporaries, the language of which is so prevalent in the *Vita nuova* (*La Prosa del Convivio*, 15).

rulers had a philosophical adviser at their sides such a reconciliation might be achieved, the purpose of his self-depiction becomes clear.[48] Dante is the man for the job!

By the latter part of Book 4 we see an interesting development. While Dante is still using his literary evolution to express his political and social views, he seems to rely less and less on the philosophical models and looks with increasing frequency to Virgil, whom he calls "our greatest poet" and this "most exalted poet," as the authority for his political and social recommendations.[49] This is especially noticeable in Chapter 26 of Book 4, the entirety of which is taken up with Dante's opinion as to how one should comport oneself at a particular age. In contrast to the first three books, wherein Dante cites a variety of sources to support his arguments, in this chapter Virgil is the only authority on which he relies.[50] While in these instances

---

[48] *Convivio* IV, vi, 18:

which is to say, "Let the philosophic be united with the imperial authority, for good and perfect government." O pitiful are you who rule at present, and most pitiful you who are ruled! For no philosophical authority is united with your governments, whether by virtue of your own study or through the counsel of others, so that to all may be applied the words of Ecclesiastes, "Woe to you, O land whose king is a child and whose princes eat in the morning!"; and to no land may the following words be said: "Blessed is the land whose king is noble and whose princes devote their time to the people's needs and not to their own wantonness."

[ciò è a dire: "Congiungasi la filosofica autoritade con la imperiale, a bene e perfettamente reggere." Oh miseri che al presente reggete! e oh miserissimi che retti siete! ché nulla filosofica autoritade si congiunge con li vostri reggimenti né per proprio studio né per consiglio, sì che a tutti si può dire quella parola de lo Ecclesiaste: "Guai a te, terra, lo cui re è fanciullo, e li cui principi la domane mangiano!," e a nulla terra si può dire quella che seguita: "Beata la terra lo cui re è nobile e li cui principi si cibano nel suo tempo, a bisogno e non a lussuria!"]

[49] *Convivio* IV, xxvi, 8: "lo maggiore nostro poeta"; IV, xxvi, 13: "questo altissimo poeta"

[50] *Convivio* IV, xxvi, 8:

Vergil, our greatest poet, shows that Aeneas was unrestrained in this way in that part of the *Aeneid* in which this age of life is allegorized, the part comprising the fourth, fifth, and sixth books of the *Aeneid*. How great was his restraint when, having experienced so much pleasure with Dido, as will be recounted below in the seventh book, and having derived from her so much gratification, he took his departure from her to follow an honorable, praiseworthy and profitable path, as is recorded in the fourth book of the Aeneid! What spurring was felt when this same Aeneas mustered the courage to enter into Hell alone with the Sibyl in search of the soul of his father Anchises, in the face of so many perils, as is described in the sixth book of the same history.

[E così infrenato mostra Virgilio, lo maggiore nostro poeta, che fosse Enea, ne la parte de lo Eneida ove questa etade si figura; la quale parte comprende lo quarto, lo quinto e lo sesto libro de Eneida. E quanto raffrenare fu quello, quando avendo ricevuto da Dido tanto di piacere quanto di sotto nel settimo trattato si dicerà, e usando con esse tanto do dilettazione, elli si partio, per seguire onesta e laudabile via e fruttuosa, come nel quarto de l'Eneida scritto è! Quanto spronare fu quello, quando esso Enea sostenette solo con Sibilla a intrare ne lo Inferno a cercare de l'anima di suo padre Anchise, contra tanto pericoli, come nel sesto de la detta istoria si dimostra!]

Convivio IV, xxvi, 11:

"As the previously named poet shows in the fifth book mentioned above, this is the love that Aeneas had when he left the aged Trojans behind in Sicily, entrusting them to the care of Acestes, and released them from their labors, and when in this same site he prepared his young son Ascanius, with the other youths, for tournament games. From this it is evident that love is necessary in this age of life, as the text states." [E questo amore mostra che avesse Enea lo nomato poeta nel quinto libro sopra detto, quando lasciò li vecchi Troiani in Cicilia raccomandati ad Aceste, e partilli da le fatiche; e quando ammaestrò in questo luogo Ascanio, suo figliuolo, con li altri adoloscentuli armeggiando. Per che appare a questa etade necessario essere amore, come lo testo dice.]

Convivio IV, xxvi, 13:

Our most exalted poet shows in the sixth book previously mentioned that Aeneas had this courtesy when he says that King Aeneas, to honor the lifeless body of Misenus, who had been Hector's trumpeter and had afterwards placed himself in Aeneas' trust, made preparations and took up his ax to help hew the wood for the fire that would be used to burn the body,

Dante does not rewrite Virgil as he did in chapters 4 and 5 of Book 4, he does, nonetheless, offer an interpretation of the *Aeneid* that differs from the generally accepted interpretation of the time and of which he was likely aware.[51] This variation indicates that Dante is prepared to offer revised readings of his

---

in keeping with their custom. From this it is quite evident that courtesy is necessary in maturity, and therefore the noble soul displays it in that age of life, as has been said.

[È questa cortesia mostra che avesse Enea questo altissimo poeta, nel sesto sopradetto, quando dice che Enea rege, per onorare lo corpo di Miseno morto, che era stato trombatore d'Ettore e poi s'era raccomandato a lui, s'accinse e prese la scure ad aiutare tagliare le legne per lo fuoco che dovea ardere lo corpo morto; come era di loro costume. Per che bene appare questa essere necessaria a la gioventute, e però la nobile anima in quella la dimostra, come detto è,]

Convivio IV, xxvi, 14:

It should suffice for him to follow the law and to take delight in following it, as the previously cited poet in the above-mentioned fifth book says that Aeneas did when he held the games in Sicily on the anniversary of his father's death, for he loyally awarded to each victor what he had promised for victory, according to their longstanding custom, which was their law. From this it is evident that in this age of life loyalty, courtesy, love, courage, and temperance are necessary, as the text presently under discussion states; and therefore the soul that is noble displays them all.

[E basti che esso seguiti la legge, e in quella seguitare si diletti: sì come dice lo predetto poeta, nel predetto quinto libro, che fece Enea, quando fece li giuochi in Cicilia ne l'anniversario del padre; che ciò che promise per le vittorie, lealmente siede poi a ciascuno vittorioso, sì come era di loro lunga usanza, che era loro legge. Per che è manifesto che a questa etade lealtate, cortesia, amore, fortezza e temperanza siano necessarie, sì come dice lo testo che al presente è ragionato, e però la nobile anima tutte le dimostra.]

[51] Vasoli cites Busnelli and Vandelli, who have noted that the interpretation of Virgil's *Aeneid* as an allegory for the human lifespan can be traced to Fabio Fulgenzio Planciade, who lived between the fifth and sixth centuries and who was a well-known author in medieval schools. His *Expositio virgilianae continentiae* equates each of the four ages of man into a particular section of the poem. Dante's allegorical interpretation of the sixth book of the *Aeneid*, for example, in the fourth book of the *Convivio*, according to

auctores to facilitate the expression of his own story. This shift in influence may have signaled even further development in Dante's literary evolution, but, because the *Convivio* is unfinished, it is impossible to say with any certainty to what extent Dante may have continued to express such a development.[52] However, this shift away from Aristotle and the apparent movement to yet another literary model might, in light of the *Comedy*, be read as evidence of Dante's dissatisfaction with rational philosophy and the reason for the *Convivio*'s unfinished state.

Vasoli, is substantially removed from that of Fulgentius, who understands Aeneas's descent into Hades as a symbol of the human initiation into "sapientiae obscura secretaque misteria" [dark and secret mysteries of knowledge (my translation)] whereas for Dante the episode is an allegory for strength or rather greatness of spirit demonstrated by the hero when he confronts the frightening secrets of the underworld. Similarly, as Vasoli notes, Dante's interpretation of the episode, in which the games are celebrated in Sicily to commemorate the anniversary of Anchise's death, differs from Fulgentius's.

For Dante, however, the episode represents the attribute of "lealtade." That Dante was aware of the accepted interpretation is evident from *Convivio* IV, xxiv, 9: "Leaving aside the allegorical meaning which Vergil applies to the different ages of human development in the *Aeneid*..." [E lasciando lo figurato che di questo diverso processo de l'etadi tiene Virgilio ne lo Eneide...]

[52] Ulrich Leo associates this shift in model with the very reasons the *Convivio* remains unfinished. In his comprehensive article "The Unfinished *Convivio* and Dante's rereading of the *Aeneid*," Leo suggests that aside from philosophical and religious reasons, there were literary and aesthetic reasons for the halt in work on what Leo posits was to have been Dante's "*Summa philosophiae* in volgare." Looking to formal shifts in the way classical authors are cited in the *Convivio*, Leo concludes, "Dante, while writing the last chapters of the fourth Book of the *Convivio*, and at the same time the end of the fragmentary *De Vulgari eloquentia*, read again, or in part for the first time classical Latin poetry and prose. Among the poetry read by him was—perhaps suggested by the allegorical explanations of Virgil used in *Conv.* IV—the sixth Book of the *Aeneid*, which tells the story of Aeneas's descent into Hell" (45).

Numerous aspects of the *Convivio* suggest that Dante saw it as a continuation of the life-writing exercise he started in the *Vita nuova*: the auto-exegetical stance and the preoccupation with *auctoritas* mark it as the next stage in Dante's accounting of his literary evolution. The influence of Beatrice, however, is substantially less noticeable and it becomes apparent that if once Dante thought the road to his own redemption, literary and spiritual, lay with his love for the now dead Beatrice, he now believes that he too has been tasked with a salvific mission. Specifically, Dante's association with the saintly Beatrice empowers him to redeem not only the authors who preceded him but also the society that rejected him. In the *Convivio* we see that it may also have engendered his auto-hagiographic impulse.

Dante's attempts to demonstrate this development, through the figure of the *donna gentile*, has caused intense discussion amongst scholars.[53] The principal difficulty lies in

---

[53] Richard Lansing takes the position that the two works and the treatment of the *donna gentile* in both are irreconcilable. Luigi Pietrobono is adamant that there is no way to reconcile the two. In *An Essay on the* Vita Nuova, Charles Singleton takes the position that Beatrice becomes an allegory in the *Convivio* and the *Comedy*. Kenneth MacKenzie, however, feels that the two versions don't contradict each other, suggesting that

> Some years later in exile, with his usual method of ascribing to real events an allegorical meaning, Dante hit upon the idea of making this lady a symbol of his philosophical studies—the idea being suggested by Boethius, who in the Book cited personifies Philosophy as a sympathizing lady. As one seeks silver and finds gold, so these studies, undertaken as a consolation, led Dante to comprehend the real nature of Beatrice. It is not necessary to make the allegory correspond in every detail with the original facts. The method of Dante, we must remember, is to start with a literal meaning and proceed thence to the allegorical; the latter being more "true" because in accord with permanent underlying principles. Understood in this way, the two accounts of the episode do not contradict each other; and the account in the *Convivio*, cannot properly be taken as proof that the *gentile donna* of *Vita nuova* was nothing but a symbol. Still less does it support the

---

view that Beatrice was a purely imaginary person; in the *Convivio* she is always spoken of as real. (*La Vita nuova*, ed. McKenzie, 128)

Francis Fergusson says he simply does not believe Dante. Bruno Nardi resolves the issue by hypothesizing revisions to the *Vita nuova* made after the *Convivio* was written:

> ...siffatta conclusione della *Vita nuova* è perentoriamente esclusa dall'autocitazione che Dante ne fa nel *Convivio*, commentando la Canzone *Voi che 'ntendendo*. La fine della *Vita nuova* cui Dante fu esplicito e preciso reiferimento nel trattato secondo del *Convivio* e che è presupposta dalla canzone *Voi che 'ntendendo* era cosa assai diversa da quella che ora vi si legge. Dunque è evidente che Dante stesso ebbe più tardi a dare alla *Vita nuova* una conclusione diversa da quella che aveva in origine. (Nardi, *Dal "Convivio" alla "Commedia,"* 7)

> [...such a conclusion of the *Vita nuova* is peremptorily excluded by Dante's self-quotation of it in the *Convivio*, commenting on the *canzone Voi che 'ntendendo* that he intends. The end of the new life to which Dante was explicit and precise reference in the second treatise of the Convivio and which is presupposed by the song *Voi che 'ntendendo* was something very different from what we now read there. Therefore, it is evident that Dante himself later gave a different conclusion to the *Vita nuova* from the one he originally had.]

Even less satisfactory is the suggestion by Gioacchino Natoli of a second Beatrice; "Filosofia è la donna gentile destinata a diventare gentilissima, o Beatrice" [Philosophy is the kind woman destined to become very kind, or Beatrice] (*Dante rivelato nel Convivio*, 70).

Cesare Vasoli provides a concise summary of the various critical options and favors the approach suggested by Barbi in which the two episodes are seen as distinct: "quali sono narrativi, prima nella *Vita nuova* e poi nel *Convivio*, in quanto 'manifestazioni d'arte di due periodi distinti e successivi' vanno tenuti separati." [these are narratives, first in the *Vita* and then in the *Convivio*, in as much as they are manifestations of the art of two distinct and successive periods, are to be kept separate.] In conformity with this approach, he distinguishes as well between the interpretation of the two episodes, noting that in the *Convivio*, "la vicenda prende il ritmo e le misure delle nuove esperienze intellettuali di Dante e il vecchio episodio, immaginato per la *Vita nuova* serve ora, come 'dichiarate finzione retorica', e giustificare l'immaginazione della filosofia come 'donna gentile', e l'uso del 'vecchio linguaggio' per parlare di un nuovo 'amore di scienza e non di creature umana' concilabile e integrabile con quello di Beatrice" [the story

Dante's differing treatment of the *donna gentile* in the two works. In the *Vita nuova*, she is presented as a purportedly real woman whom Dante ultimately abandons in order to stay true to the memory of Beatrice. In the *Convivio*, however, Dante narrates a struggle between the memory of Beatrice and his love for the same *donna gentile*—there is no doubt that he is referring to the same woman for he tells us so[54]—and chooses to stay with the latter. The key to resolving the issue, it would appear, lies in remembering that Dante explicitly tells us that in the poems of the *Convivio* the *donna gentile* represents the study of

---

takes the rhythm and measures of Dante's new intellectual experiences and the old episode, imagined for the *Vita nuova* now serves as "declared rhetorical fiction", and justifies the imagining of philosophy as a "gentle woman", and the use of the "old language" to speak of a new "love of science and not of human creatures" which can be reconciled and integrated with that of Beatrice] (*Convivio*, ed. Vasoli, xvi).

Similar in its practicality is the approach taken by Cudini: "Inutile rivedere ora la posizioni della critica.... Basti...ricordare come Dante stesso sia cosciente della diversità di modi e funzione tra le due opere (pur nella loro sotanziale continuità), spesse volte riaffermata (e più che altrove esplicita in I i 16-17)." [It is useless now to review the positions of the criticism.... Suffice it...to remember how Dante himself is aware of the diversity of modes and functions between the two works (despite their substantial continuity), often reaffirmed (and more than elsewhere explicit in I i 16-17)] (*Convivio*, ed. Cudini, 133).

[54] *Convivio* II, ii, 1: "when that gentle lady, of whom I made mention at the end of the *New Life*," [quando quella gentile donna, cui feci menzione ne la fine de la Vita nuova,]

Vasoli also notes this, saying "Dante...sembra dichiarare esplicitamente che la verità narrata nella canzone non è tale di fatto, bensì è un'invenzione poetica che gli permetterà di esprimere e communicare verità e dottrine altrimenti inaccesssibili per il pubblico al quale è destinato il *Convivio*" [Dante...seems to explicitly state that the truth narrated in the canzone is not such in fact, but is a poetic invention that will allow him to express and communicate truths and doctrines otherwise inaccessible to the audience the Convivio is intended for] (*Convivio*, ed. Vasoli, xxii).

Philosophy and that the narrative of the poems was constructed to tell this story.[55] The events, as narrated, are therefore not real, that is, they did not occur in actuality. Or at least, and perhaps more importantly, Dante wants us to perceive the events as representations. That being the case, there appears to be little difficulty in reconciling the two versions of the *donna gentile*: at the end of the *Vita nuova* Dante chose not to remain with a purportedly actual woman and instead chose the kind of love represented by Beatrice, that kind of love that finds its reward in the act of praise itself.

Moreover, what Dante *does not* say in the *Convivio* is of utmost importance. He does not say that in hindsight he realized that this woman (whom he described as an "adversary of reason" and the desire for whom he described as a "wicked desire and vain temptation") was Philosophy in the same way that he realized in hindsight that Beatrice was a nine and, therefore,

---

[55] *Convivio* II, xii, 8:

Per che io, sentendomi levare dal pensiero del primo amore a la virtù di questo, quasi marvigliandomi apersi la bocca nel parlare de la proposta canzone, mostrando la mia condizione sotto figura d'altre cose: però che de la donna di cu' io m'innamorava non era degna rima di volgare alcuna palesemente po[e]tare; né li uditori erano tanto bene disposti, che avessero sì leggiere le [non] fittizie parole apprese; né sarebbe data loro fede a la sentenza vera, come a la fittizia, però che di vero si credea del tutto che disposto fosse a quello amore, che non si credeva di questo.

[Consequently, feeling myself raised from the thought of that first love to the virtue of this one, almost in amazement I opened my mouth to speak the words of the canzone before us, revealing my condition beneath the figure of other things, because no rhyme in any vernacular was worthy to treat openly of the lady of whom I was enamored; nor were the listeners so well prepared that they would have understood the fictive words so easily; nor would they have given credence to their true meaning, as they did to the fictive, because in fact they fully believed that I was disposed toward this love, and not, as they believed, to the other.] See also *Convivio* II, i ,1; *Convivio* II, xii, 8.

a miracle.[56] What Dante does say is, "And I imagined her [referring to Philosophy] fashioned as a gentle lady."[57] Dante has simply adopted a method used often in Christian iconography, such as Saint Francis of Assisi's likening of poverty to a woman or, more telling perhaps, in Boethius's representation of philosophy as a woman.[58] Dante's choice of metaphor, the pursuit of a lover, to frame this episode underlines the popularity of love as a favorite subject or catalyst for discussions of everything from philosophy to metaphysics.[59] At the same time, it conveniently continues the motif of the *Vita nuova*, which also dealt with literary endeavor in terms of a love story.

As was the case with Beatrice, the actual existence of the *donna gentile* in the *Vita nuova* is not nearly as important as the reader's perception of her as actual. She may or may not have existed and Dante may or may not have turned to her at a time when he was otherwise inconsolable, but this uncertainty is of little consequence. What does matter is that for the purposes of the *Vita nuova*, the *donna gentile* is purportedly actual and is de-

---

[56] *Vita nuova*, Chap. XXXIX [XL], 1, 6: "Avversario de la ragione"; "malvagio and vana tentazione"

[57] *Convivio* II, xii, 6: "E immaginava lei fatta come una donna gentile."

[58] Richard Lansing notes that the personification of philosophy is likewise a familiar image, for Dante is directly indebted to the paradigm Boethius employs in *De Consolatione Philosophiae*, a work he cites as one of his two principal models. The figure of the poet as lover of an abstraction is, he continues, "a narrative device familiar to much of medieval literature" (*Il Convivio*, trans. Lansing, xiv).

Nardi notes, "Boezio ha tramito al medioevo l'immagine allegorica della filosofia che si vede ancora scolpita nelle facciate di alcune cattedrali" [Boethius conveyed to the Middle Ages the allegorical image of philosophy that can still be seen carved on the facades of some cathedrals] (*Dal "Convivio" alla "Commedia,"* 11).

[59] Vasoli refers to "l'uso emblematico del linguaggio d'amore" [the emblematic use of the language of love] (*Convivio*, ed. Vasoli, xvi).

picted as a distraction from Dante's praise of the now dead Beatrice. In the *Convivio*, Dante chooses to represent his new pursuit in the form of a character who, in the *Vita nuova*, had constituted a distraction from Beatrice and who was, therefore, a diversion from his primary pursuit at that time. In both works, the *donna gentile* represents movement beyond Beatrice and whatever she may represent. She must add to the Beatrice of the *Vita nuova* so that Dante can mark a new and broader direction, so that he can "correct," if not the error, then the shortsightedness of the earlier work and demonstrate his literary progression. In using a figure that he has previously used, he creates a continuity between the two works and revises his trajectory. At this point Dante is not prepared to attach to Beatrice the wide range of meanings with which he will infuse her in the *Comedy*. In the *Convivio*, Dante associates Beatrice only with love, not philosophy, politics, or theology. In the *Convivio*, Dante distinguishes reason and philosophy from love, so he must find another referent for them; the *donna gentile* represents one of Dante's earliest attempts at palinodic revision. The primacy of the *donna gentile* in the *Convivio* signals clearly that, at this point at least, he does not see philosophic wisdom and the language of love as compatible. If the Dante of the *Vita nuova* thought his destiny lay in the field of lyric poetry, the Dante of the *Convivio* tells him he was mistaken.

Accordingly, the literal meaning of the *Convivio* poems can be reconciled with the apparently incompatible ending of the *Vita nuova* if we read them in the same way as we read the entirety of the *Convivio*: as a continuation of the story commenced in the *Vita nuova*, relegating the *Vita nuova* and its poetry to "then" status. In this way, we can see that Dante has simply prolonged the struggle between the two forces; therefore, it seems that, although at the end of the *Vita nuova* he had decided to stay with Beatrice, the struggle continued, with the "true" ending to the episode being found in the *Convivio*. Such a reading is compatible with Dante's evident attempt to present the two works as linked and suggests as well that the meaning of the *Vita nuova* ought to be considered in light of this newer truth: Dante's new destiny is much broader than he believed it to be at the end of the *Vita nuova*.

A greater problem, however, arises from Dante's directive as to how the poems of the *Convivio* are to be interpreted.[60] If, in the *Convivio*, the poems are constructs and the events narrated in their literal level are also constructs, then what are we to make of the *Vita nuova*? Is its literal meaning also a *bella menzogna*? If so, such an interpretation could negate the divine selection implied in its events and ignores the importance Dante places on the reader perceiving Beatrice as actual. On the other hand, if the poems of the *Convivio* were interpreted as representing actual events, then it becomes even more difficult to reconcile the apparent contradiction. To suggest that the poetry of both works should be interpreted according to two different methods seems, at first, no more satisfying an explanation. However, a distinction in interpretive method is consistent with the differing moods of the two works and may be justifiable as another indication of an ideological shift in Dante's project.[61] More importantly, in either case, the significance of the poems, the allegorical meaning, which in both interpretive

[60] See *Convivio* II, i.

[61] Ulrich Leo gives a concise overview of the main positions in this respect, citing Pietrobono as a proponent of the opinion that the Dante of the *Vita nuova* is a mystic while in the *Convivio* Dante follows human reason. ("The Unfinished *Convivio*," 42). The Pietrobono position holds that in the *Convivio*, Dante's reason leads to a Christian faith but that it is a faith void of superrational illumination. The position taken by Michele Barbi also notes a distinction in mode, suggesting that while the *Vita nuova* is a highly poetic love story set on a background of reality, the *Convivio* is marked by its rationalism.

schemes is considered "true," reveals an autobiographical intent.

We see then that while the *Convivio* continues the project commenced in the *Vita nuova*, it was by no means the culmination. What we do see is a more pronounced direction in terms of strategies Dante employs to transform his story into a form not only expressing the facts as they existed but also conveying the connotation he intends to attach to them. Dante's shift in Book 4 away from commentary that is strictly tied to an interpretation of the poetry suggests an evolving vision of what form his life story should take. As the focus of the work shifts from the general view of the cosmos as a scientific entity capable of being mapped and catalogued to a politically oriented exploration of how man should exist daily within that cosmos, there is a parallel shift from a mere transfer of knowledge to an effort at solving some of the problems confronting the author.[62] This movement suggests an evolving Dante and comprises perhaps one of the most telling manifestations of his actual story. Of course, Dante abandoned the *Convivio*, and it is not until the *Comedy* that we see the form that this self-portrait will ultimately take.

[62] Vasoli notes the shift in emphasis in Book IV, suggesting that the narration shifts to resemble a "'quaestio' scholastico" [scholarly inquiry] (*Convivio*, ed. Vasoli, xvii).

Chapter 4

A Canticle of *Caritas*

AS A POETIC narrative devoid of an accompanying prose commentary, the *Comedy* immediately signals a substantial departure from the *Convivio* and the *Vita nuova*.[1] However, the distinctions between the *Comedy* and the earlier two "autobio-

[1] It is perhaps this lack of a prose commentary that has led to the great debate as to whether the journey of the *Divine Comedy* is a metaphor. Nardi, for example, has argued that Dante considered his own experience as a "visione verace" and that those who view the poem as a literary fiction misread it: "Chi considera la visione dantesca e il rapimento del poeta al cielo come finzione letteraria, travisa il senso" [Anyone who considers Dante's vision and the poet's rapture to heaven as literary fiction, misrepresents the meaning] (*Dante e la cultura medioevale*, 392).

Scholars critics have pondered whether Dante took the journey he describes, whether he did not take the journey but instead uses the journey to describe a vision he experienced, or whether the entirety of the *Comedy* is simply a fiction Dante may or may not have intended his readers to believe happened.

Charles Singleton, on the other hand, is renowned for his statement that "the fiction of the *Divine Comedy* is that it is not fiction" (*Dante Studies 1*, 62). The letter to Can Grande, whether authentic or not, is proof only of the way in which Dante suggests the events of the *Comedy* should be interpreted; that is, that the allegorical level is to be true. However, since the autobiographical story is not located expressly in the literal level of the *Comedy*, this debate is little more than incidental to the examination before us now. For the purposes of this book, the journey will be treated as a metaphor

graphical" works are not only distinctions in form. Indeed, while most scholars agree (though to differing extents) that the works are related, philosophical variations and differences in their expression have generated a large part of Dante scholarship.[2]

I would suggest, however, that one of the features that most distinguishes the *Comedy* from those earlier attempts at life-writing is a significant reconfiguration of Dante's perspective vis-à-vis the meaning of his life. In the *Comedy*, Dante uses what Evelyn Birge Vitz calls a "vertical" comparison to express the significance and purpose of his life. In the *Comedy* the extraordinary quality of Dante's experience is marked not by the things that make him different from others, but by aspects of his life that are shared with others. That is, the *Comedy* marks Dante's attempt to reconcile himself within the paradigm of the lives of others, to see the meaning of his life in an inclusive rather than in an exclusive way. This kind of comparison, found in Abelard's and in other typically medieval "autobiographies," affects not only how the *Comedy* tells Dante's stories but also how it situates itself in terms of genre.

This inclusive aspect of the *Comedy* is signaled from the

(cf. William Franke's view of the debate, "Reader's Application").

[2] Leo gives a comprehensive yet concise summary of the prevailing schools of thought with respect to the apparent philosophical distinctions between the *Vita nuova*, the *Convivio*, and the *Comedy*. He summarizes the various opinions as follows:

> While Pietrobono suggests that the *Convivio* reflects a temporary renunciation of the inspiration that produced the *Vita nuova* and a return to it with the *Comedy*, Michele Barbi sees no break between the *Convivio* and the *Comedy*, except that the form used is now poetic. Beatrice, for Barbi, symbolizes this change of expression. Etienne Gilson adopts Barbi's approach, proposing that faith and metaphysics are excluded from the *Convivio* because they had "no practical part there" though they are "at the centre of the *Comedy*" (Leo, "The Unfinished *Convivio*," 45).

moment Dante places himself "In the middle of the road of our life."[3] He enunciates first that the narrative that follows will involve the "us" of "our life." Only after he establishes that this will be the story of *our* journey does he make reference to himself ("I found myself"), suggesting that his story is a mere variant extracted from within a greater pattern, emerging upon that same road.[4] The *Convivio* raised this issue, but here the relationship between "we" and "I" is resolved through the levels of imagery, and both voices are presented much more clearly as components of a single paradigm rather than as alternative narrative voices. That is, here in the *Comedy*, "I" is presented as being included in "we" rather than being a state of existence outside of "we." Though exile in the *Convivio* begot only the unrequited desire to reintegrate, in the *Comedy* exile is transformed into the very means by which reintegration is made possible. Dante accomplishes this through the framing metaphor of the journey. In contrast to the *Vita nuova* and the *Convivio*, where Dante was writing only his own story and in which the events bore a significance particular to him, in the *Comedy* Dante presents a series of events or episodes with both particular and universal significance. The journey is still Dante's story, for Dante, like each of us, shares the universal experience of the journey of life, a passage through time and space from point to point. But the particular events of Dante's life are here distinguished within that journey by a vertical pattern of descent and ascent. If we visualize the journey as a horizontal line at the middle of which ("In the *middle* of the road"—my emphasis) a vertical descent and ascent are imposed, we find that Dante has created a cruciform narrative. While Iannucci has noted the overwhelming presence of the "*discesa*" (descent) pattern, he has

---

[3] *Inf.* 1:1: "Nel mezzo del cammin di nostra vita"

[4] *Inf.* 1:2: "mi ritrovai"

primarily associated that descent with the role of Beatrice in Dante's salvation and its typological relationship to Christian salvation.[5] What I am suggesting is that the "descent" has an even broader role than Iannucci envisaged, a role, when taken together with its counterpart, "ascent," informs the entire narrative structure of the *Comedy* and has implications for all of Dante's stories. However, while Dante's own stories are located within the vertical pattern, they are by no means independent of the basic journey structure. Indeed, the two patterns are inextricably bound. Without the journey there can be no ascent and descent and, therefore, nothing to distinguish Dante's particular story. The journey metaphor provides the canvas, the universal on which to paint the particular. It not only provides the basis for the *Comedy*'s narrative structure but also accommodates multiple layers of significance. The cruciform created by the intersection of the vertical with the horizontal affirms that the *Comedy* offers salvation not just for one but for many—and that Dante is the purveyor of that salvation.

All the theological, doctrinal, and narratological differences between the earlier efforts and the *Comedy* make sense if we consider this integrated approach as the feature that most distinguishes the *Comedy* from Dante's other "autobiographical" works. Dante's stance in the *Comedy*, his new manner of distinguishing his life, leads to a reconciliation of the issues raised by his previous efforts. This stance, therefore, reflects one of the key functions of the *Comedy*, that is, to finally resolve all the issues left open by the narrative attempts of the *Vita nuova* and the *Convivio*. In expressing his life as a particular example of a universal meaning, Dante makes sense of both his life and his

---

[5] "Strutturalmente, il processo della salvezza assume la forma di una discesa all'inferno" [Structurally, the process of salvation assumes the form of a descent into hell (my translation)] (Iannucci, *Forma ed evento nella Divina Commedia*, 65).

previous attempts at writing it. The narrative form reiterates the *Comedy*'s significance and buttresses the *Comedy*'s ultimate truth and by extension, Dante's own authority as its author.

At the same time, the new stance solves the narrative issues presented by the timing of the various works. Although the *Comedy* was written after the *Convivio* and the *Vita nuova*, the events of the *Comedy* pre-date the composition of the *Convivio*.[6] How then can the narrative of the *Comedy* be said to absorb or indeed even consider the *Convivio*? The question is easily addressed if we recognize another aspect inherent in the cruciform narrative. While the "journey of our life" embodies the temporal and spatial progression from point to point, the presence of the vertical ascent and descent pattern marks a departure that now enables Dante to assume the perspective required by the Augustinian model. He can place himself "outside" of the previous life by situating himself on a different existential plane. Accordingly, Dante's removal also removes the *Comedy* from the confines of the temporally and spatially bound narratives of the *Vita nuova* and the *Convivio*. Here in the *Comedy*, the *nunc et tunc* distinction is tied not so much to temporality but instead has its genesis in its completely different view the events of his life. It would probably be more accurate to refer to the distinction as one of "this and that" rather than "now and then." Accordingly, within this vertical pattern, the problems generated by temporal chronology cease to exist. Indeed, the further Dante ascends toward a final vision of the *Paradiso*, the more it becomes apparent that temporality is an essentially earthly concern, not the concern of the vertical plane on which the journey of the *Comedy* exists.

It is within this dual context that I will examine, over the next two chapters, how Dante continues the stories of the *Vita*

---

[6] See Leo, "The Unfinished *Convivio*," 41.

nuova and the *Convivio* to tell and reconcile his love story and the story of his political vicissitudes with his quest for *auctoritas*.[7] What will become apparent is that through a number of narrative and exegetical strategies (e.g., the use of parallel episodes[8]) Dante gradually reveals that these stories are not only variants of each other but representations of a greater truth. In the *Comedy*, Dante finally finds the structure within which to fuse his own life with that of humankind, and his own books with God's book of the universe. The *Comedy* then is truly Dante's life story, for it satisfies all the requirements set out by both modern and medieval notions of autobiography. It is a retrospective writing of the author's life in order to find meaning in it.

Moreover, as Dante increasingly uses vertical comparison to link his life to the souls in *Paradiso*, we see that his *auctoritas* has expanded such that he is no longer writing the life of an ordinary human being. We see that Dante has been authorized—indeed, called—to write hagiography and by including his own life therein has authorized himself as auto-hagiographer.

As Dante transforms his ordinary life into that of a saint, so too must he transform the narrative threads he has been weaving since the *Vita nuova*. Accordingly, we see that story of his love for Beatrice is now expressed on both planes, the horizontal and vertical. In *Inferno* 2, we learn that Beatrice herself now moves along the vertical plane, the trajectory that intersects

---

[7] Iannucci identifies three separate plot lines contained within the *Comedy*: the story of Dante's love for Beatrice, the story of Dante's political vicissitudes, and the story of Dante's development as a writer ("*Paradiso* XXXI," 470).

[8] Iannucci has referred to those episodes that act as "implicit" commentary on each other and that share common narrative structures and elements as parallel episodes (ibid., 471).

with the horizontal to form the sign of the cross. While she once walked on the horizontal road of "our" life, her death has been relocated to the vertical plane marked by the pattern of ascent and descent described by Virgil.[9] Beatrice descended from heaven, he tells us, and sent Virgil to bring Dante to her. After this foray into the underworld, she returned and ascended to heaven. Beatrice's first movement within the context of the *Comedy* is, therefore, a vertical descent expressly linked to the love story by the inclusion of the fact that it was motivated by love. Beatrice's vertical trajectory is made explicit by Virgil, who reports that he asked her, "But tell me why you have not been more prudent / descending to this center, moving from / that spacious place where you long to return?"[10] Although her corresponding ascent is not described in the narrative, clearly Beatrice did not remain in hell but, rather, ascended to heaven, returning to her place among the blessed in the Celestial Rose. Following her descent and subsequent ascent, the internal construction of *Inferno* and *Purgatorio* then necessitate Dante's descent and subsequent ascent before he can catch up to her. The *iter* of this love is made clear: to reach the object of one's love, one must first descend and then ascend. In terms of models, we note that the ascent portion of the pattern was already discernible in the *Vita nuova* where, according to Singleton, the pattern of the ascent of love closely resembled the pattern of mystic as-

[9] *Inf.* 2:70-72: "For I am Beatrice who send you on; / I come from where I most long to return; / Love prompted me, that Love which makes me speak." [Io son Beatrice che ti faccio andare; / vegno del loco ove tornar disio; / amor mi mosse, che mi fa parlare.]

[10] *Inf.* 2:82-84: "Ma dimmi la cagion che non ti guardi / dello *scender qua giuso* in questo centro / dell'ampio loco ove tornar tu ardi." [But tell me why you have not been more prudent— / descending to this center, moving from / that spacious place where you long to return?]

cent to God in the tradition of saints Augustine and Bonaventure.[11] However, it also gradually becomes evident that ascent alone will not be enough to complete the *Comedy* or complete Dante's journey of love, for the pilgrim's descent and ascent do not unite the lovers.

In fact, if we look carefully, we see that Dante's pattern of descent and ascent does not always coincide directly with Beatrice's descent and ascent. Prior to their meeting in *Purgatorio* 30, Dante is, in essence, still pursuing Beatrice. Dante's descent and ascent up to the apex of Mount Purgatory reflects the courtly love that formed the basis of his early relationship with Beatrice. In that convention, the love, however ennobling it may be, is still love of the object of desire. It is a love for a human creature, not for its creator. Indeed, it seeks something in return—the lady's love, her salutation, or at very least the ennoblement of the lover—but it always involves a pursuit on the part of the lover. This structural device is also reflected stylistically in the text as we see that Beatrice's descent into Limbo to enlist Virgil's help is described in language evocative of the courtly love poetic tradition that informed so much of the *Vita nuova*.[12] Virgil, for example, calls Beatrice "Lady of virtue," recalling the *Vita nuova* where Beatrice is described as "destroyer of every vice and queen of every virtue."[13] In particular, when Beatrice tells Virgil she will speak kindly of him to her Lord, we are reminded of the hope of recompense for one's adoration so prevalent in the doctrine of courtly love.[14]

---

[11] Singleton, *An Essay on the* Vita Nuova, 106.

[12] Both Natalino Sapegno and Amilcare Iannucci have remarked upon the *stilnovistic* flavor of the scene (*La Divina Commedia*, ed. Sapegno [1985], 22; Iannucci, *Forma ed evento nella Divina Commedia*, 65).

[13] *Inf.* 2:76: "donna di virtù"; *Vita nuova*, Chap. X, 2: "distruggitrice di tutti li vizi e regina de le virtudi."

[14] *Inf.* 2:73-74: "When once again I stand before my Lord, / then I shall

Something more is required. Dante must pass through another "inferno," the baptism of fire, before he can see Beatrice.[15] It is this spiritual trial that will unite Dante with Beatrice and allow him to ascend with her into the ranks of the blessed. The journey through *Inferno* was important to tracing the sign of the cross, but it is the final ascent that completes the figure. It is important to note as well that while Dante may empathize with sinners such as Francesca, Brunetto Latini, and Ulysses, he does not experience the punishments of the condemned. In Purgatory, however, like the martyred saints chronicled in the *Golden Legend*, Dante undergoes his own ordeal, a trial by fire, out of which he emerges unscathed. Having survived the ordeal, his sainthood has been proven. Now united, Dante and Beatrice ascend together to the final and promised heights, completing the descent and ascent pattern.[16]

After their meeting in Earthly Paradise, the relationship between Dante and Beatrice assumes a symmetry not seen either in the *Inferno* nor in *Purgatorio*. Rather than pursuing Be-

---

often let Him hear your praises." [Quando sarò dinanzi al segnor mio, / di te mi loderò sovente a lui.]

[15] At *Purg.* 27:34-6, Virgil says, "When he saw me still halting, obstinate, / he said, somewhat perplexed: 'Now see, son: this / wall stands between you and your Beatrice.'" [Quando mi vide star pur fermo e duro, / turbato un poco, disse: —Or vedi, figlio: / tra Beatrice e te è questo muro.]

[16] As we shall find out definitively in *Par.* 33:22-7, reaching Beatrice is only part of this journey; there is another and ultimate "salute" to which he aspires. "This man—who from the deepest hollow in / the universe, up to this height, has seen / the lives of spirits, one by one—now pleads / with you, through grace, to grant him so much virtue / that he may lift his vision higher still— / may lift it toward the ultimate salvation." [Or questi, che da l'infima lacuna / de l'universo infin qui ha vedute / le vite spiritali ad una ad una, / supplica a te, per grazia, di virtute / tanto, che possa con li occhi levarsi / più alto verso l'ultima salute.]

atrice, Dante now travels with her. As Beatrice ascends to Paradise so too does Dante. Their iters and trajectories have become synchronized. Accordingly, we will find this portion of narrative colored greatly by language and imagery that reflect this transformation in the nature of their relationship. In contrast to Francesca and Paolo, whose entanglement described in *Inferno* 5 keeps them forever in their descent and whose episode is so often associated with courtly love, the union of Dante and Beatrice carries them together upward toward heaven. The last line of the *Comedy* not only signals this culmination with its final ascent[17] but also testifies to its ultimate connection to Beatrice's initial descent through the use of the word "moved,"[18] which recalls our earliest notice of the love story ("love moved me").[19] Love, however, has an expanded scope in this sphere, no longer moving only lovers but also the stars themselves.[20]

Accordingly, from the double narrative emerge two layers of meaning. The earlier portion of Dante's journey, his descent into Hell and his ascent as far as the Earthly Paradise, corresponds to a particular, temporal, and earthly configuration of love. His continued ascent beyond Earthly Paradise corresponds to a more universal and timeless concept. Here particular and temporal love is revealed as a mere variant of a greater love that has universal implications. While Dante was pursuing

---

[17] Both Iannucci and Mazzotta note as well that in the closing cantos of *Paradiso* the entirety of this work (including the love story) is brought to a close (Iannucci, "*Paradiso* XXXI," 480; Mazzotta, *Dante*, 254).

[18] *Par.* 33:142-45: "Here force failed my high fantasy; but my / desire and will were moved already—like / a wheel revolving uniformly." [All'alta fantasia qui mancò possa; / ma già volgera il mio disio e 'l velle, / sì come rota ch'igualmente è mossa, / l'amor che move il sole e l'altre stelle.]

[19] *Inf.* 2:72: "amor mi mosse"

[20] *Par.* 33:145: "the Love that moves the sun and the other stars." [l'amor che move il sole e l'altre stelle.]

the particular object of his love, he could not effectively integrate himself within the universal.

The turning point of the passage from the particular, earthly, and temporal to the universal, transcendent, and timeless is found in *Purgatory* 30. In that canto we see the apex of Dante's individuality when Beatrice pronounces his name and enumerates the details of his earthly love for her. Within her rebuke, Beatrice gradually turns from Dante's past errors to a new focus, correcting the particular, then moving beyond and into the realm of the universal. As a result, the episode itself is revealed as a reflection of the cruciform structure in which the particular is merely a component of the universal and the dual focus of the love story is, therefore, dramatically highlighted. It is not surprising that so many scholars have identified this as the point in which Dante's personal story merges with the exemplum. Natalino Sapegno, for example, sees Beatrice and Dante as real creatures tied to a chronicle of highly personal intellectual and emotional experiences. At the same time, he suggests that they are figures of a reality above and beyond the senses, participants in a mystical affair, invested with an exemplary weight. Sapegno characterizes theirs as a story of an earthly love that is suddenly transferred to the plane of a universal and extratemporal lesson.[21] Theodolinda Barolini notes the *Comedy*'s "intersecting of the universal with the singular," which she says is "never more on display than in these cantos, where the pilgrim's encounter with Beatrice and personal confession are literally enfolded by universal history."[22]

How Dante arrives at this turning point, how he narrates the progress of his love story within the context of the universal,

[21] "una cronaca di esperienze intellettuali e affettive personalissime… figure di una realtà soprasensibile, partecipi di un'arcana vicenda, investite di un peso esemplare" (*La Divina Commedia*, ed. Sapegno [1955], 736).

[22] Barolini, *Undivine Comedy*, 158.

involves a series of narrative strategies. However, his reliance on the intertextual absorption of his earlier works is one of the most obvious and complex of these strategies. For example, the love story is introduced immediately, although not explicitly, into the *Comedy* through the recall of its most recent incarnation prior to the commencement of the *Inferno*; that portion recounted in the *Convivio*. The lost road of *Inferno* 1 locates the work thematically and echoes language used constantly throughout the *Convivio*,[23] recalling the earlier work in which Dante sought to redeem those who had lost their way. This time, however, he uses the language to refer to himself, individualizing his situation while also locating himself within the context of a lost group. Although the reference is applicable to the multiple narrative threads in the *Comedy*, in the context of the love story, we can understand that in being lost, he is far from

[23] *Inf.* 1:3: "the right road had been obscured" [la diritta via era smarrita]; *Convivio* IV, i, 9: "I resolved that I would cry out to those who were walking along this evil path so that they might place themselves back on the right way" [proposi di gridare a la gente che per mal cammino andavano, acciò che per diritto calle si dirizzassero]; *Convivio* IV, xii, 19: "A wise traveler reaches his goal and rests; the wanderer never reaches it" [lo buono camminatore giugne a termine e a posa; lo erroneo mai non l'aggiugne]; *Convivio* IV, xvi, 10: "the straight way leads us..." [E per lo cammino dritto è da vedere]; *Convivio* IV, xxii, 6: "so these human appetites proceed from the beginning along different paths, and there is but one path alone that leads us to our peace" [così questi umani appetiti per diversi calli dal principio se ne vanno, e uno solo calle è quello che noi mena a la nostra pace]; *Convivio* IV, xxiv, 12: "who enters into the meandering forest of this life would not know how to keep to the right path" [che entra ne la selva erronea di questa vita, non saprebbe tenere lo buono cammino]; *Convivio* IV, xxviii, 2: "that it blesses the journey that it has made, because it has been straight and good" [l'altra si è, che ella benedice lo cammino che ha fatto, però che è stato diritto e buono]. Further, the image of the "*selva oscura*" [dark wilderness or woods] in *Inferno* I recalls *Convivio* IV, xxiv, 12: "The erroneous wilderness of this life" [la selva erronea di questa vita].

the object of his love—spatially, morally, or both.[24] From this point, Dante the poet works backward in time toward that moment when he first met Beatrice, doing so through the use of language found in the earlier versions of this story. Thus, in Earthly Paradise where Dante describes the holy procession coming toward him, especially the voices singing "Hosanna," we are reminded of a similar moment in the *Vita nuova*.[25] As Hollander notes, in the next canto, *Purgatory* 30, Beatrice's angelic choir seems to pick up where it left off in the *Vita nuova*.[26] Finally, Sapegno points out, the arrival of Beatrice recalls the imagery used to describe her in the *Vita nuova*.[27]

---

[24] Iannucci suggests that, indeed, Dante's state at the opening of the *Inferno* is attributable to his having been "attratto dalla figura di sirena-Eva della donna-gentile" and, therefore, having fallen so deep into his sin that the descent of Beatrice, a Christ-figure, was all that could free him from the "*selva oscura*" (*Forma ed evento nella Divina Commedia*, 67).

[25] *Purg*. 29:49-51: "the power that offers reason matter judged / those trees to be—what they were—candelabra, and what those voices sang to be "Hosanna" [la virtù ch'a ragion discorso ammanna, / sì com' elli eran candelabri apprese, / e ne le voci del cantare "*Osanna*"]

> *Vita nuova*, Chap. XXIII, 7: "It seemed that these angels were singing in glory, and I seemed to hear the words of their song as "Osanna in excelsis"—Hosanna in the highest—and it seemed I heard nothing else." [A me parea che questi angeli cantassero gloriosamente, e le parole del loro canto mi parea udire che fossero queste: *Osanna in excelsis*; e altro non mi parea udire.]

Sapegno describes the use of Osanna thus: "it is the Hebrew augural word, entered into liturgical use through the scriptural language here. It probably alludes to the words with which Jesus was greeted upon his entrance to Jerusalem: 'Hosanna, son of David; blessed is he who comes in the name of the Lord, hosanna in the highest' (Matthew 21, 9)" (*La Divina Commedia*, ed. Sapegno [1955], 737).

[26] Hollander, *Studies in Dante*, 55.

[27] *Purg*. 30:28-33. Sapegno notes, when Beatrice appears, and "reveals herself to the eyes of her poet; silent and remote as a sacred icon, with the stylized attitude of the youthful *libello*, she is the admirable, 'the glorious',

The closer Beatrice comes, the further back in time we move so that when we finally see her clothing (*Purg.* 30:23-33), as Sapegno says, we can't help but be reminded of the red and white clothing worn by Beatrice in the *Vita Nuova*.[28] But we continue to slide back in time so that in the same canto[29] we are brought back precisely to that moment in the *Vita nuova* when Dante first met Beatrice.[30]

---

not a woman. But rather '...one of the beautiful angels of heaven,' the blessed Beatrice, the 'Beatrice beata'" (cf. *Vita nuova*, Chaps. III, 1; XXVI, 2; XXVIII, 1; XLII, 3, etc.) [rivelarsi agli occhi del suo poeta; silenziosa e remota come una sacra icona, con gli atteggiamento stilizzati del libello giovanile è la mirabile, "la gloriosa," non femmina, anzi "...uno delli belissimi angeli del cielo," la benedetta Beatrice, la "Beatrice beata" (cf. *Vita nuova*, Chaps. III, 1; XXVI, 2; XXVIII, 1; XLII, 3, ecc.)] (*La Divina Commedia*, ed. Sapegno [1955], 737).

Dante's reference to having once, in her presence, felt "wonder, trembling, dissolution" [*Purg.* 30:36: stupor, tremando, affranto] evokes the emotions he described in the *Vita nuova. Vita nuova* II, 4: "At that time, truly, I say, the vital spirit, which dwells in the innermost chamber of the heart, started to tremble so powerfully that its disturbance reached all the way to the slightest of my pulses." [in quello punto dico veracemente cho lo spirito de la vita, lo quale dimora ne la secretissima camera de lo cuore, cominciò a tremare sì fortemente, che apparìa ne li menimi polsi orribilmente]

[28] Sapegno notes that "l'accento di raffinata fantasmagorìa di certe pagine della *Vita nuova*, s'illuminano proprio per quel riferimento a un paesaggio reale di un sapore nuovo di freschezza e di verità" [The accent of refined phantasmagoria of certain pages of the *Vita nuova*, are illuminated precisely by that reference to a real landscape with a new flavor of freshness and truth] since the "vestito rosso 'sanguigno' e il bianco comparano già, portati da Beatrice, nella *Vita nuova* ['blood' red and white dress already appeared, worn by Beatrice, in the *Vita nuova*] (II, 3; III, 1 e 4; XXIII, 8; XXXIX, 1)" (*La Divina Commedia*, ed. Sapegno [1955], 736–37).

[29] *Purg.* 30:41-42: when I had not yet left / my boyhood," [prima ch'io fuor di püerizia fosse]

[30] *Vita nuova*, Chap. II, 2: "She had already been in this life long enough for the heaven of the fixed stars to have moved toward the east a twelfth of a degree since she was born, so that she was at the beginning of

Most importantly, the direct use of the words "*vita nova*" draws the reader's attention back to the earlier work.[31] Eventually, Beatrice's use of a temporal reference, "for some time,"[32] not only recalls much of the language of the *Vita nuova*,[33] but also brings us back to the present, thus completing a circle. It is Beatrice, therefore, who transforms the temporal and linear into the timeless circularity of the *Comedy*. But this circle is a closed circle, consisting of Dante's story alone. The message is clear. Love as envisaged by Dante can go no further; this individual love has reached its apex.

Here in *Purgatory*, where we have reached the summit of Dante's individuality, Beatrice too is at her most particular.

---

her ninth year when she appeared to me, and I saw her when I was almost at the end of my ninth." [Ella era in questa vita già stata tanto, che ne lo suo tempo lo cielo stellato era mosso verso la parte d'oriente de lo dodici parti l'una d'un grado, sì che quasi dal principio del suo anno nono apparve a me, ed io la vidi, quasi de la fine del mio nono.]

[31] *Purg.* 30:115-17: "when in his young life [my translation], was such—potentially—that any propensity innate in him would have / prodigiously succeeded, had he acted." [questi fu tal nella sua vita nova / virtualmente, ch'ogni abito destroy / fatto averebbe in lui mirabil prova.]

[32] *Purg.* 30:121-23: "My countenance sustained him for some time [my translation] while; / showing my youthful eyes to him, I led / him with me toward the way of righteousness." [Alcun tempo il sostenni col mio volto: / mostrando li occhi giovanetti a lui meco in menava in dritta parte volto.] Sapegno suggests that "Alcun tempo" [Some time] implies "from when he first saw me until my death, i.e., 1274–1290 (*La Divina Commedia*, ed. Sapegno [1985], 343–44).

[33] *Vita nuova*, Chap. XI, 1: "I tell you that whenever and wherever she appeared, by virtue of my hope in her marvelous greeting, no one could be my enemy; on the contrary, I became possessed by a flame of charity that made me forgive whoever had hurt me." [Quando ella apparia da parte alcuna, per la speranza della mirabile salute nullo nemico mi rimanea, anzi mi giugnea una fiamma di caritade, la quale mi facea perdonare a chiunque m'avesse offeso.] Compare as well with *Vita nuova*, Chaps. XIX, 9; XXI, 2; XXVI, 3, 10, 11.

While the entire build-up to Beatrice's arrival has been allegorical and symbolic in nature, her appearance and the way she speaks to Dante create one of the most realistic or mimetic (to use Auerbach's term) episodes in the entire *Comedy*. Beatrice's first direct discourse is stunning. The first word we hear her utter is "Dante."[34]

From a narrative perspective, in a single word, Dante has found the most effective way to identify his actual existence with the poetic "I." In a word he has removed all doubt as to the identity of the pilgrim. There is no issue here, no question as to whether the reader knows whose poetry is being glossed. The reader here is told in no uncertain terms that Dante is the empiric "I" of the narrative and it is Beatrice who makes the pronouncement. This is Dante's autobiography, but it is also his auto-hagiography.[35]

As Beatrice continues to display this intimate knowledge of Dante's writing, addressing him in words taken from his own works, she expresses disappointment in his lost potential.[36] Similarly, Beatrice's demand that Dante lift his beard, to look

---

[34] *Purg.* 30:55-57: "Dante, though Virgil's leaving you, do not / yet weep, do not weep yet;" [Dante, perché Virgilio se ne vada, non pianger anco, non piangere ancora;]

[35] Albert Ascoli has observed that throughout *Purgatory*, Dante presents his own poetry alongside paraphrases of Scripture and sacred writing to effect a transformation of his own evolving *auctoritas*. Ascoli asserts that the *Comedy* represents the "manifestation of salvation history in and through the example of Dante's own life," but at the same time denies that Dante is attempting to write a new book of the Bible. Instead he says that Dante presents himself as "an especially self-conscious signifier in God's other book, the poem of creation itself" ("Performing Salvation in Dante's *Commedia*," 96–97).

[36] *Purg.* 30:115-17: "when in his young life [my translation], was such—potentially—that any propensity innate in him would have / prodigiously succeeded, had he acted." [questi fu tal nella sua vita nova / virtualmente, ch'ogni abito destro / fatto averebbe in lui mirabil prova.]

at her, though decipherable independent of any other works, also echoes Dante's observation in the *Convivio* that a full beard is proper for a man.[37] In this way the exchange with Beatrice emphasizes the autobiographical nature of the early works, but the discourse also lends meaning to the works that may not have been evident when they were first written. Dante's reference to Beatrice's "second age"[38] for example, not only recalls the discussion of the various ages of life in Book 4 of the *Convivio*[39] but it also reinforces the temporal nature and focus of the first stages of love. Later in their exchange, Dante as pilgrim further evokes his past literary efforts. In describing his visible shame, for example, he recalls the passage in the *Convivio* where displaying shame is described as a sure sign of nobility.[40] Moreover, in placing the language of the *Convivio* alongside that of the *Vita nuova*, Dante fuses both the *Convivio* and the *Vita nuova* and relegates both to "then" as the *Comedy* becomes "now."

This fusion is further effected through Beatrice's exasperation with Dante's refusal to heed her call from the beyond,[41]

---

[37] *Convivio* I, xii, 8: "every goodness proper to a thing is deserving of love in that thing, as in masculinity to have a full beard." [ogni bontade propria in alcuna cosa, è amabile in quella: sì come ne la maschiezza essere ben barbuto.]

[38] *Purg.* 30:125: "seconda etade." Here Dante means youth ("*giovinezza*"), which, according to Dante, comes at the end of the twenty-five years (*La Divina Commedia*, ed. Sapegno [1985], 343).

[39] *Convivio* IV, xxiv.

[40] *Purg.* 30:66: "acknowledging their fault repentantly" [e sé riconoscendo e ripentiti] recalls *Convivio* IV, xix, 10: "Thus it is a good and perfect sign of nobility in children and in those not fully grown when after a fault shame is painted on their faces, for then it is the fruit of true nobility." [buono e ottimo segno di nobiltade è, ne li pargoli e imperfetti d'etade, quando dopo lo fallo, nel viso loro vergogne si dipinge.]

[41] *Purg.* 30:133-35: "Nor did the inspirations I received— / with which, in dream and otherwise, I called / him back— help me; he paid so little heed! [Né l'impetrare ispirazion mi valse con le quali ed in sogno e altrimento lo

reminding us that Dante described visions of a departed Beatrice in both the *Vita nuova* and the *Convivio*.[42] This fusion not only reinforces the link between the two works but also allows Dante to address one of the issues created by the two previous autobiographical works, that is, the issue of the *donna gentile*. When Beatrice says that Dante took himself away from her and followed another,[43] we must assume, given the nature of the discussion thus far, that she is also recalling events in these works. In the *Vita nuova* Dante told us of another woman in particular. In the *Convivio* Dante spoke of a philosophical education, his studies. Further, his *Rime* include a variety of other women.[44] Here now, Beatrice is not concerned with their pos-

rivocai; sì poco a lui ne calse!] Sapegno underlines that here Beatrice's efforts are "rappresentate come inefficaci ai fini di una duratura conversione dello scrittore" [represented as ineffective for the purpose of a lasting conversion of the writer] (*La Divina Commedia*, ed. Sapegno [1955], 745).

[42] *Vita nuova*, Chap. XXXIX, 1: "an intense imagining that seemed to see this glorious Beatrice wearing the same crimson clothes in which she first appeared to my eyes. And she seemed young, roughly the same age as when I first saw her." [una forte imaginazione in me; che mi parve vedere questa gloriosa Beatrice con quelle vestimenta sanguigne co le quali apparve prima a li occhi miei; e pareami giovane in simile etade in quale io prima la vidi.] and *Vita nuova*, Chap. XLII, 3: "Then, if it be pleasing to Him who is the Lord of benevolence and grace, may my soul go to contemplate the glory of its lady—that blessed Beatrice, who gazes in glory into the face of Him *qui est per omnia secula benedictus*." [E poi piaccia a colui che è sire de la cortesia, che la mia anima se ne possa gire a vedere la gloria de la sua donna: cioè di quella benedetta Beatrice, la quale gloriosamente mira ne la faccia di colui *qui est per omnia secula benedictus*.]; *Convivio* IV, vii, 6: "*Where it would see a lady in glorious light*, to make it understood that it is because I was certain, and still am, by reason of her gracious revelation, that she was in heaven." [Ove una donna gloriar vedia; a dare a intendere ch'è perché io era certo, e sono, per sua graziosa revelazione, che ella era in cielo.]

[43] *Purg*. 30:126: "questi si tolse a me, e diessi i altrui."

[44] Sapegno suggests the rebuke, with its reference to the *pargoletta*

sible allegorical meanings, the timing issues, or apparent contradictions.[45] She simply gathers them all together and says clearly that Dante was wrong in devoting himself to anything that distracted him from her.[46]

In one sense Beatrice is suggesting that how one characterizes one's actions is irrelevant; the truth—the real meaning as manifested in the result or effect of the action—will continue to exist. Her words have such a personal ring to them and a genuine anger that we are unconcerned about the allegorical significance of the rebuke. The dramatic effect is such that we can almost hear her saying, "I don't care what you called them elsewhere, but all of the *pargolette* and other women would never have brought you to me." Dante employs the striking realism

---

[*Purg.* 31:59: green young girl], not only can be taken as an undetermined allusion to the poet's other loves after the death of Beatrice but also recalls the existence of "una *pargoletta* appunto bella e sdegnosa" [a young girl, just beautiful and disdainful] in some of Dante's lyrics (*Rime* LXXXVII and LXXXIX) or indeed to the woman referred to as *pargoletta* in the *rime* "pietrose" [stony rhymes] (*La Divina Commedia*, ed. Sapegno [1955], 749).

[45] I am referring here to the issue referred to above in chapters 2 and 3; that is, whether the ending of the *Vita nuova* was rewritten or added after the commencement of the *Comedy*. See also Michele Barbi on the date of the *Vita nuova* (*Problemi di critica dantesca*, 104–106).

[46] Sapegno cites Buti, who suggests that this reference means "ad altri studi et amori" [to other studies and loves] (*La Divina Commedia*, ed. Sapegno [1955], 744). Sapegno, like so many other critics, suggests that this is an indetermined allusion to the *donna gentile* of the *Vita nuova* "che, secondo l'interpretazione allegorica dell *Convivio* II, XII, è simbolo degli studi filosofici, cui l'autore rivolse per consolarsi della morte di Beatrice; e anche ad altri amori e vanità, di cui è traccia nelle *Rime*." [which, according to the allegorical interpretation of *Convivio* II, XII, is a symbol of philosophical studies, which the author addressed to console himself for the death of Beatrice; and also to other loves and vanities, of which there is a trace in the *Rime*.]

noted by Auerbach to emphasize the spatial and temporal nature of the kind of love that engenders such behavior, not only on Dante's part but on Beatrice's.[47] It seems natural then that Beatrice should proceed to de-allegorize the distractions and the indulgences, exposing them as mortal, fleeting, and ultimately without a further or true meaning.

The exposition of the *donna gentile* as a negative distraction reflects a common trope in hagiography, where the saint is tempted, while sleeping, by demons in the guise of women.[48] It also follows the exposition by the "*donna santa e presta*" (a lady alert and saintly) of the so-called "*femmina balba*" in *Purgatory* 19.[49] All of the distractions, including both of the *donne gentili*, are denounced and relegated to the temporal life of the sinner. Beatrice, who has become Dante's judge or Tribunal in these matters, has summarily dismissed any attempt by Dante to give them a higher, more enduring significance. Moreover, Beatrice does not restrict her rebuke to those distractions chronicled in Dante's writing explicitly. She presents knowledge external to the text when she refers to "*altra novità*" (other novelty).[50] The

---

[47] Auerbach, *Mimesis*, 166.

[48] Perhaps the most famous of these is St. Anthony of Egypt. Jacobus De Voragine's account of the saint's life is rife with descriptions of the various temptations Anthony resisted.

[49] Theodolinda Barolini describes the "femmina balba" as the "stuttering female" of verse 7, a stuttering and deformed figure who is transformed by the dreamer's gaze into a hyper-articulate, non-stuttering, and very charismatic "dolce serena" [sweet siren] who promises complete satisfaction of desire ("sì tutto l'appago!" so completely do I satisfy him! [*Purg.* 19:24]). She presents herself as the very siren who sang to Ulysses and turned him from his path: "Io volsi Ulisse del suo cammin vago / al canto mio" [I turned Ulysses from his path with my song (*Purg.* 19:21-23)]; Commentario Baroliniano: "Epistemological Incontinence," Digital Dante, Columbia University Libraries (https://digitaldante.columbia.edu/dante/divine-comedy/purgatorio/purgatorio-19/).

[50] *Purg.* 31:58-60: "No green young girl or other novelty / such brief

meta-knowledge adds to the realism and at the same time continues to generalize Dante's experiences after her death. By not dwelling on any one incident in particular, Beatrice, in effect, dismisses them all as meaningless ventures. Similarly, in *Purgatory* 33, when she points out the inadequacy of his education, she does not focus on the education he embraced and characterized in the *Convivio* as a *donna gentile*.[51] Instead, her words, referring to a "*scola*" (school) again generalize, leaving us with an ambiguity that can as easily include not only the education of the *Convivio* but perhaps also the "*scola*" described in *Inferno* 4.[52]

The rebuke also represents one of the most obvious manifestations of Dante's program of rewriting as he attributes to earlier episodes a meaning that will contextualize them within his latest work. While at the end of the *Vita nuova* we had been led to believe that Dante reverted to the memory of Beatrice after his dalliance with the other woman, we are now told otherwise. If Dante had heeded Beatrice sufficiently in the *Vita nuova*, then the *Comedy* would be superfluous, but Beatrice clearly states that he did not heed her. Something must have occurred after the ending of the *Vita nuova*, or Dante would not have found himself in the *selva oscura* in the first place. Similarly, the love described in the *Convivio* must, in the *Comedy*,

---

delight—should have weighed down your wings, / awaiting further shafts." [Non ti dovea gravar le penne in giuso, ad aspettar, più colpi, o pargoletta o altra novità con sì breve uso.]

[51] *Purg*. 33:85: "That you may recognize," she said, "the school / that you have followed and may see if what / it taught can comprehend what I have said" ["Perché conoschi," disse, "quella scuola / c'hai seguitata, e veggi sua dottrina / come può seguitar la mia parola"]

[52] *Inf*. 4:94-96: "And so I saw that splendid school assembled / led by the lord of song incomparable, / who like an eagle soars above the rest." [Cosí vidi adunar la bella scola / di quel de l'altissimo canto / che sovra li altri com'aquila vola.]

be presented as similarly averse to the Beatrice of the *Comedy*. Otherwise, her descent into the underworld and Dante's resulting journey would not have been necessary. In this way, Dante reconciles the events of the *Vita nuova* and those of the *Convivio*, confirming that while his readers may have initially thought he returned to Beatrice at the end of the *Vita nuova*, he certainly did not remain with her. The reconciliation merges the two works, making them both mere antecedents to the narrative of the *Comedy*. The *Comedy* is the "now." The *Vita nuova* is once again, this time along with the *Convivio*, relegated to "then." But perhaps it is more accurate to suggest that, in accordance with the cruciform pattern, both works are exposed as belonging to the temporal plane, to the early part of Dante's journey in which he continued to set himself apart from humankind instead of trying to rise above it.

The significance of the episode between Beatrice and Dante can perhaps be best encapsulated in two verses. The first occurs just as Dante is beginning to sense Beatrice's approach. He says, "I recognize the signs of the old flame," thus recalling the burning heart of the first vision of the *Vita nuova* and the way he first loved Beatrice.[53] Moreover, the words are taken almost entirely from the *Aeneid* and appear at the moment Virgil disappears from the text. The comment, therefore, signals very clearly that earth-bound love, the kind felt not only by Dante but also by Dido,[54] the kind of love that could not let go of Aeneas and allow him to fulfill his divine mission, the kind of love

---

[53] *Purg.* 30:48: "conosco i segni dell'antica fiamma"

[54] *Aen.* IV, 23: "agnosco veteris vestigia flammae." Peter Hawkins notes the juxtaposition of the Virgilian poetic with the image of Beatrice as a Christ figure: "The acclamation of her arrival in the double cry of 'Benedictus qui venis!' (v. 19) and 'Manibus, oh, date lilïa plenis' (v. 21)—a Christological salutation and a Virgilian lament—alerts us to the kind of juxtaposition that the whole canto will entail, as the two worlds of discourse meet at

that cannot progress past this stage.

Next, Beatrice's use of language associated with flight and her reference to the Sirens, recalls both the imagery of the love birds and the "*folle amor*" of *Inferno* 5 as well as "*folle volo*" of Ulysses.[55] Dante's earlier description of Beatrice as an "admiral," however, suggests that she will be a more caring pilot than Ulysses, that she will counteract the madness and chaos of the temporal world, and that she will steer Dante's flight in the right direction.[56] Like Aeneas, Dante must leave the burning love behind and move on. However, within the temporal plane, Dante has gone as far as he can go; the circle is closed, and progress will require a transfer to another stage. Outside of the text,

---

an impasse to reveal the great gulf fixed between them" ("Dido, Beatrice, and the Signs of Ancient Love," 113). Hawkins also notes the summarizing effect of the language, suggesting that the appearance of Beatrice "is the rehearsal of a career in poetry that stretches from the visions of boyhood ('püerizia') up to the poem's present; it is the reworking of a lifetime" ("Poetry of Allusion," 115). Hawkins, however, notes an aspect to the insertion that is worthy of note and suggests that the inclusion of the Virgilian allusion facilitates Dante's correction of love in the *Comedy*: "Dante gives us a revision of the Virgilian script that transforms tragedy into romance, that turns the disclosure of darkness visible into the unveiling of eternal light: 'O isplendor di viva luce etterna' [O splendor of living light eternal! *Purg*. 31. 139]" (122).

[55] *Purg*. 31:55-59: "then / you surely should have lifted up your wings / to follow me, no longer such a thing. / No green young girl or other novelty— / such brief delight—should have weighed down your wings." [Ben ti dovevi, per lo primo strale / de le cose fallaci, levar suso / di retro a me che non era più tale. / Non ti dovea gravar le penne in giuso.]

Purg. 31:43-45: "Nevertheless, that you may feel more shame / for your mistake, and that—in time to come— / hearing the Sirens, you may be more strong." [Tuttavia, perché mo vergogna porte / del tuo errore, e perché altra volta, / udendo le serene, sie più forte.]

[56] *Purg*. 30:58-60: "Just like an admiral who goes to stern / and prow to see the officers who guide / the other ships, encouraging their tasks;" [Quasi ammiraglio che in poppa e in prora / viene a veder la gente che ministra / per li altri legni, e a ben far l'incora,]

we can assume that this next step is the *Comedy*. Within the text, however, that next step is represented by the pilgrim's ascent beyond the Earthly Paradise, together with Beatrice. Here where the particular and the universal intersect, Beatrice's dual nature is revealed. She is the vessel of both temporal and timeless love, particular and universal significance, of then and now.

This dual nature is also manifested in terms of Beatrice's role in Dante's evolving exegetical strategies. Whereas in the *Vita nuova* and the *Convivio* Dante's prose commentary explained the meaning of the poems and the events that led to their composition, here in the *Comedy* it is Beatrice who provides the commentary. In the moment she pronounces his name, Beatrice's role expands from the mere object of Dante's love to his exegete. Given that she has already identified herself as Dante's friend, it is clear that Beatrice need not pronounce his name to cement this relationship.[57] Rather, I believe the purpose is more structural. As Beatrice becomes the commentator, increasingly it is Beatrice who connects the poetry to the events of a mundane life outside of its record.

In the *Vita nuova*, Dante was both character and commentator, but in the *Comedy* it is Beatrice who assumes this dual role. As both character and commentator, Beatrice expresses knowledge external to the poem. She tells us of the events that led to the poetry we are reading in which she is also a character. In this way, it is Beatrice who introduces the autobiographical elements most explicitly. Similarly, in *Purgatorio* 31, Beatrice, as Dante's confessor, reveals and emphasizes Dante's sins. Sapegno calls her "the voice of Dante's conscience." Thus, as commentator Beatrice is poised to reveal and illuminate the true meaning of the poetry she glosses.[58]

---

[57] *Inf.* 2:61: "l'amico mio."

[58] "Alla visione sottentra il dramma dove Beatrice è la voce stessa della

Just as the *Vita nuova* and the *Convivio* had their respective defining moments that revealed the true meaning of antecedent events, so too does the *Comedy*. Just as in the *Vita nuova* events such as the withdrawal of Beatrice's salutation and her subsequent death moved Dante to consider the meaning of love, so too does Beatrice's appearance in Earthly Paradise effect a shift in the pilgrim's perspective. The moment Dante finally turns to face Beatrice marks a new narrative focus, moving beyond the particular and a subtle flow into the universal. As Sapegno observes, after all the spectacle and symbolism, the entire situation is gathered up and we finally arrive at the theme that gives it meaning.[59] However, the perspective that the pilgrim will gain in the *Comedy*, unlike that gained in the *Convivio* or the *Vita nuova*, is not so explicitly marked as temporal. It is temporal in the sense that there is a before and after but it is also a distinction between "in this world" and "beyond this world." By the time we arrive at *Paradiso* 3, the pilgrim has begun to recognize a distinction between then and now and its effects on his feelings toward Beatrice. He now refers to her not only as an object of his early love but also as a revelator of truth.[60] Beatrice's role has expanded beyond the object of love expressed in the flames of descent; now, as commentator, she is the illuminator of truth, associated with ascent. The events of the *Vita nuova* and the *Convivio*, now relegated to the past, are also distinguished from

---

coscienza di Dante, rimorsa del peccato e anelante alla redenzione" [The drama takes over from the vision where Beatrice is the very voice of Dante's conscience, remorseful of sin and yearning for redemption] (*La Divina Commedia*, ed. Sapegno [1985], 337).

[59] *La Divina Commedia*, ed. Sapegno (1985), 336.

[60] *Par.* 3:1-3: "That sun which first had warmed my breast with love / had now revealed to me, confuting, proving, / the gentle face of truth, its loveliness;" [Quel sol che pria d'amor mi scaldò 'l petto, / di bella verità m'avea scoverto, / provando e riprovando, il dolce aspetto;]

the issue now confronting Dante, not so much because they happened in the temporal past but because they happened on another plane within the cruciform pattern.[61] It is important to note that Beatrice illuminates a new meaning during this final ascent beyond Earthly Paradise that will differ from the type of exegesis we have seen in the past.

Throughout the *Inferno* and the *Purgatorio*, parallel episodes and typologically relevant characters express the autobiographical dimension of the *Comedy*, but in *Paradiso*, the role of Beatrice provides an additional interpretive device that lends even broader significance to the earlier stories.[62] As Beatrice's new role as commentator gradually enlightens Dante and his readers to a new reading of Dante's journey to Earthly Paradise, her role within the love story evolves so that the literal level of the story evokes the allegorical level. In *Purgatorio*, Beatrice merely enunciated the distinction between then and now; in *Paradiso* she demonstrates it. Now Beatrice has Dante look down to see how far he has come,[63] an action that reinforces the perspective prefigured by having Dante look down to see the "*varco folle*" (mad course) of the ill-fated Ulysses.[64] Here more

---

[61] *Purg.* 30:121-23: "My countenance sustained him for a while; / showing my youthful eyes to him, I led / him with me toward the way of righteousness" [Alcun tempo il sostenni col mio volto:/ mostrando li occhi giovanetti a lui / meco in menava in dritta parte volto]

[62] Robert Hollander says, "the function of the allegorical sense is to relate two historical events or things or persons, each of which has a discrete and particular historical reality in time so that the relationship between them may express spiritual significance" (*Allegory in Dante's Comedy*, 59).

[63] *Par.* 32:126-29: "before / you enter farther, do look downward, see / what I have set beneath your feet already: / much of the world is there." [prima che tu più t'inlei, / rimira in giú, e vedi quanto mondo / sotto li piedi già esser ti fei]

[64] *Par.* 27:82-84: "so that, beyond Cadiz, I saw Ulysses' / mad course and, to the east, could almost see / that shoreline where Europa was sweet

than ever the difference in perspective, the ability to see the truth, is enunciated clearly. The moral distinction is expressed vertically, for indeed suddenly, Dante and Ulysses are existing within the same temporal plane. Their difference, however, lies in their respective locations on the same vertical plane. Here then temporal distinctions are less important; the vertical casts our thoughts back to the descent / ascent pattern introduced in the *Inferno* I and contrasts with Dante's time-bound descriptions of his early experiences of love. Accordingly, we have come to understand through Beatrice that on the higher plane, temporal and spatial distinctions are not nearly as relevant as is spiritual or moral distance from heaven or hell. From here, outside of the world, Beatrice is now able to assume her new role showing Dante the true state of things and especially the true nature of love. Conversely, those matters described prior to Dante's arrival at the summit of Mount Purgatory are increasingly characterized as mere imitation. Beatrice makes this explicit in pointing out that Dante "followed counterfeits of goodness, which will never pay in full what they have promised."[65]

The subtle shift from the ascent to the peak of Mount Purgatory to its continuation above Earthly Paradise occasions considerable narrative shifts as well, most notably in the role of Beatrice. As her appearance in Earthly Paradise transformed her

---

burden." [í ch'io vedea di là da Gade il varco / folle d'Ulisse, e di qua presso il lito / nel qual si fece Europa dolce carco.]

[65] *Purg.* 30:130-32: "he turned his footsteps toward an untrue path; / he followed counterfeits of goodness, which / will never pay in full what they have promised." [e volse i passi suoi per via non vera, / immagini di ben seguendo false, / che nulla promission rendono intera.] Cfr. Boezio in *De Cons. phil.* III, pr. 9: "[res mortales et caducae] vel imagines veri boni vel imperfecta quaedam bona dare mortalibus videntur; verum autem atque perfectum bonum conferre non possunt" [the death and decay or the images of the good or imperfect goods seem to give them; it cannot be true and perfect good] (*La Divina Commedia*, ed. Sapegno [1955], 336).

from the object of his love into the critic of its expression, in *Paradiso* that role is gradually expanded to embody the means through which Dante explains the nature of all love.

At the same time, we notice a concomitant adjustment in the role of Dante the pilgrim, from the lover seeking his lady to the disciple seeking to know the very nature of love. This shift in role is also facilitated by the purging process in which the vices of *Inferno* are corrected. We see, therefore, that in the pilgrim's descent, love is most often portrayed as illicit, sexual, and conducive to jealousy, dissatisfaction, and death. It often transgresses societal rules and is most often characterized as "*folle*" (mad). Above all, it remains forever earthbound and narrow in scope. This characterization is most prevalent in *Inferno* 5 in the circle of the lustful. Structurally, Dante reinforces the particular and the universal applications of this meaning by creating within each episode the dichotomy of particular and universal characters. Accordingly, in *Inferno* 5 illicit love is personified both by Francesca, with whom Dante clearly shares a personal moment, as well as by Dido, who is widely known and belongs to the distant past.[66]

In *Paradiso*, there is a similar juxtaposition, as Dante encounters souls who are connected to him, as well as those much further from his experience in time and space. Accordingly, in *Paradiso* 3 Piccarda Donati and Costanza appear in the same canto. But here the object of both stories clearly pertains to a higher vision of love, with fewer personal implications for Dante than the love espoused by the sinners of *Inferno* and the penitents of *Purgatory*. Using a narrative construction similar to that found in *Inferno* 5, the cantos of *Paradiso* recall and contrast

---

[66] Both Gianfranco Contini and Amilcare Iannucci characterize Francesca as the diametric opposite of Beatrice (Contini, *Un'idea di Dante*, 48; Iannucci, "Forbidden Love," 105-107).

those stories of false love and cupidity with the universal true love and chastity. At the same time, we hear "*amore*" (love) less and less; instead, the word *carità* (charity) is introduced, thereby creating yet another contrast.[67] Here the flames of love are directed not at some unknowable and particular object of love but rather to the universal creator of love.[68]

As Dante and Beatrice ascend throughout *Paradiso,* the discussion and ambiance become ever more focused on the true nature of love. It becomes apparent that Dante is gradually transforming Beatrice from the object of love into love itself. In the heaven of the moon, Dante addresses Beatrice as the "beloved of the First Lover" and calls her divine,[69] signaling that she has replaced "*Amore*" of the *Vita nuova.* As they prepare for their ascent into the heaven of Mars, Beatrice tells Dante that the divine light is the only source of true love.[70] In the heaven of the sun (*Paradiso* 14), where Beatrice speaks to Dante from the center of a circle, we are reminded of the vision of the *Vita nuova* where *Amore* tells Dante love is like the center of a circle.[71] Beatrice, therefore, has taken the place of *Amore*, and Dante learns that love is indeed a circle. It is not linear; it is not a pursuit. It is a communion, a continuum. Dante has, of course,

---

[67] *Par.* 3:43: "Our charity" [La nostra carità]

[68] *Par.* 3:52-53: "Our sentiments, which only serve the flame / that is the pleasure of the Holy Ghost," [li nostri affetti che solo infiammati / son nel piacere de lo Spirito Santo,]

[69] *Par.* 4:118: "O amanza del primo amante, o diva."

[70] *Par.* 5:7-9: "Indeed I see that in your intellect / now shines the never-ending light; once seen, / that light, alone and always, kindles love." [Io veggio ben sí come già resplende / ne l'intelletto tuo l'etterna luce, / che, vista, sola e sempre amore accende.]

[71] *Vita nuova*, Chap. XII, 4: "Ego tanquam centrum circuli, cui simili modo se habent circumferentiae partes; tu autem non sic." [I am like the center of a circle, to which the parts of the circumference stand in equal relation; but you are not so.]

been preparing the reader for this revelation for some time. Beatrice, in fact, ceased to be the object of sexual love once Dante was reunited with her at the top of Mount Purgatory. There she called him "*frate*," brother.[72] Indeed by *Paradiso* 7 she is calling him "*frate*" with increasing frequency.[73] In the circle of the sun, Dante notes that there are those to whom he can give his love without arousing Beatrice's jealousy.[74] This new discourse is in stark contrast to the earlier rebuke in the last cantos of *Purgatorio* where Beatrice chastised Dante for having turned his attentions elsewhere. This new discourse underlines the distinction between the earthly love we saw before Dante encountered Beatrice in the Earthly Paradise and the kind of love that characterizes the ascent through Paradise. In keeping with this familial nature of love, Dante has also been painting Beatrice as the giver of maternal love. At the summit of Mount Purgatory, Dante describes Beatrice as the essence of motherly love, Mary.[75] In the first canto of *Paradiso*, she is likened to a mother who turns her eyes to comfort a hysterical child.[76] Just before

---

72 *Purg.* 33:23: "Brother, why not try…"

73 See for example, *Par.* 7:58, "Brother…" [Questo decreto, frate,]; *Par.* 7:130: "Brother, the angels and the pure country…" [Li angeli, frate, e 'l paese sincere].

74 *Par.* 10:55-61: "No mortal heart was ever so disposed / to worship, or so quick to yield itself / to God with all its gratefulness, as I / was when I heard those words, and all my love / was so intent on Him that Beatrice / was then eclipsed within forgetfulness. / And she was not displeased, but smiled at this," [Cor di mortal non fu mai sí digesto / a divozione e a rendersi a Dio / con tutto 'l suo gradir cotanto presto, / come a quelle parole mi fec'io; / e si tutto 'l mio amore in lui si mise che Beatrice eclissò ne l'oblio / Non le dispiacque, ma sí se ne rise.]

75 *Purg.* 33:4-6: "sighing and full of pity, Beatrice / was changed; she listened, grieving little less / than Mary when, beneath the Cross, she wept." [E Beatrice, sospirosa e pia / ascoltava sì fatta, che poco più alla croce si cambiò Maria.]

76 *Par.* 1:100-103: "At which, after a sigh of pity, she / settled her eyes

ascending to the circle of the fixed stars, she responds to Dante's childlike behavior with kindness and patience,[77] like a mother quick to reassure and comfort her child.[78] Beatrice eventually cedes to Mary, and it is a simple task to transfer the mother and child language between Dante and Beatrice to describe the new relationship between Dante and Mary. This transfer also serves to contrast the love that leads to *Paradiso* with that which pervaded the *Inferno* and *Purgatorio*, that is, courtly or sexual love. The contrast is also implied in Dante's description of Mary as the "Rose in which the Word of God became flesh."[79] Mary is still a rose, but as Iannucci points out, she is now associated with a white rose as opposed to the red rose of earthly courtly love.[80]

As Dante's guide and teacher, Beatrice will also teach him in matters other than love. She exposes the falsity of the wisdom of earthly pursuits and provides Dante with examples of the

---

on me with the same look / a mother casts upon a raving child," [Ond' ella, appresso d'un pïo sospiro, / li occhi drizzò ver' me con quel sembiante / che madre fa sovra figlio deliro,]

[77] *Par.* 22:1-3: "like a child who always hurries back to find / that place he trusts the most" [come parvol che ricorre / sempre colà dove più si confida;]

[78] *Par.* 22:4-6: "like a mother quick to reassure / her pale and panting son with the same voice / that she has often used to comfort him," [come madre che socorre / súbito al figlio palido e anelo / con la sua voce, che 'l suol ben disporre.] See also *Par.* 23:121-23: "E come fantolin che 'nver' la mamma / tende le braccia, poi che 'l latte prese, / per l'animo che 'nfin di fuor s'infiamma." [And like an infant who, when it has taken / its milk, extends its arms out to its mother, / its feeling kindling into outward flame,]

[79] *Par.* 23:73-75: "The Rose in which the Word of God became / flesh grows within that garden; there—the lilies / whose fragrance let men find the righteous way." [Quivi è la rosa in che 'l verbo divino / carne si fece; quivi son li gigli / al cui odor si prese il buon cammino]. Charles Grandgent explains that the rose is Mary, and the lilies are the Apostles (*La Divina Commedia*, ed. Grandgent and Singleton, 488).

[80] Iannucci, "*Paradiso* XXXI," 473.

truth. As a result, Beatrice's language throughout *Paradiso* affirms the truth of the things they see and the words they hear during their ascent.[81] The journey as far as the summit of Mount Purgatory is revealed as *figura*, to use Auerbach's term, whereas its continuation beyond Earthly Paradise is revealed as the fulfillment.[82] At the beginning of *Paradiso*, for example, Beatrice warns Dante that "false imagining," can impede his ability to see the truth, and the reader is reminded of layered nature of representation.[83] Having exposed the falsity, Beatrice then proceeds to illuminate the true nature of the cosmos. The inability of mortals to see past the *imitatio* is highlighted by the fact that the universe, as it is shown to Dante, is merely a representation in order to allow him to comprehend and is not the true reality.[84] In the context of Dante's love story, the explanation has

---

[81] *Par.* 4:124-26: "I now see well: we cannot satisfy / our mind unless it is enlightened by / the truth beyond whose boundary no truth lies." [Io veggio ben che già mai non si sazia / nostro intelletto se 'l ver non lo illustra/ di fuor dal qual nessun vero si spazia.]

[82] Auerbach suggests, "l'interpretazione figurale stabilisce fra due fatti o persone un nesso in cui uno di essi non significa soltanto se stesso, ma significa anche l'altro, mentre l'altro comprende o adempie il primo. I due poli della figura sono separati nel tempo, ma si trovano entrambi nel tempo, come fatti o figure reali" [The figural interpretation establishes a link between two facts or people in which one of them not only means itself, but also means the other, while the other understands or fulfills the first. The two poles of the figure are separated in time, but they are both found in time, as deeds or real figures] (*Studi su Dante*, 206; cfr. the use of "figura" in *Par.* 30, 76-78).

[83] *Par.* 1:88-90: "You make yourself / obtuse with false imagining; you can / not see what you would see if you dispelled it." [Tu stesso ti fai grosso/ col falso imaginar, sì che non vedi / ciò che vedresti se l'avessi scosso.]

[84] *Par.* 4:40-45: "Such signs are suited to your mind, since from / the senses only can it apprehend / what then becomes fit for the intellect. / And this is why the Bible condescends / to human powers, assigning feet and hands / to God, but meaning something else instead" [Così parlar conviensi al vostro ingegno, / però che solo da sensate apprende / ciò che fa poscia

the effect of exposing the *donna gentile* of the *Convivio* and the *donna gentile* of the *Vita nuova* as the mere imitations they are. But like the representations in Scripture these *donne gentili* are not entirely without value. They are not ignored or rejected; they are absorbed, transformed, and revealed in the new context. Here they are both subsumed into Beatrice, who shows Dante that she is the truth while both *donne* were pale imitations. This Beatrice is more than the *donna gentile* of the *Vita nuova*, for she represents a truer love. This Beatrice is more than the *donna gentile* of the *Convivio*, for she not only speaks of pagan philosophy but of all philosophy. Caught up in the *figurae*, Dante had not realized he was chasing false images.

Here then is how Dante reconciles the question of his relationship to the *donna gentile* and how we may also resolve the critical debate in which scholars have been long engaged.[85] Whether the *donna gentile* is another manifestation of the role fulfilled by Beatrice in the earlier works or whether she stands in opposition to Beatrice ceases to be an issue because her independent existence is not relevant. Beatrice, that is, the Beatrice of the *Comedy*, absorbs all that is right and corrects all that is wrong. Moreover, as we see throughout *Paradiso* 4, Beatrice goes beyond the philosophers, for she can see the truths that they could not. Dante's construction of a Beatrice who contains philosophy, perfects it, and therefore transcends it, reflects

d'intelletto degno. / Per questo la Scrittura condescende / a vostra facultate, e piedi e mano / attribuisce a Dio e altro intende]

[85] See also Michele Barbi in *Problemi di critica dantesca*, in particular in his essay "La questione di Beatrice" ["The question of Beatrice"], 113–37. In considering the relationship of Beatrice to philosophy in the *Convivio*, he observes, "Più tardi il pensiero di Dante circa i rapporti fra Beatrice e la Filosofia può essere stato diverso" [Later Dante's thought about the relationship between Beatrice and Philosophy may have been different] (117). He concludes, nonetheless, that for the purposes of the *Convivio*, at least, she is simply Dante's previous love interest, a corporeal woman.

Dante's engagement with the writings of Thomas Aquinas, but she also reflects certain aspects of Augustinian thought.[86] In this new sphere, Beatrice is not a mere *figura* of a single school of thought. In *Paradiso* multiple sources of wisdom are absorbed, digested, and expanded beyond the confines of Dante's descent into the Inferno. This absorption fulfills the project first attempted within the *Convivio*, that is, the reconciliation of sexual love with the love of philosophy.[87] Here on the higher plane, love and knowledge become one, and Beatrice becomes both. Beatrice's transformation into wisdom was foreshadowed as early as her appearance in Earthly Paradise, where her arrival was heralded with words taken from the Song of Solomon, "Veni de Libano, sponsa mea, veni di Libano, veni" (4:8). According to the Catholic interpretation, the "*sponsa*," (bride) is the wisdom of God.[88] Moreover, the way Beatrice is dressed, together with her crown of olive branches, evokes theological wisdom.[89] It is no coincidence, therefore, that Virgil disappears

---

[86] See Singleton, *Dante Studies 2*, 134, for a deeper discussion of this. See also Iannucci, *Forma ed evento nella Divina Commedia*, 87, who notes Thomist echoes in *Paradiso* 4. Barolini asserts that Beatrice, at times, is also the spokesperson for St. Augustine (*The Undivine Comedy*, 102).

[87] Bruno Nardi sees the pursuit of knowledge in the *Convivio* as expressed in philosophical terms. In the *Comedy*, however, the reconciliation takes the form more of that expressed by Gilson in his writings on St. Bernard and courtly love.

[88] *Purg*. 30:11, *La Divina Commedia*, ed. Sapegno (1955), 735.

[89] *Purg*. 30: 31-33: "above / a white veil, she was crowned with olive boughs; / her cape was green; her dress beneath, flame-red." [sovra candido vel cinta d'uliva / donna m'apparve, sotto verde manto vestita / di color di fiamma viva.] Sapegno notes, "i colori del velo, del manto, della veste alludono alla fede, alla speranza, alla carità: le quali tre virtù sono solo della Teologia, e per questo sono detto teologiche" [the colors of the veil, of the mantle, of the robe allude to faith, to hope, to charity: which three virtues are from Theology alone, and for this reason they are called theological (my

at this point, not just because he belongs to the earthly plane but also so that Dante can distinguish between pre-Christian and post-Christian wisdom.[90] As Beatrice speaks, her "wisdom" frequently echoes Dante's earlier statements in other works. For example, when Beatrice explains that it is not just through the natural influence of the heavens but that each seed is directed to a determined end, she echoes what Dante suggested in the *Convivio*.[91] The education continues into *Paradiso* where Beatrice is continually "confuting" and "proving."[92] (In this way, Dante cleverly attributes a certain level of authority to his own knowledge without creating an appearance of being proud.)

---

translation)] (*La Divina Commedia*, ed. Sapegno [1955], 737). He continues: The olive wreath may signify "la pace, la quale è nell'animo quando si è adornato da fede; e la vittoria imperò che niuna cosa li è poi dura a credere o intendere e operare; e la sapienza imperò che l'ulivo è consecrato a Pallade [cfr. il V. 68], che è la dia de la sapienza, la quale è corona de la santa teologia" [peace, which is in the soul when adorned with faith; and the victory impelled that no thing is then hard to believe or understand and operate; and wisdom impeded that the olive tree is consecrated in Pallas [cfr. V. 68], which is the god of wisdom, which is the crown of the holy theology] (737).

[90] *Purg.* 30:49. Sapegno sees this as denoting that moral philosophy cedes to the supernatural and to the divine, as a more noble science and one that is worthy of Beatrice (*La Divina Commedia*, ed. Sapegno [1955], 738).

[91] *Purg.* 30:109-11: "Not only through the work of the great spheres— / which guide each seed to a determined end, / depending on what stars are its companions." [Non pur per ovra delle rote magna / che drizzan ciascun seme ad alcune fine / secondo che le stelle son compagne]

Convivio IV, xxii, 7: "the disposition of Heaven for the effect may be good, better, or best (varying in accordance with the constellations which undergo continuous change), it comes to pass that a soul is created more or less pure from the seed of man and from these virtues." [la disposizione del cielo puote essere buona, migliore e ottima la quale si varia per le costellazioni che continuamente si trasmutano, incontra che de l'umano seme e di queste vertudi più pur [e men pura] anima si produce.]

[92] *Par.* 3:3: "provando e riprovando."

Later, when Dante describes the constant gaze of the angels,[93] we recall a passage in the *Convivio* that likewise described the constant gaze.[94] Within the context of this new truth, Dante is, therefore, able to continue the absorption and reinterpretation of his earlier works as we see in that passage where Beatrice shows Dante the limitations of reason and then uses enlightened reason to correct Dante's earlier theory with respect to the dark spots on the moon.[95] When Dante is perplexed and imagines that Beatrice can resolve his doubts with "*le dolci stille*"[96] (sweet drops) we cannot help but recall the *dolce stil nuovo* and the *Vita nuova*. This explicit echo serves to redirect Dante's desire for relief and suggests that the *dolce stil nuovo* praise is ap-

---

[93] *Par.* 29:76-81: "These beings, since they first were gladdened by / the face of God, from which no thing is hidden, / have never turned their vision from that face, / so that their sight is never intercepted / by a new object, and they have no need / to recollect an interrupted concept." [Queste sustanze, poi che fur gioconde / de la faccia di Dio, non volser viso / da essa, da cui nulla si nasconde: / però non hanno vedere interciso / da nono obietto, e però non bisogna / rememorar per concetto diviso.]

[94] *Convivio* III, vi, 4-5: "Then when I say Every Intelligence admires her from above, I praise her without reference to anything else. I say that the Intelligences of heaven admire her and that those who are noble down here think of her when they must have that which delights them. Here we must know that every Intelligence above, according to what is written in the book Of Causes, knows what is above itself and what is below itself." [Poi quando dico: Ogni Inteletto di là su la mira, commendo lei, non avendo rispetto ad altra cosa. E dico che le intelligenze del cielo la mirano, e che la gente di qua giù gentile pensano di costei, quando più hanno di quello che loro diletta. E qui è da sapere che ciascuno Inteletto di sopra, secondo ch'è scritto nel libro de la cagioni, conosce quello che è sopra sé e quello che è sotto sé.]

[95] *Par.* 2:51-57. Dante had considered their source in the *Convivio*.

[96] *Par.* 7:10-12: "I was perplexed, and to myself, I said: / 'Tell her! Tell her! Tell her, the lady who / can slake my thirst with her sweet drops'" [Io dubitava, e dicea 'Dille, dille!' / fra me 'dille' dicea, 'a la mia donna / che mi diseta con le dolci stille,']

propriate only when it is directed toward the creator of the object of love and not toward the object of love alone.

When Beatrice advises Dante that reason, even when supported by the senses, has short wings, she recalls both the Icarus and Ulysses episodes of the *Inferno* (cantos 17 and 26 respectively).[97] This is another example of how Dante uses parallel episodes to contrast proper reasoning with the pride and folly of both flights and to emphasize the distinction between the earthly and the transcendent. The image is also supported narratively because Beatrice and Dante are rising well above the earth, unlike Icarus, who fell, and Ulysses, who remained earthbound despite using his oars as wings. The ascent beyond Earthly Paradise thus contrasts with and corrects the descents of the Icarus and Ulysses episodes. While the argument Beatrice uses to point out Dante's error is particularly remarkable in terms of its method,[98] it is also an example of how Dante uses Beatrice's voice to express his own advanced scientific knowledge while lending Christian authority to his own logical methods by having them pronounced in heaven.

Beatrice has also, in many ways, continued the project begun toward the end of the *Convivio*, specifically in Book 4. There, Dante was moving increasingly away from a mere recital of information toward a format that more closely resembles scholastic inquiry, or *quaestio*. Whereas Dante in the *Convivio*

---

[97] *Par.* 2:51-57: "If the opinion mortals hold / falls into error when the senses' key / cannot unlock the truth, you should not be / struck by the arrows of amazement once / you recognize that reason, even when / supported by the senses, has short wings," [s'elli erra l'oppinion...de' mortali / dove chiave di senso non di serra, / certo non ti dovrien punger li strali / d'ammirazione omai, poi dietro ai sensi / vedi che la ragione ha corte l'ali]

[98] As Grandgent notes, "Beatrice enforces theory by experiment, the modern method, here praised as the fountainhead of the arts. This is remarkable in a medieval poem" (*La Divina Commedia*, ed. Grandgent and Singleton, 372).

was attempting to find answers to the cosmos in the *donna gentile* (philosophy), in the *Comedy* it is Beatrice who provides the answers. Beatrice has become the light that Dante aspired to be in the *Convivio*. But Dante can share in this light, and so too can his readers.

In the early cantos of *Paradiso*, a new relationship is thus forged between Beatrice and Dante, one in which Beatrice is the teacher and Dante is the pupil. In this respect, Dante's experience in *Paradiso* follows a pattern regularly found in the hagiographical tradition. This re-education is an integral part of the conversion of the sinner into saint. Having purged vices—especially those to which Dante himself is subject, lust and pride—the sinner then must begin to learn of what a holy life consists.

In the eighth sphere of heaven, while Dante is being examined on questions of hope, Beatrice stands by, confident she has prepared him for this final examination; indeed, Dante likens himself to a student.[99] The image highlights the deficiencies in Dante's relationships with his former masters, Virgil and Brunetto Latini, who are both confined to the netherworld. Beatrice is the true teacher, the light that he himself tried to be in the *Convivio*, not because Dante loves her but because she is love. Dante the writer has, therefore, found a way to effect the role he sought for himself in the *Convivio*, by denuding it of the pride such an aspiration implies.

What becomes evident is that the higher Dante rises, the more he becomes a participant in the discussion. He is no longer simply being lectured to; he has become part of a scholarly discussion. He is still the pupil whose responses are mostly to spur

[99] *Par*. 25:64: "As a disciple answering his master, / prepared and willing in what he knows well, / that his proficiency may be revealed," [come discente ch'a dottor seconda / pronto e libente in quel ch'elli è esperto, / perché la sua bontà si disasconda.]

on the discussion, but the nature of the relationship between Dante and Beatrice has altered considerably since the stern rebuke of *Purgatorio*; we see that this is one way that Dante continues his story of love. Beatrice will show Dante, and, therefore, Dante will show us, the readers, that the *donna gentile* of the *Convivio* was inadequate as a lover, that what Dante really needed was a dialogue with Beatrice, the true Beatrice. Beatrice could just as easily have discoursed with him on the fine points of philosophy. Similarly, Beatrice's ability to provide Dante with all the answers, and indeed all of the true answers, is in direct contrast to Virgil, who (as we have seen, especially in *Purgatorio*) is at times as lost as Dante. Gradually Beatrice's and Dante's knowledge is revealed as one. Dante had hinted at this when he called Beatrice "she from whom my need could not be hidden."[100] In the heaven of Mercury, Beatrice reads Dante's mind again and dispels his doubts concerning redemption, giving him an explanation of the difference between those created things that are corruptible and those which are incorruptible.[101] As Beatrice continually anticipates Dante's questions on theology, she performs what was formerly his self-exegesis. As the incarnation of Dante the poet, she stands in opposition to Dante the pilgrim-protagonist. Yet as the pilgrim draws nearer the summit of his ascent, this distinction fades.

The closer Dante and Beatrice come to their mutual apex,

---

[100] *Par.* 2: 26: "cui non potea mia cura essere ascosa."

[101] *Par.* 7:19-24: "According to my never-erring judgment, / the question that perplexes you is how / just vengeance can deserve just punishment; / but I shall quickly free your mind from doubt; / and listen carefully; the words I speak / will bring the gift of a great truth in reach." [Secondo mio infallibile avviso, / come giusta vendetta giustamente / punita fosse, t'ha in pensier miso; / ma io ti solverò tosto la mente; / e tu ascolta, ché le mie parole / di gran sentenza ti faran presente.] Sapegno sees *sentenza* as meaning "*di grande verità, dottrina*" [of great truth, doctrine] (*La Divina Commedia*, ed. Sapegno [1955], 955, 863).

the more they become merged within the concept of the continuum. Having received Beatrice's blessing, Dante has been imbued with the necessary grace not only to ask the questions but also to answer some of them. The message is clear; Dante was not so much wrong before as misdirected. When Beatrice speaks for Dante to spare his modesty,[102] she is not only reading his mind and correcting his sin of pride but she is also reminding us of the distinctions between this realm and that in which Dante previously existed. Her words recall the *Convivio*'s question about when it is appropriate to speak for oneself and highlight that here, in *Paradiso*, even this problem is solved. There is no need to speak for oneself to correct an injustice, for here there can be no injustice. Nor does Dante need to speak to prove the truthfulness of his testimony, for here all words are true and have exemplary value. A new equation of love and wisdom has emerged. While the particular earthly attributes such as vanity and pride were formerly the norm (and talking of oneself was the major characteristic), on this universal plane, humility is the normal comportment and there is no need to speak of or for oneself. All members of the continuum know each other's minds and all speak for each other. Love is not linear, but circular, and in contrast to the false imitation, i.e., the closed circle of the temporal, the circle here is limitless and all inclusive.

As he moves throughout the spheres of Paradise, Dante continues his conversion from *stil novista*, subtly transforming himself from aspiring *poeta-theologus* to fully-fledged *theologus-poeta*. As he makes explicit his aspirations as a poet, he simul-

---

[102] *Par.* 25:52-54: "There is no child of the Church Militant / who has more hope than he has, as is written / within the Sun whose rays reach all our ranks...." [La Chiesa militante alcun figliuolo / non ha con più speranza, com'è scritto / nel Sol che raggia tutto nostro stuolo....]

taneously adopts a narrative pattern common to the hagiographical tradition.[103] Swearing that he often makes confession and repents for his sins in order to return some day to heaven, Dante "represents himself as a sinner engaged in lamenting his sins and humbling himself in the hope of attaining eternal salvation."[104] Moreover, as Giuseppe Ledda notes, Dante also links himself to Peter Damian's "model of sacred humility, thus continuing to construct his own identity after these saints."[105]

As Dante continues his ascent into the heavenly spheres, his trajectory continues to etch the shape of a cross, matching his own iter with Beatrice's. Their mutual ascent, following their own prior descents, links their pattern to that of the risen Christ and emphasizes the similarities between Beatrice and Christ forged throughout the *Comedy*.[106]

---

[103] *Par*. 22:106-11: "So may I return, reader, to that devout triumph on whose account I ever weep for my sins and beat my breast: you would not any sooner have withdrawn your finger from the fire and put it in, than I saw the sign that follows the Bull and was within it." [S'io torni mai, lettore, a quel divoto trïunfo per lo quale io piango spesso le mie peccata e 'l petto mi percuoto, tu non avresti in tanto tratto e messo nel foco il dito, in quant'io vidi 'l segno che segue il Tauro e fui dentro da esso.]

[104] Ledda, "Truth, Autobiography and the Poetry of Salvation," 251–52.

[105] Moreover, as Ledda notes, Dante also links himself to Peter Damian who was presented in the previous canto as 'Pietro Peccator' [Peter the Sinner] (*Par.*, 21:121–23): "Dante, admitting humbly to his own nature as a sinner, links back to Peter Damian's model of sacred humility, thus continuing to construct his own identity after these saints" (ibid., 251). For the autobiographical implications of this section of *Paradiso* xxii, see also Barański, *Dante e i segni*, 347–53).

[106] Many scholars have noted a marked resemblance in the actions of Beatrice to those of Christ. Erich Auerbach, in particular, has noted how often Beatrice is presented as a "figura of Christ" (*Studi su Dante*, 221). Charles Singleton specifies that her appearance in *Purgatorio* 32 is more precisely a second coming of Christ and draws an elaborate pattern of analogy in which Virgil represents the Roman people, Dante represents Everyman,

When seen from this perspective, Beatrice's descent into Limbo to enlist Virgil's help and her implied return to heaven may be likened to Christ's appearance on earth during the Roman Empire. His mission of salvation, aimed initially at the Hebrews, was seemingly limited, or at least perceived as such. The second coming of Christ, on the other hand, has a more universal scope.[107] Beatrice's appearance to Virgil, recounted in *Inferno* 2, may be associated with the first coming of Christ in that she is still being perceived in the *stilnovistic* sense within Dante's particular story. Like the Jews who sought a terrestrial messiah and looked for the kingdom of God on earth, Dante will not find salvation in this world. Beatrice's second incarnation brings the kingdom of God, the kingdom which is not of this earth. By drawing Beatrice as a *figura christi* and by matching his own patterns to both Christ's and Beatrice's, Dante transforms the object of his love into love itself. And love itself is revealed as salvific.

---

and Beatrice represents Christ (*Dante Studies 1*, 38). And as Sapegno notes, the language of *Purgatorio* 30:19 ("*Benedictus qui venis...*") recalls Christ's entrance into Jerusalem as these are the words with which the Jews greeted him (see Matt 21:9; Mark 11:10; Luke 19:38). (*La Divina Commedia*, ed. Sapegno [1955], 735). In *Purgatorio* 33:10-12, Beatrice says, "Modicum, et non videbitis me...." These are the words of Christ to his disciples to warn them that he would soon be dead and later resurrected (John 16:16). According to Sapegno, many have understood them in this context as a prophecy of the transfer of the papal court to Avignon and together with a promise that the vacancy of the roman papal seat would not last long, but it is perhaps more opportune, says Sapegno, to attribute to them a less precise and circumscribed meaning: they say that the decadence of the church has touched its lowest point and announce the coming of a profound moral reform (*La Divina Commedia*, ed. Sapegno [1955], 767).

[107] For example, in Revelation the words of Christ are now addressed to the seven churches established among the Gentiles (Rev 2:3). Moreover, the letters speak of the "hour of trial which will come upon the whole world to test those who dwell on the earth" (Rev 3:10).

Moreover, in her role as teacher, exegete, and revelator, Beatrice is the embodiment of all of Dante's pursuits. She is knowledge and love. But more importantly, she is both at the same time. Dante need no longer choose between love and knowledge. The union seems somehow familiar, and we become increasingly aware that these two have been joined elsewhere. As we look back with the benefit of hindsight, we realize that this association was prefigured in the temporal sphere before Dante's arrival in Earthly Paradise. Ulysses's quest for knowledge and Francesca's quest for love were both expressed in terms that recalled flight.[108] But their flights were misdirected and therefore remained unfulfilled.

The final prayer of the *Comedy* in which Bernard praises the Virgin Mary represents the culmination of the love story. Now called to the table of the saints, Dante-poet is authorized to write about true love. Having joined the doctors of the church in conversation, he is qualified to write his own treatises. Here the evolution of the poet who once identified himself as one inspired by love is complete.[109] While Bernard's prayer to the true *Donna* (*Par.* 33:1-39) counteracts the perversity of Francesca's supplication to Dante in *Inferno* 5, it also provides the universal exemplum of love that leads always to wisdom and the true flight of the soul.

---

[108] *Inf.* 5:82-4: "Even as doves when summoned by desire, / borne forward by their will, move through the air / with wings uplifted, still, to their sweet nest," [Quali colombe dal disio chiamate / con l'ali alzate e ferme al dolce nido / vegnon per l'aere, dal volere portate,]

[109] *Purg.* 24:52-54: "I am one who, when Love breathes / in me, takes note; what he, within, dictates, / I, in that way, without, would speak and shape." [I' mi son un che, quando / Amor mi spira, noto, e a quel modo / ch'e' ditta dentro vo significando.] See Marchesi, "Epic Ironies," for a thorough review of the episode and its autobiographic implications.

Just as significantly, the importance of Beatrice's resemblance to Christ extends beyond the confines of the love story. Beatrice's constant exhortations to Dante to write what he sees[110] not only attribute to him a role he himself had denied[111] but also recall and legitimize those portions of the *Convivio* in which Dante attributed an apostolic role for himself. His vision in the *Convivio*, however, was blurred because he was not looking at Beatrice and the truth she could show him. Now, however, he will see the true nature of what he sought before in imitations and, therefore, will be able to fulfill the goal of the *Convivio* and of the *Vita nuova* before it. The *Convivio* and the *Vita nuova* become Dante's Old Testament, mere prefigurations, while his new work in this post-salvation context becomes the fulfillment, his own personal New Testament. The resulting narrative is a new product, informed by the Gospels, the lives

---

[110] *Purg.* 32:100-106: "Here you shall be—a while—a visitor; / but you shall be with me—and without end— / Rome's citizen, that Rome in which Christ is / Roman; and thus, to profit that world which / lives badly, watch the chariot steadfastly / and, when you have returned beyond, transcribe / what you have seen." [Qui sarai tu poco tempo silvano; / e sarai meco sanza fine cive / di quella Roma onde Cristo è romano. / Però, in pro del mondo che mal vive, / al carro tieni or li occhi, e quel che vedi, / ritornato di là, fache tu scrive.] Sapegno notes echoes of similar language in Revelation 1:11: "What you see, write in a Book and send it to the seven churches which are in Asia: to Ephesus, to Smyrna, to Pergamos, to Thyatira, to Sardis, to Philadelphia, and to Laodicea" (*La Divina Commedia*, ed. Sapegno [1955], 763). See also Revelation 1:19 ("Write the things which you have seen, and the things which are, and the things which will take place after this"); Revelation 21:5 ("Then He who sat on the throne said, 'Behold, I make all things new.' And he said to me, 'Write, for these words are true and faithful'").

I note as well *Purg*. 33:55-57: "And when you write them, keep in mind that you / must not conceal what you've seen of the tree / that now has been despoiled twice over here." [E aggi a mente, quando tu le scrivi, / di non celar qual hai vista la pianta / ch'è or due volte dirubata quivi.]

[111] *Inf.* 2:32: "I am not Paul." [Io non Paulo sono]

of the saints, and the apocryphal Gospels with which Dante was familiar.[112] In terms of how the *Comedy* treats Dante's love for Beatrice, this new work takes its structure from Paul's letter to the Corinthians. As the child, unable to see clearly, becomes a man who can see, the sinner becomes a saint, and the *Comedy*, witness to his conversion, becomes a song of praise and a treatise at the same time: a canticle of *caritas*.

As this journey of conversion moves toward its culmination, Dante's status as saint is further proven by the introduction of St. Bernard of Clairvaux. Just as the pilgrim's proximity to Beatrice[113] connects him to her sainthood, as the moment of his beatific vision approaches, this "rub off" effect, as I call it, infuses Dante with a new kind of sight. He can see as only the saints can. Now, the saints in the celestial rose and the communion of saints who made his journey possible are revealed to him. St. Lucy has been with Dante from the start,[114] and now here in *Paradiso* she is there again, shining like the light that her name signifies.[115]

But Dante's inclusion of the saints is not limited to his brief sojourn in *Paradiso*. Rather, their itineraries and cults have shaped the *Comedy* and intersected on multiple occasions with the pilgrim's own trajectory. The figure of Veronica, for example, has been with him all along. As Alessandro Vettori points

---

[112] For a thorough discussion of Dante's familiarity with the apocrypha and the Gospel of Nicodemus in particular, see Iannucci, "Beatrice in Limbo," 23–45.

[113] See Cassell, "Santa Lucia."

[114] *Inf.* 2:100-102: "Lucia, enemy of every cruelty, / arose and made her way to where I was, / sitting beside the venerable Rachel." [Lucia, nimica di ciascun crudele, / si mosse, e venne al loco dov' i' era, / che mi sedea con l'antica Rachele.]

[115] *Par.* 32:137-38: "Lucia sits, she who urged on your lady / when you bent your brows downward, to your ruin." [siede Lucia, che mosse la tua donna / quando chinavi, a rovinar, le ciglia.]

out, Dante's wonder at the beatific vision reminds us of the pilgrims in the *Vita nuova* who were also on their way to see the Veronica.[116] Even then the journey to that Rome where Christ is a Roman, was being prefigured, but Dante, then blind, could not see. Even in the marvelous darkness of *Inferno*, the saints are conspicuous if only in their absence. In *Inferno* 21, the reference to the *volto santo* reminds us of the work of St. Nicodemus, whose own gospel Iannucci identified as a possible inspiration for the harrowing of hell described by Virgil in *Inferno* 4.[117]

As his journey culminates with a beatific vision, Dante is linked with Lucy's attribute, divine sight, and is made into a saint himself by having been afforded this moment. His moment of blindness thus links him with Paul, the master poet of love[118] and avatar of conversion. Like Paul, Dante has been liberated from the limits of human sight and, with his new insight, has been commissioned to write this truly new life.

---

[116] See Vettori, "Veronica," on the role of Veronica in the *Comedy*.
[117] See Iannucci, "Beatrice in Limbo."
[118] Paul's letter to the Corinthians on love (1 Cor 12:31–13:8).

Chapter 5

Exile: The Long Way Home

JUST AS THE journey metaphor of the *Comedy* provides the framework within which Dante expresses both his love story and his concomitant evolving theory of love, so too does the metaphor furnish a narrative form within which to depict the actual political events of his life and the parallel evolution in his political thinking. Moreover, the presence of a second story not only attests to the metaphor's capacity to accommodate more than one narrative thread but also allows Dante to present his political story as analogous to his love story. In this way Dante attributes to his political journey the same salvific quality that he attributes to his experience of love.

In this respect, Dante continues his struggle to find common meaning in apparently divergent events. In the *Convivio*, Dante began his quest to forge a coherence and find a common language through which emotional love and the zeal for knowledge might be expressed and in which their affinities would be evident. It is here in the *Comedy* that he finally finds the means to effect such a reconciliation. With the journey metaphor and its component parts, Dante has created a structure capable of providing a common denominator that allows all his events and the stories that emerge out of them to be viewed through the same filter. The journey metaphor provides both a structural link and a common source of images through which both stories can be told and compared. Furthermore, the journey metaphor comes already imbued with the richness of connotation[1] necessary to support the breadth of meaning that Dante will ascribe to both stories. By creating a narrative unity in which two stories share a pattern, Dante reveals a meaning in his political thought that is consistent with his theory of love, enhancing the value of both. This chapter, therefore, will consider how the metaphor integrates Dante's political evolution into the narrative of the *Comedy*. It will also consider how his integration of the political narrative works with the other narrative threads to legitimize Dante's status as a saint.

In the context of the political story, as in the love story, the cruciform pattern created by the encounter of the particular with the universal is the key to understanding Dante's representative and exegetical project. The initial progression of the pilgrim coincides with the "journey of our life" and may be seen as linear and horizontal. However, the journey is distinguished by the narrative interruption of this unremarkable progress when another voice, the poetic "I," is superimposed. The narrative voice utters "I found myself,"[2] and the shape of this journey is changed. Instead of locating itself horizontally, this voice introduces a new paradigm of movement between two new coordinates: one below, the other above this imaginary horizontal line. The first represents the nadir of hell and the second the pinnacle of heaven. The "I" of "I found myself," therefore, introduces a second aspect to the journey, expanding its context from backward and forward to include up and down. By locating the "up / down" trajectory, his particular story, midway

[1] John Freccero, in his "Introduction to *Inferno*," discusses the close resemblance between this metaphor and the imagery used by St. Augustine in *Confessions* Book 7.

[2] *Inf.* 1:2: "Mi ritrovai"

along the "journey of our life," Dante is able to tell his own story (or stories) in a way that ensures it retains a universal significance. As John Freccero suggests, Dante's story "like Augustine's life...was meant to be both autobiographical and emblematic, a synthesis of the particular circumstances of an individual's life with paradigms of salvation history drawn from the Bible."[3] Freccero's focus on the Augustinian model, however, misses a certain subtle distinction between it and the dual scope of the *Comedy*. In the Augustinian model, events from the life of the author form the literal narrative while the universal lesson lies in the allegorical interpretation of those events. In the *Comedy*, Dante's actual life, the life outside of the text, furnishes the allegorical meaning. The result is that while in the Augustinian model the true meaning is extracted or extrapolated from the events of the author's life, in the Dantean model, the events of his life *are* the truth. They are the *veritas* or fulfillment while the narrative is the mere *imitatio* or *figura*. In the *Comedy*, Dante's actual life is the truth of which the narrative is mere representation. This distinction is crucial to understanding the way Dante proposes his story be read and how the character of the pilgrim be understood. By placing his autobiographical aspects within the allegorical level of meaning and constructing a literal narrative, Dante lends more authority to his own actual events. More importantly, he creates a relationship between the literal and allegorical levels in which the literal can be interpreted in light of its fulfillment. For example, it is only with reference to the actual events of Dante's life that the political meaning of the pilgrim's state at the inception of the *Comedy* can be fully understood. Here, while Dante has stepped out of the ranks of Everyman, he is nonetheless still located outside of the vertical descent and ascent pattern noted above. He

[3] Freccero, *Dante*, 179.

is in a state that Theodolinda Barolini characterizes as "the middle of nowhere" and "nonlocatable, a nonevent."[4] Through the use of a number of narrative strategies, what was earlier revealed as representing Dante's estrangement from Beatrice also emerges as a *figura* of his actual exile.

Given the plethora of documentary evidence attesting to Dante's exile, it would appear to be a simple matter to attribute a political connotation to this spatial location with no need to resort to complicated exegetical analysis. However, I would suggest that such documentation merely confirms what is evident from the *Comedy* itself. Moreover, to rely on the external existence of documents attesting to Dante's political focus loses sight of Dante's project of autoexegesis. Yes, the documentary evidence is consistent with the allegorical meaning, but the ultimate significance of both the literal and the allegorical meanings must be sought intertextually; the *Comedy* not only tells Dante's story but also interprets it and, therefore, provides an expanded meaning to its events. While the documentary evidence of Dante's life provides a historical record, it lacks the analysis that can be found only in the *Comedy* and which characterizes the work as autobiographical. If it is to have the significance or didactic value its author intended, the exile event must be interpreted within the context Dante creates for it. A mere reading of the documents, for example, would not assist us in terms of the role and purpose Dante proposes for his exile in the *Comedy*.[5] Alan Charity suggests that while Dante's journey may be "mythologized," this "stylizing" of Dante's life is a

[4] Barolini, *Undivine Comedy*, 21.

[5] Renato Piattoli's *Codice diplomatico dantesco* catalogues the numerous documents that attest to Dante's political career, including the charges brought against him in absentia, his conviction in absentia, and the resulting sentence of exile. See documents 83, 84, 86–88, 90–92, 95, 98, 99, 114 and 115 at pp. 94–155.

"necessary means of expressing something he felt about it."[6] Charity concludes that this stylizing or "figuring" exists "not to replace Dante's personal history but to interpret it."[7] Therefore, by presenting his mythologized story as the literal narrative of the *Comedy*, Dante can locate himself socially and express exile as an interruption of the ordinary course thus removing him from the ranks of other men. It is this exile that marks Dante's passage from Everyman to the particular and takes Dante from one paradigm to another.

At the same time, the "stylizing" tells us that his removal from the universal is not absolute because, owing to the cruciform structure, the vertical movement is always contained within a larger pattern; Dante's story is a synecdochic representation of the greater journey. This point is made clear through the gradual revelation that Dante's "particular" journey will lead back to a fusion with the universal. This mythologizing also serves Dante's auto-hagiographical intent by allowing him to present his life as that of a saint.

Within Dante's particular story, just as the death of Beatrice altered the course of his love story and provided him with a new perspective and direction, so too does exile change Dante's perspective to that of an outsider looking in and compel him to seek a new direction. By transforming the state of exile into the spatial location, "the dark woods," and himself into the pilgrim who has lost "the right way,"[8] Dante expresses the exile event within the context of the primary narrative structure of the *Comedy*, the journey metaphor; he thereby establishes a link between this story and the love story, which is expressed in the

---

[6] Charity, *Events and Their Afterlife*, 253.

[7] Ibid., 254.

[8] *Inf.* 1:2: "la selva oscura"; *Inf.* 1:3: "la diritta via"

same terms.[9] At the same time, Dante includes aspects of the actual exile that might not otherwise have been evident. When Dante writes the literal version of his allegorical meaning, he starts with imagery that he then uses to prefigure his political life, altering its components in such a way as to color the subsequent events. He is thus able to suggest a significance that will, in turn, be ascribed to the actual events, which the narrative expresses chronologically. Taking actual locations and events and reshaping them with the benefit of hindsight disguised as foresight, Dante thus transforms retrospect into prophecy.

Exile, when depicted this way, becomes part of a pattern that itself has already, in the love story, been identified with salvation. In a very significant way, the *Comedy* allows Dante to throw off the shame of his exile by transforming it into something necessary to his role as a political redeemer. At the same time, the figural character of the *Comedy* provides a means of interpreting all Dante's "subsequent" political writings so as to ensure that they present a vision consistent with that of the *Comedy*. Let us not forget that it is Dante himself who creates this "prequel" and is, therefore, able to paint what it means—not just for the reader but also for Dante, in whatever colors he chooses. As Iannucci has pointed out, "Dante's pilgrim is not just an abstract figure of the exiled Christian soul nor do his two cities belong solely to moral and spiritual categories as Augustine's do. Dante's pilgrim is modeled on the historical Dante, the exiled Florentine poet."[10] That the souls in Hell can read the future enables Dante to "pre-interpret" the people, places, and events that will also figure in his subsequent political vision. As a result, Farinata degli Uberti's prediction of Dante's exile[11]

---

[9] Within the love story, the "selva oscura" corresponded to the protagonist's alienation from Beatrice.

[10] Iannucci, "*Paradiso* XXXI," 475.

[11] *Inf.* 10:79-81: "And yet the Lady who is ruler here / will not have

lends an enhanced significance to its actual occurrence, presenting the exile as preordained as opposed to random. The fulfillment of much of this "foresight" lends an accuracy to those "predictions," which are not otherwise verifiable, such as the fate of Boniface VIII,[12] and transforms Dante's opinion into prescience. Thus, from the narrative representation of a Dante who is outside of the ordinary course, we assume the "true" version will similarly provide such a perspective. When Giuseppe Mazzotta suggests that it is Dante's exile that is the "stance affording the detached vantage point from which he can speak to the world and impose his sense of order on it," he is implicitly referring to Dante's actual exile.[13] We must not, however, forget that within the literal narrative of the *Comedy*, Dante the pilgrim has not yet been exiled, at least not politically. His political exile is, chronologically, still in the future. All that we have in the *Comedy* is the *figura* of exile. The "sense of order," to use Mazzotta's terminology, that Dante imposes upon it within the literal narrative is intended to prefigure Dante's world view, again elevating Dante's actual extra-textual view to fulfillment as opposed to *figura*. The *figura* of the *Comedy* attests to the perspective the "real life Dante" will attain from his real life exile and thereby infuse his post-exile vision with a truthfulness it might not have enjoyed otherwise.

In the same way that Dante anchored his love story primarily within the context of emotional relationships and

---

her face kindled fifty times / before you learn how heavy is that art." [Ma non cinquanta volte fia raccesa / la faccia de la donna che qui regge, / che tu saprai quanto quell'arte pesa.]

[12] *Inf.* 19:52-54: "and he cried out: 'Are you already standing, / already standing there, o Boniface? / The book has lied to me by several years.'" [Ed el gridò: "Se' tu già costí ritto, / se' tu già costí ritto, Bonifazio? / Di parecchi anni mi mentí lo scritto."]

[13] Mazzotta, *Dante*, 112.

thereby rendered certain characters emblematic, here he sets the political story within the context of civic relationships represented by cities that reveal a variety of political systems in the same way emotional relationships revealed types of love. In the love story, the movement from one type of relationship to another illustrates evolution in Dante's own personal experience and in his own theory of love; so too does the pilgrim's movement from one city to another mark Dante's own political journey and his attendant evolution in political thought. This particular journey, like the love story, finds expression in a descent and ascent pattern. The pattern commences with Dante's movement in a direction away from the horizontal line of the linear journey, to a place somewhere below, toward the point below the line in the heart of the *Inferno*. Although this place is removed geographically from the world of the living, it is not completely detached from it. Just as the bodies of the damned have been transformed into recognizable shades, at times disfigured in accordance with Dante's strategy of *contrapasso*, so here the physical city of Florence, while transformed into the City of Dis, is still recognizable.[14] Though its baptistry and churches are gone and in their place we find graveyards and woods of suicides, its gates and walls remain as a reminder of its power to exclude. Because Florence, in the world of the living, excluded the virtuous (such as Dante), its inhabitants are now limited to thieves, traitors, and murderers. The pilgrim and the reader are aware almost from the start of the descent that Dante's first destination is associated at least in some way with Florence. As early as *Inferno* 6, the reader encounters Florentines in all their shameless glory, or, as Theodolinda Barolini

[14] *Inf.* 8:67-69: "the city / that bears the name of Dis is drawing near, / with its grave citizens, its great battalions." [la città c'ha nome Dite, / coi gravi cittadin, col grande stuolo.]

has noted, "when we 'reach hell' we reach Florence as well."[15] There, in the third circle of Hell, amid the gluttons, we meet Ciacco,[16] who introduces the theme of Florence, representing its excesses. In the fourth circle, we find Florence's spendthrifts and misers, including clergymen and cardinals.[17] In the fifth circle, Filippo Argenti's wrath introduces the City of Dis, which numerous scholars have associated with Florence.[18] Iannucci points out that, in his opinion, the Florentine suicide at the end of the *Inferno* 13, "represents figuratively the whole city."[19] Perhaps the meaning of Hell in the *Comedy* was best expressed by Alan Charity, who saw the issue in terms of Auerbach's theory of *figura* and fulfillment and concluded that Hell is fulfilled in Florence.[20] Hell, then, in Dante's pre-exile journey prefigures what Florence is to become for Dante after his real-life or actual exile.

The mere likening of Hell to Florence, the suggestion that one is the fulfillment of the other, merely provides the setting and does not complete the expression of Dante's political story. It is the pilgrim's interaction with this Florence that hones its political meaning. As Dante descends into Hell, for example, his presence is marked with surprise, contempt, and exclusion. He is not welcome there. In *Inferno* 8, outside the City of Dis,

---

[15] Barolini, *Undivine Comedy*, 43.

[16] *Inf.* 6:14.

[17] *Inf.* 7:46-48: "These to the left—their heads bereft of hair— / were clergymen, and popes and cardinals, / within whom avarice works its excess." [cherci, che non han coperchio / piloso al capo, e papi e cardinali, / in cui usa avarizia il suo superchio.]

[18] *Inf.* 8:61-63. Joan Ferrante offers an extensive discussion as to the similarities between medieval Florence and the City of Dis, enumerating the "the several hints within the *Comedy*" that Dante equates Florence with Hell (*Political Vision of the Divine Comedy*, 67).

[19] Iannucci, "*Paradiso* XXXI," 478.

[20] Charity, *Events and Their Afterlife*, 245.

Dante is prohibited from entering. Although Virgil explains that Dante has been divinely chosen to take this journey, its gates remain shut. Since it has been established that Hell will be fulfilled in Florence, then we can deduce that Dante, allegorically, will not be welcome in Florence. Moreover, the descent of the angel to open its gates expands upon this to show that divine intervention will be required for Dante to reenter. The episode outside the walls is a virtual reenactment of Dante's exile. Rather than say, "I was excluded from Florence and could not get back in without divine intervention," he paints Florence as Hell, as the City of Dis, and stands outside its doors awaiting entry. Likening Hell to Florence prefigures Dante's allegorical, or actual, events and gives them meaning. Since Hell excludes the virtuous and prefigures Florence, if Florence excludes Dante, Dante must be virtuous. Concomitantly, the episode reinforces the importance of the descent and ascent trajectory to the entire structure of the poem. Here the descent of the angel is a repetition of Christ's and Beatrice's descent into Hell.[21] Reintegration will only be possible through descent and ascent. We see not only that Dante's exile is integral to his ultimate reintegration into the universal but also that his political story repeats the pattern of his love story and of Christ's story. In this way, Dante's political vicissitudes acquire hagiographical significance, and Dante's life, including his political life, is revealed as the life of a saint.

Dante's exile, of course, is not his entire political story; it is an episode, the catalyst of an evolving political book played out in the *Comedy*. While Alessandro D'Entrèves sees Dante's evolution in terms of a traceable progression[22] and Joan Ferrante

[21] For a more in-depth discussion of the episode, see Iannucci, *Forma ed evento nella Divina Commedia*, and specifically the chapter on the descent of Beatrice.

[22] Alessandro D'Entrèves discerns in Dante's writing three consecutive

suggests that Dante thought more in terms of opposing political forces,[23] both approaches are restrictive and risk missing the interpretive aspect of the *Comedy* vis-à-vis Dante's political thought. An approach that examines the extent to which Dante attempts within the *Comedy* to catalogue and characterize the various questions is more useful in interpreting the work and more in keeping with the purpose of the *Comedy*. The *Comedy* is not merely an alternative representation of Dante's political views but rather an attempt to reap meaning from his own vicissitudes while consolidating and reconciling his own, at times, seemingly divergent political theories. To that end, Dante uses the cruciform pattern to create a mechanism through which he can divide political issues into those with temporal or earthly significance and those with eternal or spiritual significance. Within this scheme, each political issue is relegated to a particular location within the narrative pattern. To a large extent, this approach coincides with the descent and ascent pattern of the love story since the thinking that Dante locates prior to his arrival at the summit of Mount Purgatory tends to correspond to the earthly[24] while that above it, in *Paradiso*, is timeless. Accordingly, his focus on Florence in the *Inferno* does not merely

---

stages of political thought: an initial concern with the issue of the city as a state, followed by a growing concern with the larger issue of the place of the empire, and then, after he suffered substantial disappointment and disillusionment with the notion of empire, the question of how the church might figure in the governance of man. He labels these stages Civitas, Imperium, and Ecclesia, respectively (*Dante as a Political Thinker*, 1, 26, 52).

[23] Ferrante approaches the issues in terms of opposing interests: city versus empire, church versus state, and corrupt versus ideal society (Ferrante, *The Political Vision*).

[24] Barolini suggests that "Spatially, hell is treated as tangible and concrete, while temporally, the fact that it is eternal means only that it will last forever, that its torments are perpetual. Eternity in the context of hell signifies duration" (*Undivine Comedy*, 15). She thus distinguishes it from *Paradiso*

reflect Dante's view of Florence. It also situates the stage in his political thought that related to the local issues of the city state and thereby assigns it both value and meaning.

This function is also served by certain characters that Dante inserts into the literal narrative. Their location conveys the relationship Florence bears to Hell and underlines the highly local and temporal nature of the issues involved in governing a city state. Farinata degli Uberti (*Inferno* 10) is the epitome of this intertextual gloss and the encapsulation of the political meaning of Florence as Hell. Certainly not the only character to provide political commentary, Farinata is the anthropomorphosis of the essence of Florence and its sins. While other characters speak of replaced statues, brazen women, and expanding city limits, it is in Farinata that these are all fused into a single characteristic: shortsighted pride. Farinata's epicureanism is merely symptomatic of a greater caustic feature. Florence's pride has blinded it to the destruction and trauma it has wrought and is symptomatic of its myopic view of the world. This myopia is the quintessence of political thought that focuses too much on the city state and local concerns. Farinata's apparent ignorance of his surroundings and his inability to see the present confirm this lack of vision, and as such, prefigure the fate of those who similarly limit their vision.

In his encounter with Farinata, Dante shares this pride to some extent. Dante the pilgrim smugly tells Farinata of the ultimate defeat of the Ghibellines, taking part in the political tit-for-tat that has become the bane of Florence. How do we explain this? The answer lies in remembering that Dante spent much of his time early in his exile trying to regain entry to Florence and continuing to consort with other exiles. Notwithstanding Dante's exile and the bitterness he felt toward Florence

---

of which "[t]ranscendence of space and time is the essence" (171–72).

because of it, he still wished to be there. In the depths of the *Inferno*, Dante, still mired in his Florentinism, has not yet turned his back on Florence in search of a new direction. Dante has, therefore, depicted the pilgrim as the figural representation of his own political behavior. It is for this reason that Dante enters into the debate with Farinata. The issue of who will hold the reins of power in Florence is the essence of the local and timebound character of Dante's early political thought. It reflects Dante's youthful ideas regarding the city state and factionalism. Dante's discussion with Farinata and where it takes place make clear the value Dante now places on such discourse. Additionally, Dante's own political myopia also resituates the *Convivio*, placing its thought alongside those who still concern themselves with what are, essentially, timebound or minor issues in the grand scheme of things. Dante's descent into Hell, therefore, figures not only in his exile but also in the early steps of his own political journey.

While Florence expresses Dante's personal entanglement with local politics, the lesson does not end there. Deep within the dark places of Hell, alongside the "well-ordered" city on the Arno, Dante paints the shadows of another city blinded by pride and concerned with its own self-importance, Babylon.[25] Iannucci has commented substantially on the presence of Babylon in the *Inferno* and in the circle of the lustful (*Inferno* 5), in particular where, he says, the souls have "forged on earth the realm of cupidity" instead of a world of charity and "perpetuated the

[25] Dante's ironic reference in the *Comedy* to Florence as the "well-ordered" city underlines the poet's negative view of such confines. *Purg.* 12:101-102: "where over Rubaconte's bridge there stands / the church that dominates the well-ruled city," [dove siede la chiesa che soggioga / la ben guidata sopra Rubaconte]

chaos of Babylon."[26] Iannucci's study of "forbidden love" considers the presence of Babylon primarily with respect to the connotation it has in terms of Dante's love story, but its significance extends into the political realm as well.[27] The civic hubris of Babylon serves as a universal exemplum of the destructive pride that Dante ascribes to Florence, the particular.[28] The particular, personal nature of Dante's infernal Florence is signaled by the characters he encounters; they refer to Florentine landmarks and speak of families and local struggles.

In contrast, Dante's contact with those sinners most closely associated with Babylon is much more limited. Even so, their presence in Hell suggests an even broader story that shares meaning with Dante's. Belonging to that level of universal significance, Babylon provides a lesson for all, including Florentines. Seen from this perspective, Hell can be both Florence and Babylon because they are types of each other. Although their implications differ somewhat, both stories share and teach the same lesson: man-made cities will not reach heaven, and those who foster a closed, myopic, prideful preoccupation with the

[26] Iannucci, "Forbidden Love," 99.

[27] Iannucci suggests that Babylon, through the figure of Semiramis in this scheme, represents the *civitas mundi*, the corrupt, degenerate society that Augustine says opposes the *civitas Dei*. Semiramis, according to Iannucci, "typifies lawlessness, or better, how passion creates its own laws" (ibid., 100).

[28] Genesis 10:8-10 describes the generations of Noah. At verse 8 we reach Nimrod: "Cush begot Nimrod; he began to be a mighty one on the earth. He was a mighty hunter before the Lord; therefore it is said, 'Like Nimrod the mighty hunter before the Lord.' And the beginning of his kingdom was Babel, Erech, Accad, and Calneh, in the land of Shinar." These "families of the sons of Noah," i.e., the nations "divided on the earth after the flood" (10:32), dwelt on a plain in the land of Shinar and there decided to build a "a city, and a tower whose top is in the heavens" (11:4). The Lord came down to see the "city and the tower, which the children of men built" (v. 5). To stop them doing what "they propose to do" (v. 6), "the Lord scattered them abroad...and they ceased building the city" (v. 8).

city will travel nowhere but down. This pairing also anticipates Dante's sixth epistle, written to the Florentines, in which he calls the Florentines a second race of Babylonians and berates their failure to support the emperor.[29]

We see again how Dante's particular journey is at all times a part of a broader universal lesson. As Dante's story of Florence suggests an even greater story, the literal narrative takes the pilgrim ever closer to the nadir of Hell, where he encounters the assassins of Julius Caesar.

The juxtaposition of this political betrayal with Judas's betrayal of Christ extends Dante's political story into the spiritual realm. Excessive loyalty to the city, he tells us, with its resulting ignorance and ultimate betrayal of the empire, shares meaning with the betrayal of Christ. Betrayal of the empire is, therefore, the earthly equivalent of the betrayal of God and recalls a paradigm introduced by Augustine in *The City of God*.

For Augustine, both realms, the City of God and the Earthly City, exist concomitantly, and man freely chooses his path, deciding his own destination. Dante's earthly cities, Babylon and Florence, correspond loosely to Augustine's *civitas mundi*, just as *Paradiso* does to Augustine's vision of *civitas Dei*. However, while Augustine associates Rome with Babylon,[30] in the *Comedy*, Dante associates Florence with Babylon. Many of

---

[29] Written to the Florentines, March 31, 1311: "Wherefore, then, stirring up so vain a thought as this, do ye, a second race of Babylonians, desert the compassionate empire and seek to establish new kingdoms, making the civic life of Florence one and that of Rome another?"

[30] See also Peter Bruegel the Elder's 1563 *The (Great) Tower of Babel*. The painting shows a tower, which looks remarkably like the architecture of the Roman Colosseum. The parallel of Rome and Babylon had a particular significance for Bruegel's contemporaries: Rome was the Eternal City, intended by the Caesars to last forever, and its decay and ruin were taken to symbolize the vanity and transience of earthly efforts.

the condemned are accused of corrupting Rome, but he still exalts Rome as the New Jerusalem. For Dante, Rome is a continuum where "Christ is a Roman," that is, the City of God.[31] While the characterization of certain cities as infernal and others as paradisaical may find its roots in Augustinian thought, in the *Comedy*, Dante uses only Augustine's method, not Augustine's judgments, to further his own political agenda.

In terms of the cruciform pattern, the pilgrim's first trajectory takes him away from the City of God and toward the *civitas*

---

[31] This revision of Augustine's concept is evident in the closing cantos of *Paradiso* where Dante describes his stupor upon seeing the white rose.

Par. 31:31-40: "If the Barbarians, when they came from / a region that is covered every day / by Helice, who wheels with her loved son, / were, seeing Rome and her vast works, struck dumb / (when, of all mortal things, the Lateran / was the most eminent), then what amazement / must have filled me when I to the divine / came from the human, to eternity / from time, and to a people just and sane / from Florence came!" [Se i barbari, venendo da tal plaga / che ciascun giorno d'Elice si cuopra, / rotante col suo figlio ond'ella è vaga, / veggendo Roma e l'ardua sua opra,/ stupefacíensi, quando Laterano / a le cose mortali andò di sopra; / io, che al divino da l'umano, / a l'etterno dal tempo era venuto, / e di Fiorenza in popol giusto e sano / di che stupor dovea esser compiuto!]

Dante asserts that the city that is "just and sane" is Rome and that its antithesis is Florence. This reiterates his invective against Florence in *Inferno* 26:1-12: "Rejoice, Florence, you are great indeed, / for over sea and land you beat your wings; / through every part of Hell your name extends!" [Godi, Fiorenza, poi che se' sì grande / che per mare e per terra batti l'ali, / e per lo 'nferno tuo nome si spande!]

As Iannucci notes, this "radical revision" of the Augustinian paradigm of the two cities is discernible as early as *Inferno* IV, in Limbo. There, says Iannucci, the castle in which the classical authors are segregated "is a projection of pagan Rome and the *pax romana*, which prepared for the coming of Christ and the establishment of the Church." Here, as in other places noted by Iannucci, Dante "disassociates Rome from Babylon and assimilates it to Jerusalem: 'quella Roma onde Cristo è romano' [that 'Rome in which Christ is / Roman' (*Purg.* 32.102; cf. *Par.* 31.31-40)]" ("Forbidden Love," 99).

mundi. While the pilgrim protests, "For I am not Aeneas, I am not Paul" and would have us believe that his descent is not of his choosing, it becomes clear that he has chosen this route, or at least the descent, through his own sinfulness.[32] The pilgrim, like Adam, has sunk so low that only Christ's descent into Hell can save him, and he must become like Christ if he is to be saved. The journey is, therefore, a necessary part of the redemption process. As he descends into the history of humankind entombed in Hell, he must come to terms with his own sinful past. This reckoning is at the heart of all autobiography, but this emulation of Christ moves the pilgrim's story into realm of hagiography.

Autobiographically, the descent corresponds to Dante's actions in the early days of his exile when he sought yet again to embroil himself in factional strife by allying with the exiled Ghibellines. This correspondence helps Dante to contextualize his actions and to consider them in the context of his ongoing political journey.

To move away from this realm, to progress toward God, the pilgrim literally and figuratively must turn around. If we visualize his trajectory in terms of the cruciform, the pilgrim can go no further. If the pilgrim is to progress, he must change direction and embark on a long upward journey from the pit of Hell to the shores of Mount Purgatory. The similarities in the imagery at the beginning of *Purgatorio* and the beginning of *Inferno* emphasize the futility of his earlier conduct that led only to the earthly city.[33] In this moment, it appears that the pilgrim

---

[32] *Inf.* 2:32-33: "For I am not Aeneas, am not Paul; / nor I nor others think myself so worthy." [Io non Enea, io non Paulo sono: / me degno a ciò né io né altri 'l crede.]

[33] Compare *Inf.* 1:22-27: "And just as he who, with exhausted breath,/ having escaped from sea to shore, turns back / to watch the dangerous waters he has quit, / so did my spirit, still a fugitive, / turn back to look intently at

is no further ahead spatially. He has barely escaped death and stands again on a deserted shore looking up to a seemingly insurmountable peak. There are, however, indications that the next foray, this next attempt to scale the mountain, will have a different focus and orientation—and a different outcome.[34] Although Dante's expedition will still take place below the horizontal line and, therefore, still in the realm of the temporal, there will be a different destination. Dante will still be situated in the temporal, but this time he faces in a different direction and travels on a different trajectory, one that will ultimately take him to the City of God. There he will find that, just as love in and of itself was not wrong—it was merely misdirected—neither is Florence, per se, evil. However, Florence's myopic inability to look beyond itself and correct its sins dooms it to damnation. Dante's own turning—or conversion—demonstrates that the choice between damnation or salvation depends upon perspective, direction, and scope.[35] When, for example, Dante encounters his ancestor Cacciaguida in the heaven of Mars, we

---

the pass / that never has let any man survive" [E come quei che con lena affannata / uscito fuor del pelago a la riva / si volge a l'acqua perigliosa e guata, / così l'animo mio, ch'ancor fuggiva, / si volse a retro a rimirar lo passo / che non lasciò già mai persona viva" and *Purg.* 1:4: "leaving behind herself a sea so cruel" [che lascia dietro a sé mar sì crudele]. Compare *Inf.* 1:5: "savage forest" [la selva *selvaggia*] and *Purg.* 2:52-53: "bewildered by the place" [*selvaggia* / parea del loco] (emphasis mine).

[34] *Purg.* 1:4-6: "and what I sing will be that second kingdom, in which the human soul is cleansed of sin, becoming worthy of ascent to Heaven" [e canterò di quel secondo regno / dove l'umano spirito si purga / e di salire al ciel diventa degno] and *Purg.* 1:118-20: "We made our way across the lonely plain, / like one returning to a lost pathway, / who, till he finds it, seems to move in vain." [Noi andavam per lo solingo piano / com' om che torna a la perduta strada, / che 'nfino ad essa li pare ire invano.]

[35] The importance of looking in the right direction is omnipresent in the *Comedy*. Bolzoni notes the multitude of examples in which the "guardare fisso" figures in *Purgatorio* and *Paradiso* ("Costruire immagini," 64–65).

see a different kind of Florentine, one distinguishable from Farinata degli Uberti. Cacciaguida looks beyond Florence and its confines, toward God, and has, therefore, found a place in Paradise. On the other hand, the unrepentant city of Florence cannot become a City of God. We will return to Cacciaguida below.

This different focus corresponds to and "prefigures" not only Dante's journey but also his evolving political focus. While it may be tempting to equate this shift in Dante's political thought with what D'Entrèves terms *Imperium*, it important to bear in mind where Dante locates such thoughts. In the opening scenes of *Purgatorio*, Dante is once again located outside Hell and now outside the gate that leads to the mountain. He is also well outside *Paradiso*. He is, therefore, in neither the *civitas dei* or the *civitas mundi*. Consequently, the journey back will still be concerned with and informed by his perspective of exile. However, now he also will be concerned with issues of restoration and regaining lost ground. In *Purgatorio* the issue is no longer confined to Dante's desire to return home but includes returning to a home made better than it was before.

The theme of paradise lost was introduced early in the *Inferno* with the inclusion of the old man of Crete (*Inf.* 14:94). Giuseppe Mazzotta links Virgil's explanation that the "rivers of Hell have their origin in the cracks in the weeping statue of the Old Man of Crete" to Dante's vision of salvation. Suggesting that the "renewed" man is not Christ but an old man drawn from the secular order, says Mazzotta, accords with Dante's notion of man's *restauratio* referred to in the *Convivio*.[36] When the old man of Crete weeps for the corruption of society, we are reminded not only of Adam and paradise lost but also of Fran-

[36] Mazzotta, *Dante*, 14–18.

cesca's lament that there is nothing sadder than in times of unhappiness to remember happiness[37]—a reminder once again of how Dante intertwines multiple narrative threads. By locating Florence in Hell where the sinners bemoan the loss of a Golden Age and yearn for past happiness, Dante deftly associates Florence with the infernal theme of paradise lost. The infernal voyage away from God looks back rather than forward and, therefore, is similarly associated with being turned around and looking the wrong way. This imagery recalls the tragic fate of Lot's wife, or equally, the pagan Orpheus, and is rooted in the sin-filled atmosphere of *Inferno* where there exists no hope of redemption.[38] The tone changes considerably from a preoccupation with the past to anticipation of the future when Dante starts the arduous journey up through *Purgatorio*. Dante's own preoccupation with the past is corrected at the mountain's peak when Beatrice's voice finally turns Dante around to look at her instead of back to see where Virgil has gone.[39]

Logically, this moment also coincides with Dante's arrival in a paradise regained. It is important to note, however, that paradise has also been renewed and transformed. As Theodolinda Barolini observes, "In the *Comedy*, too, God makes things new: by causing the Apocalyptic end of the purgatorial journey to coincide with Eden, the place of our beginnings, Dante

---

[37] *Inf.* 5:121-23: "Nessun maggior dolore / che ricordarsi del tempo felice / ne la miseria.

[38] "But [Lot's] wife looked back behind him [toward Sodom and Gomorrah], and she became a pillar of salt" (Gen 19:26). Orpheus disobeyed Hades and turned to look back at Eurydice, only to see her dissolving.

[39] *Purg.* 30:61-66: "(I'd turned around when I had heard my name— / which, of necessity, I transcribe here), / I saw the lady who had first appeared / to me beneath the veils of the angelic / flowers look at me across the stream." [quando mi volsi al suon del nome mio, / che di necessità qui si registra, / vidi la donna che pria m'apparïò / velata sotto l'angelica festa, / drizzar li occhi ver me di qua dal rio.]

causes mankind's first place to transform from the oldest place ('primus') to the newest of places—'novissimus' (not coincidentally does the poem's only use of 'novissimo' belong to these cantos)."[40] It quickly becomes evident as well that Earthly Paradise is not the Florence for which Dante once yearned.

In terms of the political story, regaining paradise also coincides with Dante's new political vision. In this new trajectory, Florence with its local, earthbound focus has been left behind. Dante has moved away from the nadir of locality and climbed back up to the point on the horizontal line where the particular and universal coincide. He is back at the point on the line from which he started his descent and can this time choose God's city or man's city. But this is a second beginning, occasioned by his descent, which Charity calls a "fore-having" of death."[41] That this terminus is marked by the garden motif is not coincidental; it serves as a sign that the pilgrim has moved from one state to another. Iannucci notes the structural importance of the garden motif: "The major way stations on the pilgrim's journey through the afterlife are set in garden-like places, and usually bring into focus a structurally defining spiritual condition: paradise lost and regained, or about to be recovered."[42] Dante's reference to Rome as the "Garden of the Empire"[43] discloses the nature of this new Paradise: if Rome is a garden and Paradise is a garden, then Rome is Paradise. Thus we move from a city that tries to stand alone (Florence) to a city that provides the cornerstone of a greater structure. Both Rome and Florence are cities, but

[40] Barolini, *Undivine Comedy*, 159.

[41] Charity, *Events and Their Afterlife*, 246.

[42] Iannucci, "*Paradiso* XXXI," 474.

[43] *Purg*. 6:103-105: "For both you and your father, in your greed / for lands that lay more close at hand, allowed / the garden of the Empire to be gutted." [Ch'avete tu e 'l tuo padre sofferto, / per cupidigia di costà distretti, / che 'l giardin de lo 'mperio sia diserto.]

where Rome's focus is outward, Florence's is inward and ultimately sterile. A message emerges: a narrow political focus can lead to Hell, but a broader, more expansive view can reverse that trajectory. If the city provides the road to Hell, then the empire provides the road to Heaven.

It is important to note, however, that Rome is not located at the top of Mount Purgatory—neither is Earthly Paradise, Rome, or the empire. What is restored in Earthly Paradise is a new locus from which the voyage to Rome can start. Purgatory, if anything, is an anti-*Inferno* representing the journey back to the place where we can begin again. It represents transition in thought and is the literal manifestation of Dante's long journey back from his concern for city politics and his growing engagement with the issues of empire. Just as the culmination of *Inferno* reveals a spiritual aspect to the political lesson, so too does the culmination of *Purgatorio* reveal a broader connotation. As Giuseppe Mazzotta suggests, the Earthly Paradise is the "point of convergence between nature and grace; here, memory of the Fall and quest for redemption mingle."[44] It is the new starting point, the clean slate.

If we focus for a moment on the pilgrim's movement in terms of the cruciform pattern, we see more clearly why the journey to his ultimate destination, the pinnacle of *Paradiso*, is twice as long as the journey to the center of *Inferno*. Having descended to the lowest point below the horizontal line, the pilgrim must first make his way back up to the point from which he started before he can embark upon the final ascent to heaven. In terms of the intersecting journeys of the individual and the universal, this means that Dante's initial descent must be reversed by a corresponding ascent before his particular journey

[44] Mazzotta, *Dante*, 115.

can again intersect with the universal. Accordingly, Dante's descent into Hell takes up only a third of the narrative of the *Comedy*. His ascent through *Purgatorio* constitutes the next third. From Earthly Paradise, departing from the regained ground, Dante can start the voyage away from the realm of the temporal and the earthly, and travel vertically above the line and onto the true way toward God.

By keeping the empire at a prospective distance rather than materializing it within the context of the *Purgatorio*, Dante is able to suggest that the quest for empire is not earthly; instead it is a necessary step on the road to Heaven, to a heavenly kingdom. Moreover, he distinguishes it from the earthbound local politics of Florence and suggests that his theory of empire belongs in the timeless and endless space of Paradise. Finally, by placing the issue of empire here, Dante is able to connect the earthly (but not earthbound) particular empire, Rome, and the heavenly universal empire, Jerusalem.[45] Joan Ferrante notes the interplay between the two kingdoms stating, "The rose is the heavenly city (30.130), the joyful kingdom (31.25), the just and pious empire (32.117) whose emperor is God; it is the model for the political and moral life on earth."[46] Perhaps more to the point, Ferrante recognizes the dependence of one model on the other: "On earth, the model of the ideal society can be realized within the secular sphere only in the empire."[47] By situating the empire beyond the earthly realms, Dante is able to situate the earthly empire alongside Augustine's heavenly city, thus radically redefining Augustine, who had identified pagan Rome with the *civitas mundi*. It is important to reiterate that for Dante, Rome, although earthly, is not earthbound. For him, the

---

[45] Iannucci suggests that *Paradiso* is the typological fulfillment of Jerusalem ("*Paradiso* XXXI," 475).

[46] Ferrante, *Political Vision of the Divine Comedy*, 253.

[47] Ibid., 255.

fact of being earthly is not inherently bad; of more concern is the direction of one's focus. Therefore, while the Roman Empire[48] has existence in time and space as much as Florence does, it exists on a different trajectory and on a different path. In the *Comedy* Dante expresses this distinction by associating Rome with the realm of the timeless and locating it on the road to God. This association also provides a basis for Dante's political position that the empire is not subordinate to the Roman Church but instead divides jurisdiction with it. This association also glosses *Monarchia* III, xv, and suggests that directing temporal power to God is as essential to peace as limiting the power of the church to spiritual matters. More importantly, this peaceful division of power justifies the rapt tone taken in his fifth epistle where he attributes a divine authority to Henry VII.[49] At the same time this division of power dismisses the possible reading of the same letter that might suggest Henry's rule depended upon the permission of the papacy and concentrates more on the division of power treated at the end of the letter.[50] For Dante, the journey to Rome and the journey to Jerusalem take place along one road. To travel to one is to travel to the other, hence the constant mingling of the language used to in-

[48] In *De Monarchia* (trans. Shaw), Dante defines his "empire" (I, ii, 2) as a temporal monarchy, "a single sovereign authority set over all others in time, that is to say over all authorities which operate in those things which are measured by time" (9).

[49] The letter was written October 1310 whereas the *Monarchia* was probably written at very earliest in 1314. In the letter, Dante likens Henry to the "bridegroom," a term used frequently in Scripture to describe Christ.

[50] "He it is whom Peter, the vicar of God, extorteth us to honor, whom Clement, the present successor of Peter, doth illuminate with the light of the apostolic benediction; that where the spiritual ray sufficeth not there the splendor of the lesser luminary may give light" (Epistle V, 30, written to the princes of Italy).

dicate the journey of the pilgrims. This confluence is first introduced in *Purgatorio* in the song of the new arrivals "*In exitu Isräel de Aegypto*," which recalls the journey of the Hebrews from the slavery of Egypt to the Promised Land.[51] In the *Convivio* and in his letter to Can grande,[52] Dante argues that the Exodus event signifies anagogically the exodus of the soul from sin.[53] At the same time, Dante links this journey to Rome, when he notes that "Tiber's water" marks the start of the sea journey to

---

[51] *Purg.* 2:46-48: "*In exitu Israel de Aegypto*," / with what is written after of that psalm, / all of those spirits sang as with one voice." ['*In exitu Isräel de Aegypto*' / cantavan tutti insieme ad una voce / con quanto di quel salmo è poscia scripto.] These are the first words of Psalm 113 and refer to the liberation of the people of Israel from the slavery of Egypt.

[52] I do not intend to enter into the debate about whether the epistle was Dante's; there has been little evidence that would compel me to discount his authorship.

[53] *Convivio* II, i, 6-7:

> The fourth sense is called anagogical, that is to say, beyond the senses; and this occurs when a scripture is expounded in a spiritual sense which, although it is true also in the literal sense, signifies by means of the things signified a part of the supernal things of eternal glory, as may be seen in the song of the Prophet which says that when the people of Israel went out of Egypt, Judea was made whole and free. For although it is manifestly true according to the letter, that which is spiritually intended is no less true, namely, that when the soul departs from sin it is made whole and free in its power.
>
> [Lo quarto senso si chiama anagogico, cioè sovrasenso; e questo è quando spiritualmente si spone una scrittura, la quale ancora [sia vera] eziandio nel senso litterale, per le cose significate significa de le superne cose de l'etternal gloria: sì come vedere si può in quello canto del Profeta che dice che, ne l'uscita del popolo d'Israel d'Egitto, Giudea è fatta santa e libera. Che avvegna essere vera secondo la lettera sia manifesto, non meno è vero quello che spiritualmente s'intende, cioè che ne l'uscita de l'anima dal peccato, essa sia fatta santa e libera in sua potestate.]

See also *Epist.* XIII, 21.

Purgatory's shores.[54] Mazzotta equally observes that "in *Purgatorio* the language of secular history ('qui sarai tu poco tempo silvano / e sarai meco sanza fine cive/ di quella Roma onde Cristo è Romano.' *Purgatorio* XXXII, 100–102) is used to prefigure the City of God at the end of time."[55]

The connection that Dante introduced in the *Vita nuova* between the journey to Rome and the journey to God is now made explicit.[56] As Dante compares his stupor upon seeing the celestial city to that of a pilgrim seeing Rome, he connects the pilgrim's destination and this celestial vision. He also recalls the Veronica, the famous relic that the pilgrims at the end of the *Vita nuova* were traveling to see. Although the pilgrim will reach Rome in heaven, it must be remembered that, just as the Earthly Paradise at the top of Mount Purgatory was different from the Earthly Paradise from which man had been expelled so many years before, neither is this empire the same as that which was the glory of ancient Rome. Yes, it is still Rome, but

---

[54] *Purg*. 2:101: "at which the Tiber's waters mix with salt," [dove l'acqua del Tevero s'insala.]

[55] Mazzotta, *Dante*, 115. *Purg*. 32:100-103: "Here you shall be—awhile—a visitor; / but you shall be with me—and without end— / Rome's citizen, the Rome in which Christ is / Roman;" [Qui sarai tu poco tempo silvano; / e sarai meco sanza fine cive / di quella Roma onde Cristo è romano.]

[56] In the *Vita nuova*, for example, Dante includes the image of pilgrims on their way to Rome to see the relic known as the "Veronica."

Vita nuova, Chap. 29: "After this tribulation, at that time when many people go to see the blessed image that Jesus Christ left us as an imprint of his beautiful visage, which my lady sees in glory, it happened that certain pilgrims were passing along a street that runs virtually straight through the middle of the city where that most gracious of women was born, lived, and died." [Dopo questa tribulazione avvenne, in quello tempo che molta gente va per vedere quella imagine benedetta la quale Iesu Cristo lasciò a noi per essemplo de la sua bellissima figura, la quale vede la mia donna gloriosamente…]

a Roman Empire that has been transformed and Christianized. The old Rome was a *figura* of this Rome. Nowhere is this made more clear than in Dante's use of the Virgilian model on which Dante relies to reinforce the providential nature of Rome's imperial power. The journey of Aeneas is, for Dante, the epic model of exile that ends in the founding of a divinely predestined civilization, the Roman Empire. Aeneas's journey, therefore, suggests typologically Dante's own voyage to this new Rome. The connection in *Inferno* 2 between the two journeys is unambiguous, and Dante reminds the reader of this connection through the inclusion of intertextual references to Virgil's hero.[57] Aeneas's exile and journey, like Dante's, was necessary to bring about the founding of an empire. We must always remember that Aeneas was a pagan, as was the Rome he founded. This crucial fact is the feature that anchors the Virgilian model to the temporal and earthly. The Virgilian voyage cannot infiltrate the secondary level; it cannot move above the line that separates the earthly from the transcendent and the temporal from the eternal. Virgil's voyage cannot reach the City of God; at most it can prefigure that voyage. The confines of this voyage are found at the Earthly Paradise where everything is made new, including Rome, and it is here where Virgil slips out of sight.

The voyage that, on the other hand, will culminate in a new empire will be more akin to that of Paul, for Paul reached Rome and, in his attempts to Christianize it, he ultimately made the heavenly kingdom possible. If, as Charity explains, the purpose of typology as used by Dante is "not to replace Dante's personal

[57] *Inf.* 2:32-33: "For I am not Aeneas, I am not Paul; / nor I nor others think myself so worthy." [Io non Enea, io non Paulo sono: / me degno a ciò né io né altri 'l crede.]

history, but to interpret it," then we can see here what interpretation Dante is urging upon the reader.[58] Specifically, he presents himself as a new Paul, Christianizer of an empire, one who can bring about the kingdom of God and implicitly be the redeemer he sought to be in the *Convivio*. Here then do we see the purpose of Dante's hagiographical project. The purpose of the journey is not just to convert Dante the sinner but also to reveal Dante's ultimate mission—savior of the Christian empire.

D'Entrèves observed that, in his later years, Dante turned his sights more toward the issue of the church, and D'Entrèves distinguished between Dante's theory of empire and his theory of church, but I would argue that the *Comedy* demonstrates that Dante saw the issues as two sides of the same coin. Dante imagines that within a corrected Roman Empire, the City of God can be realized and peace can reign in this world as it does in the next. In this vision Dante describes the City of God not so much in accordance with Augustine's but in accordance with his own political vision, transforming his views into *figurae* of their own fulfillment. While in *Monarchia* Dante relied on Aristotle, albeit through Christian eyes, to justify his theory of empire, in the *Comedy*, the vision of the *Monarchia* is fulfilled.[59] As Ferrante suggests, Dante's *Paradiso* conforms to his vision of the empire and to his vision of the ideal society. Narratively, he expresses this through the "gran mar de l'essere" which, Barolini

[58] Charity, *Events and Their Afterlife*, 254.

[59] *De monarchia*, I, v. "So the first question is this: is temporal monarchy necessary for the well-being of the world? That it *is* necessary can be shown with powerful and persuasive arguments, and neither reason nor authority provides any strong counter-argument. The first of these arguments may be taken from the authority of Aristotle in his *Politics*" (*De Monarchia*, trans. Shaw, 9).

suggests, "effectively absorbs the many into the oceanic one."[60] There can be no mistake then; Dante believes that peace is only possible through the absorption of the many into the one. As Barolini suggests, "This theme is carried forward in the *Monarchia*, where the need to justify a single ruler leads to the explanation that what can be done by one—'per unum'—is better done by one than by many—'per plura.' Dante goes on to align oneness—'unum'—with goodness and multiplicity—'multa'—with evil." At the same time, *Paradiso* represents an attempt on Dante's part to provide a solution as to how "oneness" can coexist with multiplicity. Or as Barolini sees the issue, "The posture of the *Paradiso*...reflects a willingness to accommodate difference as an essential aspect of the created universe."[61] In this sense, Dante's Jerusalem stands in direct contrast to Babylon, which was emblematic of linguistic chaos and the concomitant loss of societal cohesion. In *Paradiso*, through a series of discourses, Dante illustrates the kind of peace that is ultimately attainable among those of difference, illustrating that there can be peace in diversity. The theme was introduced as early as the *Purgatorio* 6 where Sordello represents political unity.[62] The idea is affirmed in *Paradiso*, where earthly law is transformed into a divinely ordained rule. Here Dante takes his political vision out of the realm of the particular and beatifies it, giving it the divine seal of approval, rewriting his *Monarchia* with the divine hand of God, and echoing the ultimate significance of the narrative cruciform. The merger of the particular with the uni-

[60] Barolini, *Undivine Comedy*, 176.
[61] Ibid., 181.
[62] Barolini, *Dante's Poets*, 161.

versal effects reconciliation and, through reconciliation, redemption. Like St. Matthew,[63] Dante the sinner has been chosen for this task, and Beatrice's mandate that he write what he has seen is fulfilled.[64]

In *Paradiso* Dante expresses this reconciliation through the pilgrim's interaction and relationship with the characters and the destination itself. In contrast to the reception the pilgrim encountered in the *Inferno*, in *Paradiso* he is welcomed. His presence in *Paradiso* is of no surprise to its denizens. Dante takes part in discussions, with not only particular or local characters but also with those of more universal renown. The pilgrim here is part of both paradigms. In *Paradiso* Dante's particular story merges with the universal story. Dante's story, therefore, is not simply another type of a lesson with universal application, Dante's story, here in the realm above the Earthly Paradise, *is* the universal. The temporal has found its fulfillment in the timeless and the particular in the universal. The pilgrim is home.

Thus in *Paradiso*, as in the *Inferno*, Dante will continue to meet Florentines, but now they have a different focus and broader significance. In the case of Cacciaguida, in contrast to

---

[63] Among the early followers and apostles of Jesus, Matthew is mentioned in Matthew 10:3 as a publican (KJV) or tax collector (NIV), who, while sitting at the "receipt of custom" (9:9 KJV) in Capernaum, was called to follow Jesus. He is also listed among the Twelve but without identification of his background in Mark 3:18, Luke 6:15, and Acts 1:13. In passages parallel to Matthew 9:9, both Mark 2:14 and Luke 5:27 describe Jesus' calling of the tax collector Levi, the son of Alphaeus, but Mark and Luke never explicitly equate this Levi with the Matthew named as one of the Twelve.

[64] *Purg.* 33:52-55: "Take note; and even as I speak these words, / do you transmit them in your turn to those / who live the life that is a race to death. / And when you write..." [Tu nota; e sì come da me son porte, / così queste parole segna a' vivi / del viver ch'è un correre a la morte quando tu le scrivi,]

Farinata, this Florentine warrior is not linked merely to the Florence that Dante associates with Hell. Instead, he recalls Florence's glorious past and, like Dante, laments the city's descent into licentiousness. Rather than continue stubbornly to engage in petty local turf wars, Cacciaguida enlisted in a bigger struggle, the Crusades. Cacciaguida gave his life not for the Guelph or Ghibelline cause but for the cause of Christendom. In this way Dante uses Cacciaguida as an exemplum of Christians united against a common enemy and underlines Dante's condemnation of papal aggression in Rome.[65] Boniface VIII's local war against the Colonna family is thus revealed as an infernal perversion of a truer, universal war: the crusade to recover Jerusalem. Thus in *Paradiso*, Dante demonstrates how the local or particular can, if properly directed, be integrated into the universal, as Cacciaguida transcends the *campanilismo* of Florence and finds his place in heaven.

Cacciaguida's episode does more than illustrate Dante's political evolution. Structurally, the episode creates an immediate backward glance to the other Florentine who predicted Dante's exile, Farinata. That both conversations discuss family fates only reinforces the parallel. The two episodes help interpret each other in that similarities in the episodes highlight the contrasts. We see then that Florentines are not inevitably damned, but rather that perspective of focus and direction of energies determine their fates. Florentines, and presumably Florence, can be saved if they look beyond themselves, just as

[65] *Inferno* 27:85-90: "The prince of the new Pharisees, who then / was waging war so near the Lateran— / and not against the Jews or Saracens, / for every enemy of his was Christian, / and none of them had gone to conquer Acre / or been a trader in the Sultan's lands—" [Lo principe di novi Farisei, / avendo guerra presso a Laterano, / e non con Saracin né con Giudei, / ché ciascun suo nimico era Cristiano, / e nessun era stato a vincer Acri / né mercatante in terra di Soldano.]

lovers can be saved if they look beyond the object of their love. The episodes, therefore, also reinforce the narrative structure of the *Comedy* in their conformity to the parallel, or perhaps more accurately, opposing trajectories of the cruciform narrative in which the temporal journey is the antithesis of the journey through *Paradiso*. Moreover, the episodes are also structurally determining, as the term is used by Iannucci, inasmuch as they represent the focus of Dante's particular political story. Farinata is the embodiment of all that Dante sees wrong with Florence, yet, as the episode makes clear, Dante's own life is inextricably bound up in its people and its intrigues. Farinata is also the touchstone of the despair and the seemingly inescapable downward spiral of Hell and the city state. Cacciaguida, on the other hand, is at once the paradise that was lost and paradise regained. He represents the hope of redemption both personal and civic, and together with Farinata he presents a microcosm of the structure of Dante's political story.

These parallel episodes, moreover, serve a structural and exegetical function beyond Dante's particular narrative thread. The two parallel characters who represent the two faces of Florence, one turned to face the wrong way (inward and downward) and one turned to face the right way (outward and upward), mirror the presence of the two kinds of love presented in the love story, figured by the *donna gentile* and by Beatrice. Dante's love was not wrong; it was simply directed at the wrong object. The affinity between the two stories is forged through the revelation of similar significance to both the Farinata / Cacciaguida relationship and the *donna gentile* / Beatrice parallel. Though these relationships exist within different contexts, both reveal that salvation is a matter of direction. It is not the action so much as the object to which the action is directed that counts. The revelation of the shared meaning aligns the political story with the love story. Indeed, they almost can be substituted for one another. More importantly, this shared meaning reinforces Dante's use of his stories as exempla of the way to spiritual salvation. In Charity's terms, both narrative threads, the love story and the political story, function as types of each other.

Moreover, Dante's narrative representation of his political vision urges a retrospective reading of his political works in which his theory of the empire is not exclusively secular. Rather, by reconciling the apparently divergent interests of the kingdom of God and the earthly empire, Dante's vision is linked to spiritual salvation. At the same time, the *Comedy* situates Dante's political writing and theories vis-à-vis the empire within the allegorical level and ascribes to them a truth akin to that ascribed to Scripture. Dante as the bearer of that truth is equally resituated as *theologus-poeta*.

Dante, of course, was not the first to use the journey metaphor to represent spiritual progression, nor was he the first to use a celestial city to represent the ultimate destination of the soul or to use exile to depict the state of the soul before it reaches heaven.[66] What Dante does is relate these familiar motifs, in particular, the voyage of the soul, to his own political voyage. By creating a narrative that echoes the voyages of Aeneas, Paul, and Christ, Dante presents his own actuality as a new testament, one whose meaning is revealed by those earlier journeys and is the fulfillment of those other stories. Charity explains the purpose of the inclusion of the other stories: "Without the historical basis, the myth would be meaningless, with it Dante's

---

[66] "Behind the image of Paradise as a city lies the medieval *topos* of the Christian as an exile, which we find, for example, at the beginning of St. Augustine's *De civitate Dei*" (Iannucci, "*Paradiso* XXXI," 474). As John Freccero suggests, Dante the pilgrim may be seen as the symbol in Platonic thought for "the return of the soul to its heavenly *patria* by the exercise of philosophical wisdom" (*Dante*, 137).

claim can be made: this Dante may say, is my own self-conforming with Christ, Christ's truth has become mine, and I believe that my truth points to his."[67] Dante has put two of his own stories, the love story and the political story, into the same vessel, a vessel that by itself signifies redemption. In this way he achieves a synthesis of his various stories and illuminates the connection between their meanings, showing that the narrative threads interact as "types." When Iannucci notes that only with the help of Beatrice can Dante reacquire his true *patria*, not the city of Florence but the city of God in the Empyrean,[68] he is recognizing the typological connection between the love story and the political story.

Ultimately, it becomes clear that although the sins and virtues of the souls of the *Comedy* may fall into different categories, they share common characteristics. Those condemned to Hell, or who require purging in *Purgatorio*, typically loved the wrong things or loved the wrong way. As opposed to loving God the creator, they were loving his creations (in the case of the love story) or the things of the Earthly City (in the case of the political story). The love story, for example, speaks of lust, which is in stark contrast to the charity described in Augustine's *De doctrina christiana*.

Politically, this misdirected focus translates into loyalty to the wrong causes. The souls in Hell and Purgatory served the Earthly City or rendered misguided service to the City of God, seeking for such service a reward they should not desire.[69] Both

---

[67] Charity, *Events and Their Afterlife*, 254.

[68] Iannucci, *Forma ed evento nella Divina Commedia*, 138.

[69] As Gilson observes, "This distinction has its genesis in Augustine, who refers to the ensemble of men that lead the existence of the 'homo vetus', of the terrestrial man and those who find themselves united by their common love of the temporal things from the earthly city as distinguished from that ensemble of men who are united by the chain of divine love and

types of misdirected energies are synthesized on the fourth and fifth terraces of Purgatory, first with the discussion on the nature of love and then with Hadrian V's description of his own avarice for which he is now punished.[70]

As the pilgrim approaches the summit of Mount Purgatory, Dante signals the fusion of these multiple threads. When Virgil miters and crowns the pilgrim,[71] he not only bestows upon him the outward signs of imperial and ecclesiastical authority but also responds to the pilgrim's earlier concerns that he is neither Paul nor Aeneas. Dante's mission—soon to be revealed to him by Beatrice—will continue both Aeneas's and Paul's providential missions. Sanctioned now to save those who have gone astray both politically and spiritually, Dante the writer, through Dante the pilgrim, will show them the right way, turn them in the right direction, and, once they are converted, take them all to that Rome where Christ is a Roman.

---

thereby forming a second city the City of God" (Gilson, *Introduzione allo studio di Sant'Agostino*, 200).

[70] *Purg.* 18; *Purg.* 19:112: "Until that point I was a squalid soul, / from God divided, wholly avaricious; / now, as you see, I'm punished here for that." [Fino a quel punto misera e partita / da Dio anima fui, del tutto avara: / or, come vedi, qui ne son punita.]

[71] *Purg.* 27:139-42: "Await no further word or sign from me: / your will is free, erect, and whole—to act / against that will would be to err: therefore / I crown and miter you over yourself." [Non aspettar mio dir più né mio cenno; / libero, dritto e sano è tuo arbitrio,/ e fallo fora non fare a suo senno: / per ch'io te sovra te corono e mitrio.]

Epilogue

Dante Legend

DANTE'S SKILLFUL FUSION of his multiple stories serves two of the clearly personal goals of the *Comedy*: to rehabilitate himself in the eyes of the Florentines and to fulfill his own dreams of becoming a famous *auctor*. While Dante has chosen himself for this experience, the broader purpose of the journey and the meaning of this vision are not as immediately evident. The culminating vision, however, reveals the reason he has been brought to this point, and the series of prophecies and dreams throughout the *Comedy* now make perfect sense: Dante, by recording what he has seen, will right the wrongs occasioned by the well-intentioned but ultimately disastrous Donation of Constantine.

In particular, the prophecies and guidance of those characters most personal to the poet, Virgil and Beatrice, that spur Dante along on this quest, give shape to the mandate that has been assigned to him. Beatrice's prophecy of the "DXV,"[1] her

---

[1] *Purg*. 33:40-45: "for I can plainly see, / and thus I tell it: stars already close / at hand, which can't be blocked or checked, will bring / a time in which, dispatched by God, a Five / Hundred and Ten and Five will slay the whore / together with that giant who sins with her." [ch'io veggio certamente, e pero' il narro, / adarne tempo già stelle propinque, / secure d'ogn'intoppo e d'ogni sbarro, / nel quale un cinquecento diece e cinque, /

announcement that someone is coming who will avenge the great error of the Donation, must surely then be read as part of a gradual revelation to Dante of the true purpose of his journey through this "other world." In contrast to the many interpretations proposed over the centuries, perhaps the simplest and most logical solution to the enigma is to recognize that Beatrice's prophecy, like most of the prophecies in the *Comedy*, speaks to Dante's personal future.[2] If we accept this proposition, then it follows that Dante himself is the DXV. His descent into Hell and purification in Purgatory, we learn, are to prepare him for the final examination of faith in Paradise that will determine whether Dante is fit for the challenge that awaits him after the final vision of *Paradiso*. His journey through the three realms is thus a *figura* that will be fulfilled when Dante returns to the living and completes his mission—to reconcile the two great lights, restore the New Jerusalem, and turn the backward Eagle[3] the right way around, to

---

messo di Dio, anciderà la fuia / con quel gigante che con lei delinque.]

[2] It is not my intention to enumerate all the prophecies found throughout the *Comedy*. It is, however, worth noting that the other seemingly unsolvable enigmatic prophecy, that of the *veltro* in *Inferno* 1:100-14, might equally be interpreted as identifying Dante himself or at least his poetic output as salvific. Claudia Rattazzi Papka has argued that "Virgil's prophecy of the *veltro* is fulfilled in the composition of the *Commedia* itself, not yet born in the first canto of *Inferno*, but still seeking to restore health to a morally ravaged Italy" ("'Tra Feltro E Feltro,'" 42).

[3] Dante refers to Constantine as he "who made himself Greek."

Par. 20:55-60: "The next who follows—one whose good intention / bore evil fruit—to give place to the Shepherd, / with both the laws and me, made himself Greek;" [L'altro che segue, con le leggi e meco, / sotto buona intenzion che fé mal frutto, / per cedere al pastor si fece greco: / ora conosce come il mal dedutto / dal suo bene operar non li è nocivo, / avvegna che sia 'l mondo indi distrutto.]

I am greatly indebted to Alessandro Vettori, Zygmunt Baranski, Giuseppe Mazzotta, and Walter Stephens, all of whom provided invaluable input and helped me see the flaws in and strengths in this argument, which

once again follow the sun.

In support of this interpretation, we may look at the way in which Beatrice's history lesson in Earthly Paradise interacts with a similar canto in *Paradiso*, where Justinian recounts the history of the Roman Empire.[4] The canto is naturally linked to Constantine by virtue of its content, but it may also be linked to Dante's role vis-à-vis Constantine, through the pervasive use of deictic references. In same sense that the entirety of *Paradiso* may be considered the fulfillment of the rectification prefigured throughout the *Inferno* and the *Purgatorio*, the Justinian canto may be considered an exemplum of the same process in the context of imperial history. Justinian's conversion, moreover, from a heretical to an orthodox view of Christianity makes Justinian an apt figure of correction.[5]

There is also a role Justinian plays that links him even more specifically to Constantine, who turned the empire from its natural course. It is Justinian who, after the fall of the western empire, one might say, embarks on a wholesale mission to recover the west. Justinian's actions then, in trying to retake the lost Western Roman Empire, are recuperative acts making him the emperor who sought to turn the backward Eagle around.

---

is explored in further depth in my article "Dante and Constantine: A Backwards Eagle and the DXV."

[4] Zygmunt Baranski notes that his colleague pointed out that Beatrice's lessons in the closing cantos of *Purgatorio* anticipate the way Justinian recounts the story of the Eagle in Paradise. Because Baranski's work focused on a different aspect of the canto, he does address the issue of Constantine, and, although Baranski's remarks are tangential, they are sufficiently tantalizing to merit mention (*Dante e i Segni*, 148n3).

[5] Reynolds provides the following description of Justinian's conversion: "Having previously held the heretical view that only the divine nature, not also the human, existed in Christ, Justinian was converted to the truth that he now sees as clearly as it can be seen that of two contrary positions one must be true, one false" (*Dante*, 350).

Justinian's project and Dante's have a shared goal and by aligning his views with those of an emperor, one that is in heaven, no less, Dante is able, as Barbara Reynolds notes, to secure assent to his political convictions by setting them within the framework of the universe.[6] Justinian is, therefore, an exemplum of personal conversion; he also prefigures the rectification, the turning the right way around of the empire, that Dante aspires to effect with his cruciform narrative. Dante's hope to correct the empire urges the reader to speculate that the messianic DXV (i.e., five hundred, ten, and five, transliterated into Roman numerals) is none other than Dante himself.

To propose that DXV refers to Dante is, like so many other interpretations, speculative at best, but it is certainly consistent with his view or projection of himself as divinely elected. Again, while speculative, it bears noting that DXV forms an appropriate acronym easily attributable to Dante: "Dante Xristo Vincet" ("Dante through Christ shall triumph," or equally "Dante with the cross[7]—symbolized by X—will triumph.") In this case, the cross is his *Comedy*. It also links Dante's mission to the figure of Constantine and his legendary vision of a cross in the sky with the message "In hoc signo vinces." It has also been anticipated by the moment in Dante's arrival in *Purgatorio* when the pilgrim turns to the right to see the four stars in the sky.[8] Similarly speculative, but consistent with this interpretation, is Claudia Rattazzi Papka's position that Virgil's

---

[6] Reynolds, *Dante*, 349.

[7] For a deeper exploration of the imagery of the cross as it relates to the construction of the *Comedy*, see Watt, *The Cross that Dante Bears*.

[8] *Purg*. 1:22-23: "Then I turned to the right, setting my mind / upon the other pole, and saw four stars / not seen before except by the first people." [I' mi volsi a man destra, e puosi mente / a l'altro polo, e vidi quattro stelle]

prophecy of the *veltro* is fulfilled in the composition of the *Comedy* itself, not yet born in the first canto of *Inferno*, but still seeking to restore health to a morally ravaged Italy.

Such theorizing aside, Dante has provided the reader with the essential elements of the hagiographical tradition. By writing the *Comedy*, his canticle of *caritas*, Dante becomes the savior saint of a country as dilapidated as the church in a similar vision experienced by St. Francis.[9] In addition to the crown and miter, with the continual references to his writing project, Dante adds another attribute to his hagiographical self-portrait: the sacred book to which "heaven and earth have set hand."[10] Not insignificantly, many early illustrations of the *Comedy* show Dante in the act of writing. Probably the best known of these is Domenico di Michelino's fifteenth-century painting *La commedia illumina Firenze* in the Florentine duomo.[11] Similarly, given Dante's belief that the saint's name often coincides with his meaning, the inclusion of his own name, an abbreviation of "lasting" ("*durante*"), atop Mount Purgatory was no doubt helpful to fulfilling his auto-hagiographical aspirations.[12]

[9] For a thorough study of Franciscan imagery and traditions in the *Comedy*, see Herzman, "'Io Non Enëa, Io Non Paolo Sono,'" 23–69.

[10] *Par.* 15:1-3: "this sacred poem— / this work so shared by heaven and by earth / that it has made me lean through these long years" ['l poema sacro / al quale ha posto mano e cielo e terra, / sì che m'ha fatto per molti anni macro]

[11] See Giovanni di Paolo's miniature illuminated manuscript of Dante being expelled from Florence and of Dante composing his poem in exile (Catalogue of Illuminated Manuscripts, British Library, http://www.bl.uk/catalogues/illuminatedmanuscripts/ILLUMIN.ASP?Size=mid&IllID=56-966). For more on Domenico Michelino's fifteenth-century painting, see di Fonzo, "Dante e l'interpretazione iconografica di domenico di Michelino," 107–14.

[12] *Purg.* 30:55-57: "Dante, though Virgil's leaving you, do not / yet weep, do not weep yet; you'll need your tears / for what another sword must yet inflict." [Dante, perché Virgilio se ne vada, / non pianger anco, non

Given the depth and complexity of the *Comedy*, the enormity and longevity of Dante studies are not surprising. It would seem that almost any episode, canto or indeed individual line of the great poem, could easily engender an entire study. Perhaps it is this richness, combined with the inevitable urge to understand each small thing that Dante says, that has produced the meticulous and microscopic examination of the most minute details that characterize the classic and enduring *Lectura Dantis*. Such an approach, however, runs the risk of missing the forest for the trees. Even the broader approaches, which look at particular aspects from a global perspective, such as Barolini's work on the poetic influences in the *Comedy*, *Dante's Poets: Textuality and Truth in the "Comedy,"* Freccero's *Dante: The Poetics of Conversion*, and Iannucci's *Forma ed evento nella Divina Commedia*, do not directly confront the broad question of the autobiographical or auto-hagiographical intent of the *Comedy*. This is not to say these works are lacking, for they more than adequately respond to the questions they pose; it is just that, to my knowledge, no one thus far has considered that Dante's primary purpose in writing the *Comedy* was to create a comprehensive and lasting record of his own life.

As I have suggested, the reluctance to consider the *Comedy* as substantially autobiographical is likely because it bears little resemblance to modern autobiography. However, as I have shown, the *Comedy* follows many of the conventions belonging to an earlier life-writing tradition, and to a variety of medieval models, and ought not to be excluded from the genre of autobiography on the basis of narrative style or structure. In any event, the *Comedy*, like the medieval model to which it adheres, does exhibit features integral to "modern" autobiography—

---

piangere ancora; / ché pianger ti conven per altra spada.]

most importantly, the need to reconcile the meaning of apparently arbitrary and unrelated events within the context of a greater significance. It is this feature that underlies the entire narrative structure of the *Comedy* and that most characterizes the work as autobiographical. This attempt to contextualize and interpret the events of a single life within a greater context is initially highlighted by the intersection of Dante's own journey, "I found myself," with the journey of "our life," but it is also present in the structure of the *Comedy* through Dante's use of what Iannucci termed "parallel episodes."[13] Such episodes extend the meaning of events beyond their particular settings and across the broader spectrum of the entire *Comedy*. But the quest to contextualize and interpret events is perhaps most evident in the *Comedy*'s persistent adoption of literary models, its absorption of other literary works, and its revision of Dante's earlier attempts at chronicling his life.

Thus we see that in each of the *Vita nuova*, the *Convivio*, and the *Comedy*, Dante looks to classical and biblical sources as well as religious writing in order to interpret and contextualize the events he narrates. In the *Vita nuova*, the presence of techniques and stylistic elements borrowed from the secular lyric (most noticeably, the prosimetric form, which recalls the inclusion of *razos* and *vidas*) situates the work in terms of genre. However, Dante's use of the Augustinian model takes the *Vita nuova* beyond the lyric tradition and expresses a conversion aspect to the story that unfolds within its pages. Further, biblical allusions hint at a redemptive role of the love, which the *libello* chronicles, a spiritual and mystical redemption not contemplated in the *dolce stil nuovo*. This first "Life of Dante," therefore, not only marks a young writer's debut on the literary scene but also represents an attempt to make sense of the devastating

[13] Iannucci, "*Paradiso* XXXI," 471.

passion of love and to find in it a greater meaning.

The absorption of the *Vita nuova* into the post-exile *Convivio* continued Dante's quest for meaning in love but infused that quest with a new dimension. In the *Convivio*, Dante's use of biblical allusion broadens the scope of the *libello* and looks to find meaning in the political events of Dante's life. The image of Dante, hosting a banquet and meting out knowledge, allows him to forge a new identity as a redeemer. At the same time, Dante struggles to reconcile this role and the events that precipitated it with the role he carved out for himself in the *Vita nuova*, where he was the redeemed and where redemption came from the mystical love experience and the rejection of the *donna gentile*. Dante attempts to solve this apparent contradiction in roles through the fusion of love and knowledge. By introducing philosophy as the object of his love, Dante proposes that he can be both redeemed and redeemer. This redemption has a decidedly secular tone notwithstanding its biblical imagery, and its palinodic approach to the *donna gentile* of the *Vita nuova* fails to neatly resolve the apparently different treatment of love in the two works.

It is only in the *Comedy* that Dante satisfactorily reconciles the personal issue of love, the political aspects of his life, and his earlier attempts at life-writing. The framing metaphor allows Dante the breadth of scope he needs to adequately address any inconsistencies he may have created between the *Vita nuova* and the *Convivio*, between his role as redeemer and redeemed, and between the secular and spiritual meaning of the events that comprise both his love story and his political story. Dante's struggle to present an orderly integration of the dominant concerns of his life, his love story, and his political story is also facilitated by the journey metaphor, which provides a unifying force through which Dante interprets these stories.

Within the journey metaphor, the intersection of Dante's

journey with the journey of Everyman is essential to this reconciliation, but it is the pattern of descent and ascent that Dante superimposes on this juncture that is the key to understanding it. Dante's descent into Hell and ascent through Purgatory and Paradise create a narrative grid upon which Dante is able to locate the events of his life, including his previous literary efforts. At the same time, the strong presence and import of this vertical movement within the *Comedy* reflects, narratively, a conventional medieval mode of self-expression. As we have seen, in medieval life-writing the trend was to define oneself in comparative terms, a type of comparison William Spengemann and Evelyn Birge Vitz referred to as "vertical."[14] That is, the medieval autobiographer sought only to distinguish himself comparatively; in relation to any given attribute, the distinction is expressed in terms of more or less, greater or smaller, but not in terms of uniqueness. Dante of the *Comedy*, in his downward and upward journey, typifies this convention and at the same time illustrates how much he is like Everyman even while surpassing him. While Dante's encounters along this journey contain a multitude of messages and reflect a variety of agendas, each of which deserves critical attention, they are all, to a certain extent, subordinate to the greater narrative structure of the *Comedy*, which is essentially autobiographical. Accordingly, the frequently noted exemplum aspect of the *Comedy* ought not to overshadow that the story used as an exemplum, the journey toward the divine community, is nonetheless Dante's own. While Dante's intention is that we read the story as representative of Everyman, it is Dante's individual presence that provides the source of his narrative and is the bedrock upon which the entire *Comedy* is based.

[14] Spengemann, *Forms of Autobiography*, 36–37; Vitz, *Medieval Narrative*, 19.

Finally, Dante's adoption of the vertical scale of comparison demonstrates clearly that he has found a way to include himself in the cosmos and to end the estrangement he encountered in his love life and in his political life. The exercise in personal reconciliation is, therefore, a microcosm of a broader quest, the reconciliation of one's life with the cosmic community of all souls, a quest that is expressed through the intersection of the universal with the particular. The final vision of the *Comedy* is the most telling in terms of the ultimate purpose of the work. In the *Paradiso*, all of Dante's stories meld into one. The vision of God completes the fusion and provides closure to Dante's life. It affirms his decisions, forgives his trespasses, and prophesies his afterlife. He may never return to earthly Florence and may never be united with the corporeal Beatrice, but he will reach the City of God, and he will know love.

As the *Comedy* picks up where the *Vita nuova* and the *Convivio* left off, it represents the culmination of Dante's lifelong project of self-examination. The *Comedy* presents Dante's encyclopedic vision of both world history and his own history. In the *Comedy* Dante catalogues, critiques, and predicts the outcome of not only the lives of others but also his own life. His exploration of the purpose for which he was created and the reason for the suffering he has endured represents the essence of autobiography, medieval or otherwise. Moreover, this self-portrait, fashioned in the style of the hagiographies included in the popular compendia of his time, presents this exploration as a "Life of Dante." As a kind of personal myth,[15] Dante's own "golden" *legenda* presents its author, perhaps not so much as he was, but as he would have us read him: *theologus* and *poeta* of divine love, patron saint and savior of Rome.

---

[15] Charles Mauron has called this kind of autobiography "personal myth" (*Des Métaphores obsédantes au Mythe Personnel*, 9).

Bibliography

Abailard, Pierre. *The Story of Abelard's Adversities. A Translation with Notes of the* Historia Calamitatum. Translated by J. T. Muckle. Toronto: The Pontifical Institute of Medieval Studies, 1954.

Aquinas, Thomas. *Summa Theologiae.* Accessed April 1, 2021, https://aquinas101.thomisticinstitute.org/st-index.

Ascoli, Albert Russell. "Palinode and History in the Oeuvre of Dante." In *Dante: Contemporary Perspectives*, edited by Amilcare A. Iannucci, 23–50. Toronto: University of Toronto Press, 1997.

———. "Performing Salvation in Dante's *Commedia*." *Dante Studies* 135 (2017): 74–106.

Auerbach, Erich. *Studi su Dante.* Milan: Feltrinelli, 1966.

———. *Mimesis.* Princeton: Princeton University Press, 1968.

Augustine. *The City of God.* Translated by Marcus Dods. New York: Random House, 1950.

———. *The Works of Aurelius Augustine, Bishop of Hippo. A new translation.* Vol. 1 of *The City of God*, edited by Marcus Dods. Edinburgh: T. & T. Clark, 1871. Project Gutenberg. Released April 8, 2014. https://www.gutenberg.org/files/45304/45304-h/45304-h.htm.

———. *Confessions.* Translated by Vernon J. Bourke. New York: Fathers of the Church, 1953.

———. *Confessions.* Translated by Henry Chadwick. Oxford: Oxford University Press, 1991.

———. *Contra academicos de beata vita necnon de ordine libri.* Edited by William M. Green. Antwerp: Spectrum, 1961.

———. *De doctrina Christiana.* Edited and translated by R. P. H. Green. Oxford: Clarendon Press, 1995.

———. *De ordine.* Vol. 4 of *Bibliothèque augustinienne*, edited by R. Jolivet. Bruges: Brepols, 1939.

———. *La Trinité (livres VIII–XV).* Vol. 16 of Bibliothèque Augustinienne, edited and translated by P. Agaesse. Ouevres de Saint Augustin 2me série: Dieu et son oeuvre. 2. Les Images. Paris: Desclée de Brouwer, 1955.

———. *King Alfred's Old English Version of St. Augustine's Soliloquies, Turned into Modern English* by Alfred, King of England, 849–99. Translated by Henry Lee Hargrove. New York, H. Holt and Company, 1904. Accessed January 5, 2021. http://www.gutenberg.org/files/40341/40341-h/40341-h.htm.

Avalle, D'Arco Silvio. *Modelli semiologici nella "Comedy" di Dante.* Milan: Bompiani, 1975.

———, ed. *Poeti del Duecento, La Letteratura Italiana.* Vol. 2. Verona: Valdonega, 1960.

Baranski, Zygmunt G. *Dante e i segni. Saggi per una storia intellettuale di Dante Alighieri.* Naples: Liguori, 2000.

Barbi, Michele. *Vita di Dante.* Florence: Sansoni, 1963.

———. *Problemi di critica dantesca. Prima Serie. (1893–1918).* Florence: Sansoni, 1985.

Barolini, Teodolinda. "Dante and Cavalcanti (On Making Distinctions in Matters of Love): *Inferno* v in Its Lyric Context." *Dante Studies, with the Annual Report of the Dante Society* 116 (1998): 31–63. Accessed January 5, 2021. https://www.jstor.org/stable/40166521.

———. *Dante's Poets: Textuality and Truth in the* "Comedy." Princeton: Princeton University Press, 1984.

———. *The Undivine Comedy: Detheologizing Dante.* Princeton: Princeton University Press, 1992.

Barthes, Roland. "An Introduction to the Structural Analysis of Narrative." *New Literary History* 6/2 (Winter 1975): 237–72. Accessed January 5, 2021. https://www.jstor.org/stable/468419.

Basile, Maria Adelaide. "Al mattin del ver si sogna: i sogni di Dante nelle albe del *Purgatorio.*" *Dante: Rivista Internazionale Di Studi Su Dante Alighieri* 3 (2006): 41–68. Accessed January 5, 2021. https://www.jstor.org/stable/26480903.

Black, Max. *Models and Metaphors.* Ithaca: Cornell University Press, 1962.

Bodei, Remo. "Riflessioni sul tempo e gli intrecci temporali nella narrazione storica." In *Scienza, narrazione e tempo. Indagine sociale e correnti storiografiche a cavallo del secolo*, edited by Mariuccia Salvati, 339–56. Milan: Angeli, 1985.

Boitani, Piero. "Dream and Vision." In *English Medieval Narrative in the Thirteenth and Fourteenth Centuries*, translated by Joan Krakover Hall, 71–113. Cambridge: Cambridge University Press, 1982.

Bolzoni, Lina. "Costruire immagini. L'arte della memoria tra letteratura e arti figurative." In *La cultura della memoria*, edited by Lina Bolzoni and Pietro Corsi, 57–97. Bologna: Mulino, 1992.

———, and Pietro Corsi, eds. *La cultura della memoria.* Bologna: Mulino, 1992.

Bonaventure, St. *Itinerarium mentis in Deum.* Vol. 2 of *Works of St. Bonaventure*, edited by Philotheus Boehner and Zachary Hayes. New York: Franciscan Institute, 2002.

Brooke, Christopher. *From Alfred to Henry III: 871–1272.* New York: Norton, 1961.

Browning, Oscar. *Dante: His Life and Writings.* 1891. Reprint, New York: Haskell Books, 1972.

Carrasco, Magdalena. "Sanctity and Experience in Pictorial Hagiography: Two Illustrated Lives of Saints from Romanesque France." In *Images of Sainthood in Medieval Europe*, edited by Renate Blumenfeld-Kosinski and Andrea Szell, 33–66. Ithaca: Cornell University Press, 1991.

Carruthers, Mary J. *The Book of Memory: A Study of Memory in Medieval Culture.* Cambridge: Cambridge University Press, 1990.

Casadei, Alberto. "Incipit Vita Nova." *Dante Studies, with the Annual Report of the Dante Society* 129 (2011): 179–86. Accessed January 5, 2021. https://www.jstor.org/stable/23390452.

Cassell, Anthony K. "Santa Lucia as Patroness of Sight: Hagiography, Iconography, and Dante." *Dante Studies, with the Annual Report of the Dante Society* 109 (1991): 71–88. Accessed January 5, 2021. https://www.jstor.org/stable/40166438.

Charity, Alan C. *Events and Their Afterlife.* Cambridge: Cambridge University Press, 1966.

Clark, Arthur Melville. *Autobiography: Its Genesis and Phases.* Edinburgh: Oliver & Boyd, 1935.

Comparetti, Domenico. *Vergil in the Middle Ages.* Translated by E. F.

M. Benecke. London: Allen & Unwin, 1895.

Contini, Gianfranco. *Un'idea di Dante.* Turin: Einaudi, 1976.

Corbett, George, and Heather Webb, eds. *Vertical Reading in Dante's Comedy: Volume 1.* Cambridge: Open Book Publishers, 2015.

Corti, Maria. "Dante e la Torre di Babele: una nuova «allegoria in factis»." In *Il viaggio testuale*, edited by Maria Corti, 243–56. Turin: Einaudi, 1978.

———. "Il modello analogico nel pensiero medievale e dantesco." In *Dante e le forme dell'allegoresi*, edited by M. Picone, 11–20. Ravenna: Longo, 1987.

———, ed. *Il viaggio testuale.* Turin: Einaudi, 1978.

D'Andrea, Antonio. "L' 'Allegoria dei poeti': Nota a *Convivio* II.1." In *Dante e le forme dell'allegoresi*, edited by M. Picone, 71–78. Ravenna: Longo, 1987.

Dante Alighieri. *Il Convivio (The Banquet).* Translated by Richard H. Lansing. Garland Library of Medieval Literature, 1990.

———. *Convivio.* Translated by William Walrond Jackson. Oxford: Clarendon Press, 1909.

———. *Convivio.* Edited by Piero Cudini. Milan: Garzanti, 1980.

———. *Convivio.* Edited by Cesare Vasoli and Domenico de Robertis. Vol. 1, part 2, of *Opere minori.* Milan: Ricciardi, 1988.

———. *Epistole.* Testo critic della Società Dantesca Italiana. Edited by Ermengildo Distelli. Florence: Società Dantesca Italiana, 1960. Accessed April 1, 2021, https://dante.princeton.edu/pdp/epistolae.html.

———. *La Divina Commedia.* Edited by Charles Hall Grandgent and Charles S. Singleton. Cambridge: Harvard University Press, 1972.

———. *La Divina Commedia.* Edited by Natalino Sapegno. Milan: Ricciardi, 1955.

———. *La Divina Commedia.* Edited by Natalino Sapegno. 3 vols. Florence: La Nuova Italia Editrice, 1985.

———. *La Commedia secondo l'antico vulgata.* Edited by Giorgio Petrocchi. 4 vols. Milan: Mondadori, 1966–1967.

———. *Monarchia.* Edited by Bruno Nardi. Milan: Ricciardi, 1979.

———. *De monarchia.* Translated by Prue Shaw. Cambridge: Cambridge University Press, 1996.

———. *Rime.* Edited by Gianfranco Contini. Turin: Einaudi, 1946.

———. *Tutte le opere.* Edited by Fredi Chiappelli. Milan: Mursia,

1965.
———. *La Vita nuova*. Edited by Domenico De Robertis. Milan: Ricciardi, 1984.
———. *De vulgari eloquentia*. Edited by Pier Vincenzo Mengaldo. Vol. 2 of *Opere minori*. Milan: Ricciardi, 1979.
———. *Vita Nova*. Translated by Andrew Frisardi. Evanston: Northwestern University Press, 2012.
———. *La Vita Nuova: Di Dante Alighieri*. Edited by Kenneth McKenzie. Boston: Heath, 1922.
Davis, Robert Glenn. "Hierarchy and Excess in Bonaventure's *Itinerarium Mentis in Deum*." *Journal of Religion* 95/4 (October 2015): 433–53. Accessed January 5, 2021. https://www.jstor.org/stable/10.1086/682321.
D'Entrèves, Alessandro Passerin. *Dante as a Political Thinker*. Oxford: Clarendon Press, 1952.
De Robertis, Domenico. *Il libro della "Vita Nuova."* Florence: Sansoni, 1970.
De Voragine, Jacobus. *Medieval Sourcebook: The Golden Legend (Aurea Legenda). Compiled by Jacobus de Voragine, 1275, Englished by William Caxton, 1483*. Fordham University Center for Medieval Studies. Accessed January 5, 2021. https://sourcebooks.web.fordham.edu/basis/goldenlegend/.
Di Fonzo, Claudia. "Dante e l'interpretazione iconografica di Domenico di Michelino." *Dante: Rivista Internazionale Di Studi Su Dante Alighieri* 3 (2006): 107–14. Accessed January 5, 2021. https://www.jstor.org/stable/26480906.
Doreski, William. "Dante and the Roman Poets in Robert Lowell's "History." *Modern Language Studies* 18/2 (Spring 1988): 47–59. Accessed January 5, 2021. https://www.jstor.org/stable/3194765
Farnell, Stewart. *The Political Ideas of the Divine Comedy: An Introduction*. Lanham: University Press of America, 1985.
Fergusson, Francis. *Dante*. New York: Collier Books, 1966.
Ferrante, Joan M. *The Political Vision of the Divine Comedy*. Princeton: Princeton University Press, 1984.
Franke, William. "Reader's Application and the Moment of Truth in Dante's *Divine Comedy*." In *Dante: Contemporary Perspectives*, edited by Amilcare A. Iannucci, 259–80. Toronto: University of Toronto Press, 1997.

Fraser, James E. "Hagiography." In *Edinburgh History of Scottish Literature: From Columba to the Union (until 1707)*, edited by Clancy Thomas Owen, Pittock Murray, et al., 103–109. Edinburgh: Edinburgh University Press, 2007. Accessed January 5, 2021. https://www.jstor.org/stable/10.3366/j.ctt1g09vfd.

Freccero, John. *Dante: The Poetics of Conversion.* Cambridge: Harvard University Press, 1986.

———. "Introduction to *Inferno*." In *Cambridge Companion to Dante*, edited by Rachel Jacoff, 172–91. Cambridge: Harvard University Press, 1993.

Gilson, Etienne. *Introduzione allo studio di Sant'Agostino.* Translated by Vincenzo Venanzi Ventisette. Casale Monferrato: Marietti, 1983.

Gross, Karen Elizabeth. "Scholar Saints and Boccaccio's *Trattatello in laude di Dante*." *MLN* 124/1 (January 2009): 66–85. Accessed January 5, 2021. https://www.jstor.org/stable/29734481.

Guglielminetti, Marziano. *Memoria e scrittura: l'autobiografia da Dante a Cellini.* Turin: Einaudi, 1977.

Guillaume de Lorris et Jean de Meun. *Le Roman de la Rose.* Edited by Félix Lecoy. Classiques du Moyen Age. 3 vols. Paris: Champion, 1965–1970.

Gusdorf, Georges. "Conditions and Limits of Autobiography." Translated by James Olney. In *Autobiography: Essays Theoretical and Cultural*, edited by James Olney, 28–48. Princeton: Princeton University Press, 1980.

Harrison, Robert P. *The Body of Beatrice.* Baltimore: Johns Hopkins University Press, 1988.

Hawkins, Peter S. *Dante's Testaments: Essays in Scriptural Imagination.* Stanford: Stanford University Press, 2000.

———. "Dido, Beatrice, and the Signs of Ancient Love." In *The Poetry of Allusion: Virgil and Ovid in Dante's Comedy*, edited by Rachel R. Jacoff and and Jeffrey T. Schnapp, 113–30. Stanford: Stanford University Press, 1991.

Herzman, Ronald. "'Io Non Enëa, Io Non Paolo Sono': Ulysses, Guido Da Montefeltro, and Franciscan Traditions in the Commedia." *Dante Studies, with the Annual Report of the Dante Society* 123 (2005): 23–69. Accessed January 5, 2021. http://www.jstor.org/stable/40166582.

Hollander, Robert. *Allegory in Dante's Comedy.* Princeton: Princeton

University Press, 1969.

———. "Dante's Poetics." *Sewanee Review* 85/3 (Summer 1977): 392–410. Accessed January 5, 2021. https://www.jstor.org/stable/27543260.

———. "Dante 'Theologus-Poeta.'" *Dante Studies, with the Annual Report of the Dante Society*, 94 (1976): 91–136. Accessed January 5, 2021. http://www.jstor.org/stable/40166210.

———. "Le opere di Virgilio nella *Commedia* di Dante." In *Dante e la "bella scola" della poesia: autorità e sfida poetica*, edited by Amilcare A. Iannucci, 247–343. Ravenna: Longo, 1993.

———. *Studies in Dante.* Ravenna: Longo, 1980.

———. *Il Virgilio dantesco: tragedia nella "Commedia."* Florence: Olschski, 1983.

Iannucci, Amilcare A. "Beatrice in Limbo: A Metaphoric Harrowing of Hell." *Dante Studies, with the Annual Report of the Dante Society* 97 (1979): 23–45. Accessed January 6, 2021. http://www.jstor.org/stable/40166271.

———. "Forbidden Love: Metaphor and History (*Inferno* 5)." In *Dante: Contemporary Perspectives*, edited by Amilcare A. Iannucci, 94–112. Toronto: University of Toronto Press, 1997.

———. *Forma ed evento nella Divina Commedia.* Rome: Bulzoni, 1984.

———. "*Paradiso* XXXI." *Lectura Dantis* 16/17 (Spring–Fall 1995): 470–85. Accessed January 6, 2021. http://www.jstor.org/stable/44806619.

———, ed. *Dante e la "bella scola" della poesia: autorità e sfida poetica.* Ravenna: Longo, 1993.

———, ed. *Dante: Contemporary Perspectives.* Toronto: University of Toronto Press, 1997.

Jacoff, Rachel, ed. *The Cambridge Companion to Dante.* Cambridge: Cambridge University Press, 1993.

———, and Jeffrey T. Schnapp, eds. *The Poetry of Allusion: Virgil and Ovid in Dante's Comedy.* Stanford: Stanford University Press, 1991.

Ledda, Giuseppe. "Truth, Autobiography and the Poetry of Salvation." In vol. 2 of *Vertical Readings in Dante's* Comedy, edited by George Corbett and Heather Webb, 237–58. Cambridge, England: Open Book Publishers, 2016. Accessed January 6, 2021. https://www.jstor.org/stable/j.ctt1sq5vb5.17.

Leo, Ulrich. "The Unfinished *Convivio* and Dante's Rereading of the *Aeneid*." *Mediaeval Studies* 13 (1951): 41–64.

Looney, Dennis. "Negro Dante." In *Freedom Readers: The African American Reception of Dante Alighieri and the* Divine Comedy, 65–104. Notre Dame: University of Notre Dame Press, 2011.

Lynch, Kathryn L. *The High Medieval Dream Vision: Poetry, Philosophy, and Literary Form*. Stanford: Stanford University Press, 1988.

———. "Robert Henryson's 'Doolie Dreame' and the Late Medieval Dream Vision Tradition." *The Journal of English and Germanic Philology* 109/2 (April 2010): 177–97. Accessed January 6, 2021. https://www.jstor.org/stable/10.5406/jenglgermphil.109.2.0177

Marchesi, Simone. "Epic Ironies: Poetics, Metapoetics, Self-translation ('Inferno' 18.1, 'Purgatorio' 24.52, 'Paradiso' 1.13)." *Dante Studies, with the Annual Report of the Dante Society* 131 (2013): 99–117. Accessed January 6, 2021. http://www.jstor.org/stable/43490492.

Marie de France. *L'espurgatoire Seint Patriz*. Edited by Thomas Atkinson Jenkins. Philadelphia: Ferris, 1894.

Mastrobuono, Antonio C. *Dante's Journey of Sanctification*. Washington: Regnery Gateway, 1990.

Mauron, Charles. *Des Métaphores obsédantes au Mythe Personnel: Introduction à la Psychocritique*. Paris: Carti, 1962.

Mazzotta, Giuseppe. *Dante, Poet of the Desert. History and Allegory in the "Divine Comedy."* Princeton: Princeton University Press, 1993.

———. "Life of Dante." In *Cambridge Companion to Dante*, edited by Rachel Jacoff, 1–13. Cambridge: Harvard University Press.

Namier, Lewis B. "History: Its Subject Matter and Tasks." *History Today* 2/3 (March 1952): 160–62.

Nardi, Bruno. *Dal "Convivio" alla "Commedia" (Sei saggi danteschi)*. Rome: Istituto Borromini, 1960. Reprint, Rome: Istituto Storico Italiano per il Medio Evo, 1992.

———. *Dante e la cultura medievale: Nuovi saggi di filosofia dantesca*. Bari: Laterza, 1949.

Natoli, Gioacchino. *Dante rivelato nel Convivio*. Rome: Società Editrice Dante Alighieri, 1954.

Olney, James. "Some Versions of Memory/Some Versions of *Bios*: The Ontology of Autobiography." In *Autobiography: Essays Theoretical and Cultural*, edited by James Olney, 236–67. Princeton: Princeton University Press, 1980.

———, ed. *Autobiography: Essays Theoretical and Cultural.* Princeton: Princeton University Press, 1980.

Padoan, Giorgio. "La 'mirabile visione' di Dante e l'Epistola a Cangrande." In *Il pio Enea, l'empio Ulisse*, 30–63. Ravenna: Longo, 1977.

Papka, Claudia Rattazzi. "'Tra feltro e feltro': Dante's Cartaceous Apocalypse." *Dante Studies, with the Annual Report of the Dante Society* 117 (1999): 35–44. Accessed January 6, 2021. http://www.jstor.org/stable/40166536.

Pascal, Roy. *Design and Truth in Autobiography.* London: Routlege & Kegan Paul, 1960.

Peck, George Terhune. *The Fool of God, Iacopone da Todi.* Alabama: University of Alabama Press, 1980.

Pepin, Jean. *Dante et la tradition de l'allégorie.* Montreal: Inst. d'Etudes Médiévales, 1970.

Petrocchi, Giorgio. *Biografia. Attività politica e letterarie.* In vol. 6 of *Enciclopedia Dantesca*, 1–53. Rome: stituto dell'Enciclopedia Italiana, 1978.

———. *Vita di Dante.* Bari: Laterza, 1976.

Piattoli, Renato. *Codice diplomatico dantesco.* Florence: Società Dantesca Italiana, 1950.

Picone, Michelangelo. "Dante and the Classics." Translated by Susan Iannucci. In *Dante: Contemporary Perspectives*, edited by Amilcare A. Iannucci, 51–73. Toronto: University of Toronto Press, 1997.

———. "L'Ovidio di Dante." In *Dante e la "bella scola" della poesia: autorità e sfida poetica*, edited by Amilcare A. Iannucci, 107–44. Ravenna: Longo, 1993.

———. *'Vita Nuova' e tradizione romanza.* Padua: Liviana, 1979.

———. "La *Vita Nuova* fra autobiografia e tipologia." In *Dante e le forme dell'allegoresi*, edited by Michelangelo Picone, 59–69. Ravenna: Longo, 1987.

Pietrobono, Luigi. *Saggi danteschi.* Turin: Società Editrice Internazionale, 1954.

Prince, Gerald. *Narratology. The Form and Function of Narrative.* Berlin: Mouton, 1982.

Radice, Betty, trans. *The Letters of Abelard and Heloise.* Harmondsworth: Penguin Books, 1974.

Raffa, Guy P. "Saint Dante." In *Dante's Bones: How a Poet Invented Italy*, 106–34. Cambridge: Belknap Press of Harvard University Press, 2020.

Raimon de Miraval. *Les poésies du troubadour Raimon de Miraval.* Edited by L. T. Topsfield. Paris: Nizet, 1971.

Reynolds, Barbara. *Dante: The Poet, the Political Thinker, the Man.* London: I. B. Tauris, 2006.

Robert of Flamborough. *Liber poenitentialis.* Edited by J. J. Francis Firth. Toronto: Pontifical Institute for Medieval Studies, 1976.

Ruiz, Juan. *Libro de buen amor.* Toulouse: Privat, 1901.

Sales, Marco M., ed. *La Sacra Bibbia.* Vol. 1. Turin: Lega Italiana Cattolica Editrice, 1949.

Salimbene de Adam. *The Chronicle of Salimbene de Adam.* Edited by Joseph L. Baird, Giuseppe Baglivi, and John Robert Kane. Binghamton, NY: *Medieval Renaissance Texts and Studies*, 1986.

Salimbene da Parma. *Cronica.* Edited by Ferdinando Bernini. Bari: Laterza, 1942.

Salvati, Mariuccia, ed. *Scienza, narrazione e tempo. Indagine sociale e correnti storiografiche a cavallo del secolo.* Milan: Angeli, 1985.

Sapegno, Natalino. *Frate Iacopone.* Naples: Libreria Scientifica Editrice, 1969.

Segre, Cesare. *Le strutture e il tempo. Narrazione, poesia, modelli.* Turin: Einaudi, 1974.

Shaw, James Eustace. *Essays on the* Vita Nuova. Princeton: Princeton University Press, 1929.

Singleton, Charles S. *An Essay on the* Vita Nuova. Cambridge: Harvard University Press, 1949.

———. "Dante's Allegory." *Speculum* 25/1 (1950): 78–86.

———. *Dante Studies 1: Elements of Structure.* Cambridge: Harvard University Press, 1965.

———. *Dante Studies 2: The Journey to Beatrice.* Cambridge: Harvard University Press, 1967.

Solerti, A. *Le vite di Dante, Petrarca e Boccaccio scritte fino al secolo XVI.* Milan: Vallardi, 1904.

Spengemann, William C. *The Forms of Autobiography.* New Haven: Yale University Press, 1980.

Speroni, Charles. "Dante's Prophetic Morning-Dreams." *Studies in Philology* 45/1 (January 1948): 50–59. Accessed January 7, 2021.

http://www.jstor.org/stable/4172830.

Spitzer, Leo. "Note on the Poetic and Empirical 'I' in Medieval Authors." *Traditio* 4 (1946): 414–22.

Suso, Henry. *Das Buch von dem Diener (The Life of the Servant).* Edited by K. Bihlmeyer, *Heinrich Seuse. Deutsche Schriften*, 1907. In Frank Tobin, trans., *The Exemplar, with Two German Sermons.* New York: Paulist Press, 1989.

———. *The Life of Blessed Henry Suso by Himself.* Translated by Thomas Francis Knox. London: Burns, Lambert and Oates, 1865.

Thomas Aquinas, Summa Theologiae. https://aquinas101.thomisticinstitute.org/.

Took, John F. *Dante: Lyric Poet and Philosopher. An Introduction to the Minor Works.* Oxford: Clarendon Press, 1990.

Toynbee, Paget Jackson. *Concise Dictionary of Proper Names and Notable Matters in the Works of Dante.* Oxford: Clarendon Press, 1914.

———. *Dante Alighieri: His Life and Works.* New York: Harper Torchbooks, 1965.

Uc de Saint Circ. *Poésies de Uc de Saint Circ.* Toulouse: Privat, 1913.

Vallone, Aldo. *La Prosa del Convivio.* Florence: Felice le Monnier, 1967.

Vance, Eugene. "Augustine's *Confessions* and the Grammar of Selfhood." *Genre* 6/1 (1973): 1–28.

Vettori, Alessandro. "Veronica: Dante's Pilgrimage from Image to Vision." *Dante Studies, with the Annual Report of the Dante Society* 121 (2003): 43–65. Accessed January 7, 2021. https://www.jstor.org/stable/40166627.

Virgil. *The Aeneid.* Translated by W. F. Jackson Knight. London: Penguin, 1958.

———. *Eclogues.* In vol. 1 of *Virgil with an English Translation by H. Rushton Fairclough in Two Volumes.* Cambridge: Harvard University Press, 1938.

———. *Georgics.* In vol. 1 of *Virgil with an English Translation by H. Rushton Fairclough in Two Volumes.* Cambridge: Harvard University Press, 1938.

Vitz, Evelyn Birge. *Medieval Narrative and Modern Narratology.* New York: New York University Press, 1989.

Vossler, Karl. *Medieval Culture, An Introduction to Dante and his Times.* Translated by William Cranston Lawton. New York: Frederick

Ungar, 1929.
Watt, Mary. *The Cross that Dante Bears. Pilgrimage, Crusade, and the Cruciform Church in the* Divine Comedy. Gainesville: University Press of Florida, 2005.
———. "Dante and Constantine: A Backwards Eagle and the DXV." *Quaderni danteschi ungheresi* 12 (2016): 51–81.
West, Francis James. *Biography as History*. Sydney: Sydney University Press, 1973.
Winslow, Donald J. Life-Writing: A Glossary of Terms in Biography, Autobiography and Related Forms. 2nd. ed. Honolulu: University of Hawaii Press, 1995.
Yates, Frances A. *The Art of Memory*. London: Routledge and Kegan Paul, 1966.
Zingarelli, Nicola. *La vita, i tempi e le opere di Dante*. Milan: Vallardi, 1931.
Zumthor, Paul. "Autobiography in the Middle Ages?" *Genre* 6/1 (1973): 29–48.

Acknowledgments

This book is the result of conversations and collaborations over many years with many wonderful colleagues, far too numerous to mention. I am grateful to all of them. I have learned from their scholarship and been inspired by them to explore my own theories with respect to Dante's literary projects. I am grateful also to Marc Jolley, my kind and enthusiastic editor, for his patience and his faith in this project.

Finally, I could not be where I am, nor who I am, without my beloved husband, Joe. His unfailing belief in me, in my dreams and aspirations, has given me the courage to start over many times, to see life as a continuous process of writing and rewriting, and to look forward always to the next chapter.

Index